iPod
Fully Loaded

If You've Got It, You Can iPod It

iPod
Fully Loaded

If You've Got It, You Can iPod It

Andy Ihnatko

Wiley Publishing, Inc.

iPod® Fully Loaded: If You've Got It, You Can iPod It
Published by
Wiley Publishing, Inc.
111 River Street
Hoboken, N.J. 07030
www.wiley.com

Published by Wiley Publishing, Inc., Indianapolis, Indiana
Published simultaneously in Canada

Library of Congress Control Number: 2006932682

ISBN: 978-0-470-04950-1

Manufactured in the United States of America

10 9 8 7 6 5 4 3 2

1B/QZ/RQ/QW/IN

For general information on our other products and services or to obtain technical support, please contact our Customer Care Department within the U.S. at (800) 762-2974, outside the U.S. at (317) 572-3993 or fax (317) 572-4002.

Wiley also publishes its books in a variety of electronic formats. Some content that appears in print may not be available in electronic books.

Acknowledgments

Well, y'got the Mom and the Dad, obviously.

We then proceed smartly to my agent, Carole McClendon, who can take me from idle musings of "You know what would make a good idea for a book?" to a signed contract before I have a chance to protest, "But what about that opera I wanted to write?"

Onward to Mike Roney. Formerly Friend and Editor, now singly a Friend.

While we're discussing editors, let's not blow straight past Carol Person, who edited this book and was a real good sport about the airbag deployment, though I still insist that the cornering performance on our rental car wasn't up to the published spec. Layout guru Galen Gruman did honor by his pike and his halberd.

My good pal Chris Breen — a true Iron Chef of iPod — was gracious with support, both moral and not.

And finally, a huge shout-out to all my BFFs at the Drama Club, whose hard work on the costumes and the sets will make this the best darned production of *Gentlemen Prefer Blondes* that St. Albans Junior High has ever seen. *Go Wolverines!!!*

Credits

Acquisitions Editor
Kim Spilker

Project and Layout Editor
Galen Gruman,
The Zango Group

Editor
Carol Person,
The Zango Group

Editorial Manager
Robyn B. Siesky

**Vice President &
Executive Group Publisher**
Richard Swadley

**Vice President and
Publisher**
Barry Pruett

Business Manager
Amy Knies

**Product Development
Supervisor**
Courtney Allen

Production Designer
Jonathan Woolson,
thinkplaydesign

Book Designer
Marie Kristine Parial-Leonardo

Interior Illustrator
Joyce Haughey

Cover Image
Michael E. Trent

**Copy Editing, Proofreading,
and Indexing**
The Zango Group

About the Author

Andy Ihnatko describes himself as "the world's 42nd most-beloved industry personality" because "it's vaguely credible but utterly impossible to prove or disprove, and thus precisely the sort of tagline I was looking for."

An unabashed geek ("The bashings ended when I left high school for Rensselaer Polytechnic, thank God"), Andy's been writing about tech since 1989. In the past, he's written for every single magazine or Web site with the word "Mac" in it, highlighted by ten years as *MacUser*'s and then *Macworld's* back-page opinion columnist. He's currently the *Chicago Sun-Times'* technology columnist.

In his pursuit of "heroically stupid applications of technology," Andy has built an animatronic Darth Vader doll that could be controlled over the Internet via telepresence to hassle his roommate's cats and has written and published a complete set of plans and instructions for converting any Classic-style Macintosh into a fully-functional 2.5-gallon aquarium. *The Original MacQuarium* was one of the Internet's first e-Books and can be downloaded from several sites after a quick Google search.

This is Andy's sixth book. Andy lives in Boston with his two goldfish, Click and Drag. He invites you to visit his aptly named "Colossal Waste of Bandwidth" at www.andyi.com.

Contents

Appendixes

Bonus Material

But wait, there's more! For a convenient summary of the book's key advice, download the bonus Appendix C, available as a PDF file, from www.wiley.com. Just search for "iPod Fully Loaded" at the Wiley site to get to this book's Web page, then click the Bonus Materials link.

Appendix C: The Super Skim

Chapter 1: iPod Startup

Chapter 2: Ripping CDs

Chapter 3: LP, Tapes, and Whatnot

Chapter 4: Ripping DVDs

Contents

➤   ➤   ➤

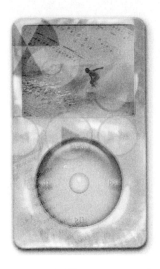

Introduction

Welcome to My Book

A book introduction is dedicated to a very specific and very special breed of reader: the moocher.

Yes, the moocher. The lollygagger. The browser. The person who hunches his shoulders and buries his face in the book like he's all anonymous and innocent even though he knows fully well that *he* was the person the bookstore owner was speaking to when she yelled out, "Hey, this isn't a *library*, you know!!!"

No, I'm not angry. Honestly, my hat's off to you.

Yes, Bookstore Browser and So-Called Friend Who Clearly Has Little Intention of Ever Returning This Book to the Co-Worker You Borrowed It From, you are the focus of this introduction. I have a thousand words or so here in which to lay out the reasons why the book you are now holding is the critical pivot point between The Dark Age and The Moment When Everything Started Going Right for You.

The iPod is an all-too-rare triple-convergence product. For once, the item that represents the pinnacle of technology and the acme of style is also the best-selling thing on the market. It's slick and sexy. Speaking as a tech columnist who gets to play with any and every gadget that gets thrown at a fearful and defenseless populace, I can certify that it's hands-down the most trouble-free player out there. From the iPod itself to the iTunes software that keeps its hard drive fresh, fed, and funky, everything's designed to put the lowest resistance to your efforts to be entertained, whether you're interested in music or videos.

But!

▷ As good as iTunes is, there's a lot more to ripping a CD than just slapping it in the drive and clicking a button. What you'll actually be able to do with your music library after you've ripped disc #718 depends on the settings that iTunes has been working with since disc #1.

▷ The iTunes Music Store is so utterly crammed with wonderfulness that the only way to adequately put across its monumental coolness would be to compare it to a Wiffle Ball made out of Nerf. Absolutely. But if your only sources of iPod content are the CDs that you rip and the music and video you buy through the iTunes Music Store, you're only enjoying a fraction of the entertainment an iPod can provide.

▷ What about TV shows that either (a) aren't available through the iTunes Music Store or (b) aren't worth paying $1.99 an episode for? And what about DVDs that you've already paid for? How about free videos that you can download — *legally* — from the Web?

▷ And why are we thinking of the iPod as just an entertainment device? Can it do more for you than just play music and video? What about news, and Web sites, and books, and e-mail? Presentations? Office work?

This book assumes that you've already read through iTunes' built-in tutorials. I'm even willing to assume that you might have already bought a book about iTunes and the iPod. You know, the sort of book that explains the history of the device and the technology inside it, how to best charge the battery, and what sort of lie you should rehearse for the guy at the iTunes store's customer-support desk when he asks you, "When did your iPod stop working?" and the worst possible answer is the truth ("Sometime between the rinse and spin cycles, I guess").

There are some wonderful books like that already. And in case you need an accelerated course in iPod 101, Chapter 1 reviews the basics of iPod-ology.

No, *this* book is all about filling your iPod with as much content as possible. With the tools, tricks, and techniques I've so kindly delineated within these pages, there's very little of your world that you *won't* be able load and enjoy on your iPod.

Yes, there's a whole multiplex out there waiting to be strip-mined. This book is eager to provide you with precisely the sort of heavy-diesel machinery that gets the Sierra Club all irked up when its raised against hills, streams, and forests. Luckily, you'll be using it on sources of entertainment and information, so we're all in the clear.

The point is that you have as much as 60 gigabytes of storage there on your iPod. The thing weighs the same whether it contains just five tracks from *Frampton Comes Alive* or it's crammed with 300 albums, fifty podcasts, the most recent ten broadcasts of *Late Night with David Letterman*, all six *Star Wars* films, the entire (landmark) seventh season of *The Simpsons*, all the photos you shot during your trip to the International Mustard Convention and Exhibition, two PowerPoint presentations you need to give, all the readable content from a Ferrari-restoration blog, every e-mail you've received in the past month, and the complete contents of the Documents folder on your PC.

Peter Frampton crafted a perennial classic. I'm not dissing Peter Frampton here. I'm just saying that if that's all you have with you, you're missing out on something rather special and that you desperately need to purchase this book.

Just don't steal it. This book isn't about stealing things that never belonged to you in the first place. All the tools and techniques I describe are perfectly legal.

Besides, shoplifting is wrong. And lastly, this business about talking directly to you here in the bookstore was all just a ruse to stall you while I alerted store security to your presence. Oh, they're *on* to you now, cowboy. I think the only way to prove beyond a shadow of a doubt that you never intended to steal this book is to walk to the counter in a non-threatening manner — keeping the book in plain sight at all times — and pay for it.

Tough love, I know. But trust me: This book is for your own good.

Conventions Used

Well, I can't say I'm a fan of conventions because they are so … er … conventional. But even I, despite all my Special Powers, must bow to conventions. Like for all those geeky aspects inevitable in a book that talks about computyer technology, so you know what I mean when I diverge from good ol' English. Wherever possible, I've kept the book free of weird computer symbols and geeky icons. But some insisted on being used, so here are their conventions.

MOUSE CONVENTIONS

Here's what I mean when I talk about using the mouse:

- Click: Most Mac mice have only one button, but some have two or more; all PC mice have at least two buttons. If you have a multibutton mouse, quickly press and release the leftmost mouse button once when I say to click the mouse. (If your mouse has only one button — you guessed it — just press and release the button you have.)

- Double-click: When I say to double-click, quickly press and release the leftmost mouse button twice (if your mouse has only one button, just press and release twice the button you have). On some multibutton mice, one of the buttons can function as a double-click (you click it once, the mouse clicks twice); if your mouse has this feature, use it — it saves strain on your hand.

- Right-click: A Windows feature since Windows 95, right-clicking means clicking the right-hand mouse button. On a Mac's one-button mouse, hold the Control key when clicking the mouse button to achieve the right-click effect. On multibutton Mac mice, Mac OS X automatically assigns the righthand button to Control+click.

> Drag: Dragging is used for moving and sizing items in a document. To drag an item, position the mouse pointer on it. Press and hold down the mouse button, and then slide the mouse across a flat surface to drag the item. Release the mouse button to drop the dragged item in its new location.

The commands that you select by using the program menus appear in this book in normal typeface. When you choose some menu commands, a related pull-down menu or a pop-up menu appears. If I describe a situation in which you need to select one menu and then choose a command from a secondary menu or list box, I use an arrow symbol. For example, "Choose Edit   Paste" means that you should choose the Paste command from the Edit menu.

KEYBOARD CONVENTIONS

In those rare cases where I get into nitty-gritty computer comands, I'll provide both the Macintosh and Windows shortcuts throughout, with the Mac shortcut first. In most cases, the Mac and Windows shortcuts are the same, except for the names of the keys, as follows:

> The Mac's Command key (⌘) is the most-used shortcut key. Its Windows equivalent is Ctrl.

> Shift is the same on the Mac and Windows. In many Mac program menus, Shift is displayed by the symbol ⇧.

> The Option key on the Mac is usually the same as the Alt key in Windows. In many Mac program menus — including iTunes — you'll see the symbol ⌥ used.

> The Control key on the Mac has no Windows equivalent (it is not the same as the Windows Ctrl key). Many Mac programs indicate it with the symbol ^ in their menus.

> The Tab key is used both to move within fields in panes and dialog boxes and to insert the tab character in text. iTunes and many other Mac programs indicate it in menus with the symbol ⇥.

> The Return key (Mac) or Enter key (Windows) is used to apply a dialog box's settings and close the dialog box (equivalent to clicking OK or Done), as well as to insert a hard paragraph return in text. In many Mac programs, it is indicated in menus by the symbol ↵. Note that there is another key labeled Enter on most keyboards, in the numeric keypad. This keypad Enter usually works like the regular Return or Enter.

> The Delete key (Mac) and Backspace key (Windows) deletes text, one character at a time, to the left of the text-insertion point. On the Mac, programs like iTunes use the symbol ⌫ to indicate Delete. Windows also has a separate Delete key that deletes text, on character at a time, to the right of the text-insertion point. The Mac's Clear key, although in the same

position on the keyboard, does not delete text.

If you're supposed to press several keys at the same time, I indicate that by placing plus signs (+) between them. Thus, Shift+⌘+A means press and hold the Shift and ⌘ keys, then press A. After you've pressed the A key, let go of all three keys. (You don't need to hold down the last letter in the sequence.)

I also use the plus sign (+) to join keys to mouse movements. For example, Option+drag means to hold the Option key while dragging the mouse on the Mac, and Alt+drag means to hold the Alt key while dragging the mouse in Windows.

Rarely, I indicate programming code or text you must enter as is into some dialog box or other program interface. I do that by formatting the text in a typewriter-like font: `like this`.

Okay, enough of this techno mumbo-jumbo. Onto the good stuff!

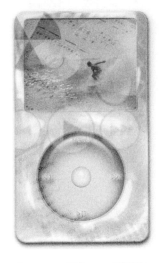

PART I

The Real World According to iPod

iPod Startup

The Skim

I will start not at the beginning, but *before* the beginning. First, because there's a lot more parking available, but mostly to make sure that as you make your way through this book and rush off to apply what you've learned, you're not stymied by fundamentals. Yes. I'm the sort of geek who believes that converting a DVD into a movie file is enormously entertaining merely as an intellectual exercise, and I have a very firm opinion on whether Batman could beat Captain America in a hand-to-hand situation, but market research strongly suggests that most of you want to actually *play* the thing on your iPod.

Herewith I present the Basic Rules of the iPod on loading files into iTunes and your iPod. To assume full Jedi mastery of the iPod and iTunes, I suggest you speak with your guidance counselor regarding a two-year degree program at an area junior college, or simply explore iTunes' Help menu.

The basic path from having a file on your hard drive to having a *thing* on your iPod that you can click and enjoy in your car, on the beach, or during a dull bit of a wedding service goes like this:

▷ You import the file into iTunes, which adds the file to your computer's ever-expanding catalog of music and video.

> You organize your content in playlists.

> Your iPod is updated with fresh content when you hook it up to your computer. iTunes can update the iPod automatically at the very moment it realizes that the iPod has been plugged in. Or, if you're a control freak, the sort of universally-disliked office manager who won't let an employee take a freakin' pad of sticky notes out of the supply cabinet without filling out a form, you can explicitly tell iTunes to update the iPod right *now*.

IMPORTING FILES INTO ITUNES

iTunes isn't a simple music player that just plays a file off your hard drive and then forgets that it ever existed. No, iTunes is grabby and ambitious: It's a Media Content Library Management System. When you import a music or video file into iTunes, all sorts of information about it are added to a master database so that you can locate one song among thousands in an instant (A seven-minute version of "Anarchy in the U.K." recorded by Buddy Ebsen) and unless you've explicitly told iTunes not to do so — aack, those control freak issues yet again — iTunes will also copy the file into its own special

music directory so your collection is kept nice and tidy and all in the same place.

There are two ways to add files to your iTunes library:

Method the First: The Add To Library Command

This method is easy, if you like using menus:

1. Choose File ⇨ Select Add To Library.

   In the Windows edition of iTunes, there are two Add To Library menus. Add File allows you to select one specific file. If you select Add Folder, iTunes will scan through the contents of a selected folder and automatically add any music or video files that it's capable of playing.

   In the Macintosh version of iTunes, a single command handles both tasks.

   Either way, you'll find yourself looking at your computer's standard file/folder browser.

2. Select a music or video file, or a folder containing music and videos.

3. Click the highlighted button. On a Mac,

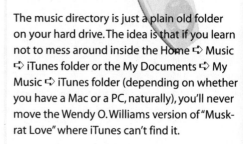

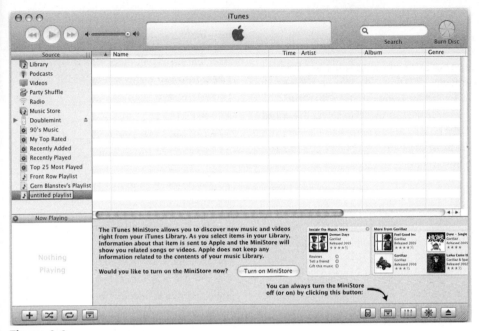

Figure 1-1
A new playlist takes its first breath.

it'll be Choose. If you're selecting a file on a PC, it'll be OK, or Open if you're using the Add Folder command.

iTunes will percolate for a minute. When it's done, all the selected files that iTunes knows how to deal with will appear in the iTunes library.

Method the Second: Just Drag It

This method is easy if you like working with your hands instead of menus: If you're in Windows Explorer or the Mac Finder and you can see the name or icon of the files you want to import, you can just drag the files straight into iTunes without any further ado.

Drag them into the iTunes window, or drag them into iTunes' desktop icon or its tile in the Windows taskbar or the Macintosh Dock. However you do it, if the music or video is in a format iTunes thinks it understands, a plus sign (+) will appear next to your mouse pointer when you enter iTunes' airspace. Release, and iTunes will take it from there.

ORGANIZING YOUR MUSIC INTO PLAYLISTS

A playlist is a simple concept: It's just a list of songs you've selected and arranged in the order you'd like to hear them. You can make as many playlists as you want, tailored to nearly any situation: music for your workouts, music to put on when a blind date heads for extra innings, or the perfect soundtrack for piloting your souped-up Dodge Charger down rural back roads at breakneck speeds with Boss Hogg in close pursuit. Play-

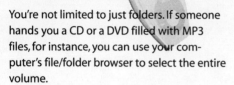

lists also help you to manage the problem of having more music and video on your computer than you have space for on your iPod. I mean, the whole goal of this book is to help you stuff that device until it's ready to explode and rely on playlists to make sure that iTunes doesn't simply choose ten hours of doo-wop music to tide you over during a trans-Atlantic flight.

iTunes offers two different flavors of playlists. There's the plain-vanilla variety, through which you manually pick and choose specific bits of music and video. And there're Smart Playlists, which are way more powerful. Smart Playlists allow you to describe the *sort* of music you'd like to hear: "Twenty rock songs, but nothing I've listened to in the past month," for example. And then iTunes works out the specifics on its own.

Plain Old Playlists

You can create a new playlist either by choosing File ➪ New Playlist or by clicking the plus (+) button at the bottom of the iTunes browser window. Either way, an untitled playlist will appear in iTunes' list of music sources (see Figure 1-1).

The default playlist name, Untitled Playlist, is highlighted and awaits your creative genius. Type in something memorable. "Just

Drive" is my usual playlist of stuff I want to hear in the car.

And that's really all there is to it. Any song I drag into Just Drive will be added to the playlist. To wit:

1. Click Library in the iTunes window's Source list. A list of all the music and video in your iTunes library appears.

2. Select one or more items from your library.

3. Drag the selected items to the playlist's name.

Incidentally, when you copy items into a playlist, the only thing you're actually copying is the items' information. All the actual music and video files remain in your iTunes' library, which means that any music track or video can be in many playlists at the same time. I mean, what sort of life would it be if you could only enjoy "The Cockroach That Ate Cincinnati" in one playlist?

If you click the playlist's name, iTunes' browser window will show you a list of all the playlist's tracks. You can change the play order of those items by just dragging them around, and you can remove items by selecting them and hitting the Backspace or Delete key on your keyboard.

Figure 1-2
A Smart Playlist for my morning constitutional

Smart Playlists

Some apps have certain features that are so good they make me want to stick five bucks in an envelope and mail it to the company. iTunes' Smart Playlists is definitely one of those features.

Smart Playlists let you create a playlist without being specific about its contents. You describe the *sort* of content you want, and iTunes makes the selections for you. iTunes stores a lot of information about all the items in its library — including how frequently and recently you've been playing that stuff — which means that it's easy to get iTunes to make some fairly sophisticated choices on your behalf.

For instance: I buy lots of music through the iTunes Music Store, representing all kinds of artists and genres. And every morning when I take my hour-long constitutional — I'd like to call it a *morning jog* but that would imply an ability to run faster than the average man can walk on his hands — I want to listen to my freshest music.

I could either religiously move tracks in and out of a manual playlist or I could just define a Smart Playlist by choosing File ➪ New Smart Playlist (see Figure 1-2):

Each line represents a different "rule" to apply when iTunes chooses songs for this

playlist; to add a new one, I click the plus (+) button at the end of any rule. This Smart Playlist says:

> Choose only "protected" songs — copy-protected songs are songs purchased through the iTunes store.

> Don't choose spoken-word recordings or books-on-tape. Neither my metabolism nor my enthusiasm for exercise are great enough to keep my legs moving during 45 minutes of Alan Greenspan's memoirs.

> For that matter, don't select any music over six minutes long, either.

> If I've played this song any time in the last three days, don't bother playing it again.

Below the list of rules, you specify how much music you'd like, and how you'd like iTunes to make the selection. One hour will do me just fine, although you can alternatively tell iTunes to limit by number of songs or the amount of space the collection will take up. I've also told it to select the newest songs.

Alternatively, I could also ask iTunes to pick songs at random, songs I haven't heard recently, or select from an abundance of other options.

Once I click OK, the new playlist will be automatically populated with items that match the rules I laid out.

One of the (many) terrific features of Smart Playlists is that the list is "live." If I buy new music, the Smart Playlist will automatically add them to the playlist, kicking out older songs to make room. And remember, both iTunes and your iPod keep track of what songs and videos you've been watching.

When I get home from my constitutional and plug my iPod into the computer, iTunes immediately knows which songs I've heard since the last time the iPod was connected. Songs that no longer pass the "Last Played is not in the last 3 days" test are automatically removed from the playlist and replaced.

> **TIP**

Let's revisit that "My iPod is no longer big enough to store all my music and videos" problem. I have a 30-gigabyte iPod and about 80 gigabytes of music. So, I've set up a collection of individual Smart Playlists that automatically fill the iPod with content from this library, with each genre of music chosen in different proportions. "Five gigabytes of Rock, chosen at random"; "3 gigabytes of Country"; "5 gigs of Classical." Result: I always have a broad swatch of my 10,000-track iTunes library represented. And by telling the playlists to favor music I haven't heard recently, it's always fresh stuff.

UPDATING YOUR IPOD

When you connect your iPod to your computer, it automatically appears in iTunes' list of music sources. What happens after that depends on the iPod options you've set. You can open the iPod Options window by either clicking the iPod button at the bottom of the iTunes window or right-clicking the iPod's name and selecting iPod Options from the contextual pop-up menu. Mac users who don't own a two-button mouse can reveal the contextual menu by holding down the Control key while clicking the iPod's name. You wind up with a window like the one you see in Figure 1-3.

iTunes can update the iPod's contents automatically every time you plug it in, as follows:

> If you click Automatically Update All Songs and Playlists, iTunes will always attempt to mirror the entire contents of your iTunes library onto your iPod. If there isn't enough space on your iPod for that stuff, iTunes will warn you and then (at your discretion) try to fit in as much as possible.

> The Automatically Update Selected Playlists Only option does what it says. Instead of trying to cram *everything* in there, it'll just update the songs and videos that are in the playlists you've checked. Plain playlists, smart playlists — it's all the same.

> The Manually Manage Songs and Playlists option means that iTunes will leave the task of updating your iPod completely up to you. The iPod will behave exactly like an iTunes playlist: Drag tracks and playlist to add them, select them and press Backspace (Windows) or Delete (Macintosh)

to remove them. You're a control freak, and you'll never change. The iPod is cool with that. The iPod doesn't judge people. Why can't we all be more like the iPod? And if I want to parade around in my Spider-Man costume, that's my business, isn't it?

There's another tweak to all this: the Only Update Checked Songs checkbox. Each track of video in every iTunes window has a checkbox next to it. With this option enabled, any item that *does not* have its checkbox checked would *not* be synched to your iPod, which makes it easy to *point and shoot* certain items that you never want to hear in the car.

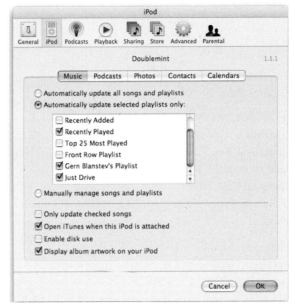

Figure 1-3
The iPod Options window

Automatic updates only take place when you plug in your iPod. You can also tell iPod to update this iPod *right freaking now* by selecting Update Songs from the iPod's contextual menu. You use this contextual menu option if you've selected Manually Manage Songs and Playlists in the iPod Options window (remember, the Manual option means that iTunes will never update the iPod on its own), or if you've added new

▶TIP

Automatically Update Selected Playlists Only is by far the most useful way to manage your iPod's content. You get the convenience of an update that happens automatically as soon as you plug your iPod into a dock or a cable, with the power and control of playlists.

items or playlist to your iTunes library since plugging in your iPod. Automatic updates only take place when the iPod is first plugged in.

All these options are fine and dandy, but there's no dancing around the fact that there's nothing on your iPod yet and at the moment you have a $200 device that tells you the time and plays "Breakout," which just doesn't seem right. Let us now step forward toward the goal of converting every last scrap of media into iPod-studly formats and loading that thing up until it reaches its Mr. Creosote Point. (That means it's time to go to the Chapter 2.)

▷ ▷ ▷

Ripping CDs

The Skim

I kid you not. I have the most bizarre audio component ever conceived by God or man: a 20-cassette changer. You fill it up with tapes, the carousel spins around like the barrel of something violent, and a cozy 45 seconds after you pressed the Change button, there you are, listening to something else. It's probably one of the ten most awesome things I've ever bought, and I only paid $10 for it.

I bring this up for the benefit of you kids out there: You have no earthly idea how difficult it was, in the days before digital music formats and 60-gigabyte players, to push a button and abort to a whole other album any time an Abba song accidentally came on.

Ripping CDs into music files is certainly one of the most basic aspects of this whole iPod stuffing thing. Which is a *bit* of a shame, because it's all so automatic that you don't even really think about the choices iTunes is making on your behalf. Today, you're just eager to get a little Green Day on your new iPod; besides, you're still suffering from the vague lightheadedness that always clings to you for six or seven hours after a visit to an iTunes store. Five years from now, when you've ripped *every CD you've ever purchased,* will you still be happy with iTunes' out-of-the-box, automatic choices?

So here's the basic plan for this chapter: first, I'll show you how simple

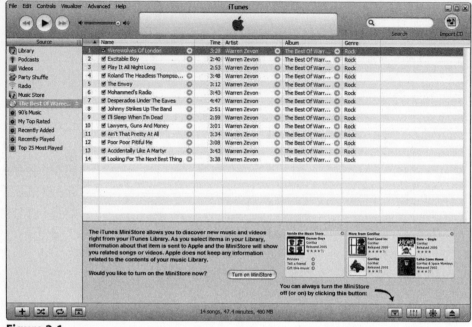

Figure 2-1
Opening a CD in iTunes

the CD-ripping process is from start to finish. And then I'll ruin the Zen-like simplicity of the chapter with glorious blobby heaps of acronyms and technical details that will leave you numbly wandering the streets of a strange city without shoes.

No need to thank me; I'm a geek. This is what I do.

THE RIP

Okey doke. Just stick a CD in the drive and after your machine has taken a moment to comprehend that it now has to deal with a copy of Howard Jones' *Greatest Hits*, iTunes opens the CD for playback and presents you with a list of tracks (see Figure 2-1).

If you push iTunes' Play button, it'll play these tracks straight off the CD, but we're living in the exciting Push-Button World of Tomorrow, not the leaden gaslight-and-spats era of the

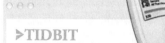

>TIDBIT

Nobody is impressed with the speed of your new computer. Honest. They're feigning interest while they scan the room for someone else to talk to. Your friends used to think this behavior was amusing, in a tragic sort of way, but now they can no longer sit by and watch you strike out again talking about your new laptop, your hybrid car, the new watch you bought for marathon training, et cetera. "The best way to talk is to listen," they urge you. I concur heartily. They're not trying to embarrass you. They just don't want you to be so terribly lonely, that's all.

Figure 2-2
The Import button, a.k.a. All You Need to Know.

	▲	Name		Time	Artist		Album
1	⊘	☑ Werewolves Of London	○	3:28	Warren Zevon	○	The Best Of Warr...
2	⊘	☑ Excitable Boy	○	2:40	Warren Zevon	○	The Best Of Warr...
3	⊘	☑ Play It All Night Long	○	2:53	Warren Zevon	○	The Best Of Warr...
4	⊘	☑ Roland The Headless Thompso...	○	3:48	Warren Zevon	○	The Best Of Warr...
5	⊘	☑ The Envoy	○	3:12	Warren Zevon	○	The Best Of Warr...
6		☑ Mohammed's Radio	○	3:43	Warren Zevon	○	The Best Of Warr...
7		☑ Desperados Under The Eaves	○	4:47	Warren Zevon	○	The Best Of Warr...

Importing "The Envoy"
Time remaining: 0:01 (12.6x)

Figure 2-3
The status of an ongoing rip

mid-Nineties: We want to make music files.

Turning all those tracks into digital music files is a complicated process consisting of:

1. Push the button marked Import CD, found in the upper-right corner of the iTunes window (see Figure 2-2).

2. Optional: Go down to the kitchen and microwave a Hot Pocket or something while iTunes converts the tracks into music files and adds them to your music library.

Because honestly, that's all there is to it.

All right, in truth, I desperately wanted to reduce this process to one step, so I wantonly glossed over the fact that if there are tracks on this disc that you don't want, you can just uncheck the checkbox next to the tracks' names. I mean, on the off chance that the artists who created this CD failed

to ensure that every single track was a timeless classic.

As you enjoy your Hot Pocket and glance at your computer screen, you might take note of some of the things going on in the iTunes window:

> The window's status display shows which track is currently being imported, how far along the process has come, and, if you like to brag about how fast your computer is, the speed of the rip. In Figure 2-3, iTunes is pleased to report that it's converting the track fifteen times faster than the time it'd take to play it.

> On the left side of the track list, next to the track numbers, you'll see little green checkmark icons that represent completed tracks, an orange one next to the track that's being ripped, and colorful expanses of absolutely nothing next to those tracks

Figure 2-4
Spit it out, son; ejecting a disc.

If you're ripping dozens or hundreds of discs instead of a handful, iTunes has a hidden feature to speed things along. Open the iTunes Preferences panel (located under the Edit menu in Windows, and under the iTunes menu in the Mac OS). Select the Advanced tab, and then click the Importing subtab (see Figure 2-5).

Choose the On CD Insert menu and you'll reveal a frisky item named Import Songs and Eject. It's tailor-made for processing CDs in bulk. With this feature enabled, iTunes will automatically start ripping the entire contents of the disc the moment you insert it. And when the last track has been ripped, iTunes will spit the disc out, impatient for more.

You can rip a 1,000-CD collection with little visible effort by merely keeping a stack of discs near the computer and sticking a new disc in there whenever a ripped disc is sticking out of the drive.

that have yet to be processed.

> There's a tiny X button on the right side of iTunes' status display. Click it to abort the rip-in-progress and cancel all the tracks due to be ripped.

> iTunes will start playing the ripped tracks as soon as the first one is complete (unless you've turned this feature off in iTunes' Preferences panel). Click the Stop button to knock off the noise.

After iTunes has finished ripping the CD, you can eject it by clicking the little Eject button next to the CD's name on the left side of the iTunes window (see Figure 2-4). Using the Eject button on your keyboard or on your CD drive will accomplish the same thing.

And I'm proud to say that here, 95 percent of my job as an instructionalist writer is complete. Nothin' left for me to do here but clear up a few trims and ends, most of which orbit the theme of "Why Did This (Possibly)

Go Wretchedly Wrong?"

TROUBLESHOOTING

But this world is a vale of tears, and even in a simple, flawless, and foolproof process like ripping a CD in iTunes, a little rain must fall.

The Disc Didn't Appear in iTunes

If the disc doesn't show up in iTunes, there are usually only two possible answers:

> The disc is way too scratched, baffed, and dinged-up for your CD drive to recognize it. I mean, for heaven's sake, man: you felt

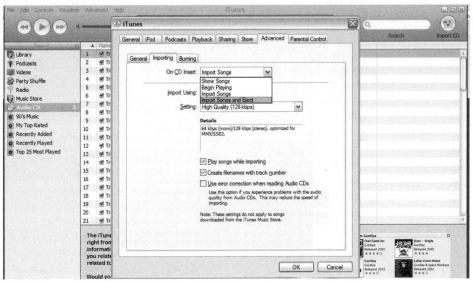

Figure 2-5
Rip-O-Matic: the best way to convert a pile of CDs at once

your chair roll over it *twice*, and yet you went over it a third time before you picked it up. That's going to cost you a new copy of *Rubber Soul*, my friend.

➤ The disc isn't an audio CD.

Not an audio CD, eh? Interesting.

Usually, this means that the publisher chose to save you a little time by burning a CD-R or a DVD-R of digital music files. Open the disc in Windows Explorer or the Mac OS Finder and see what files are there.

If it has documents with .MP3 or .AAC or other music-ish filename extensions, then just drag those files straight into the iTunes window and they'll be added to your music library without any further ado.

Sometimes, though — and if you listen carefully, you can hear my teeth grinding as I type these words — it's because the CD

has been intentionally corrupted by the publisher. Which brings us to …

Dealing with "Copy-Protected" CDs

And I put those words in quotes because it's

> **TIP**
>
> Ripping your first disc is simple. It's the remaining 992 in your collection that are going to sting. Fortunately, there are lots of services out there that will rip all your CDs *for* you. You ship 'em the discs, they ship 'em all back accompanied by a few DVDs filled with iTunes-compatible music files. These services are popping up all over the place, but if you want to check out pricing, Rip-Topia (www.riptopia.com) and MusicShifter (www.musicshifter.com) are both good places to start.

>TROUBLE

One major publisher hid a *major* piece of spyware on all their major releases. It didn't just prevent you from copying tracks, it also kept tabs on your listening habits. And the kicker: It was installed using a technique that made the software (a) difficult to detect, (b) almost impossible to remove without destroying your whole system, and (c) the source of a major security hole that could allow no-goodniks to break into your PC via your Internet connection.

Naturally, hackers discovered this weakness and started to deploy malicious software of their own, designed to exploit the gaping hole created by the record company's spyware. Idiots! They deserve to go through life in itchy underwear. And to have something heavy dropped on them from a great height.

nonsense. If you've legally purchased a CD, then you have the right to rip its tracks into digital music files. Period. It's a right granted by the Supreme Court, who realized even in those hoary old videotape days (remember them?) that people had the right to make copies for personal use. Moreover, the music industry has tried time and time again to weaken this provision or specify cases in which it doesn't matter, and time and time again, the courts have smacked them in their collective nose with a rolled-up newspaper and told them to sleep outside tonight.

So the recording industry's response to these defeats has been to "corrupt" some of their most popular titles just enough so that computers don't recognize them as audio CDs. Which, in itself is a fool's errand. The CD standard is called a "standard" for a good reason:

because when a CD fails to conform to the standard, it no longer meets the standard. Duh.

There's also a good chance this "corrupted" disc won't play in a car CD changer, or the CD boom box that you bought two years ago, or any audio CD player anywhere.

And *why* are they going to all of this trouble? I don't know. I've never drunk a pint of raw ether, so I lack the ability to process thoughts in quite the same way as a music company executive.

"To prevent piracy" is the usual smokescreen, but in truth the goal is to assert more control over what you can do with the CDs you own. I bought one copy of The Who's *Who's Next* CD fifteen years ago, and because I never lost or ruined it, and I've converted the disc to crisp, perfect digital files, I'll likely never buy another copy. This presents a problem for the record industry.

Onward.

There are limits to how angry I can get about copy-protected CDs because none of the systems currently in play actually work. There are ways to get around nearly any copy-protection scheme.

Windows Protection Avoidance

If you're a Windows user: Hold down the Shift key while inserting the CD. And you're done. Most anti-copying schemes work by sticking an invisible piece of Windows software on the disc that runs automatically when Windows loads in the CD. The sole purpose of this app is to prevent the disc's contents from being ripped. But holding down the Shift key tells Windows to ignore any auto-run software on the disc.

You should also refuse to install any "bonus"

Figure 2-6
The Compact Disc logo: Ask for it by, er, name.

software included on the disc. Often, the "special video footage" or the "special access to an exclusive Web site" offer is actually a Trojan horse, a program that secretly does Bad Things to your computer, or at least Secret Things You Don't Want. The CD will also install a permanent piece of software on your PC that will eternally look out for CDs published by that company and prevent you from ripping its tracks into your music library.

Macintosh Protection Avoidance

If you're a Mac user, the solution is simpler still: … Yeah, you don't have to do anything at all. These copy-prevention schemes are almost always keyed to work on Windows machines only. Macs will mount the disc and rip its tracks without any complaint.

Avoiding Copy-Protection Altogether

Have I done a good job concealing my moral contempt for so-called "copy-protection" schemes? That's thanks to discipline — no other word for it.

This sort of thing annoys me so much that I carefully examine every CD I buy for the familiar (and trademarked) "Compact Disc"

logo (see Figure 2-6).

If this logo appears on a disc's packaging, it means that the CD conforms to the international audio CD standard. If the publisher corrupted it, the CD can't bear this imprint.

More than once, I have taken a CD back to the store — after having opened it — and received a refund based on that argument. That logo is an implied warranty that there's no funny business standing between you and a folder full of unlocked digital music files.

Mind you, lack of a logo doesn't imply copy-corruption, but its presence means that you can stride back into that store armed with the full power of unbridled arrogance. Feel free to quote Samuel L. Jackson's big line from *Pulp Fiction* — you know, that impressive Bible passage out of Ezekiel.

If nothing works, you simply sigh, spend a moment reflecting upon the fact that this is an imperfect world and that humans are flawed vessels of Logic and Wisdom and just hook up a conventional audio CD player to the audio inputs of your PC.

Following the instructions found in Chapter 3 (which explains how to convert music via your computer's audio inputs), you can record the content using a desktop audio app.

And this method is absolutely foolproof. There's no way that a record company can prevent this technique from working. No matter what the record company does to a disc to prevent legal copies from being made, the disc *still* has to play audio on a standard CD player. And if a CD player can send analog sound into your headphones or a pair of speakers, it can send it into the recording

>TIP

If you select more than one track before choosing File ⇨ Get Info, iTunes will (after a curt warning that doing so might be a bad idea) allow you to edit the info for all those tracks at once. The album, year, genre, and maybe even the artist and composer won't change from track to track, so it's a good way to save some time. But you need to dismiss that window and edit each track individually to add the specific track titles.

inputs of your computer.

All the Tracks Are Untitled

Usually, iTunes magically fills in the title of the CD and the names and artists of each

track for you.

This particular mojo is powered by the Gracenote CD database, what I like to call the CDDB. If you have an Internet connection, iTunes automatically connects to Gracenote's database, asks it, "Have you ever heard of this CD before?" and grabs the info it needs.

If something goes wrong, you'll see the unhappy state of affairs represented in Figure 2-7.

If you didn't have an Internet connection available when you ripped the disc, don't sweat it. The next time you're Net-studly, select those tracks and then choose Advanced ⇨ Get CD Track Names (see Figure 2-8).

It's possible, however, that you are the first human on this planet to ever purchase and rip this specific CD. If so, the CDDB doesn't *have*

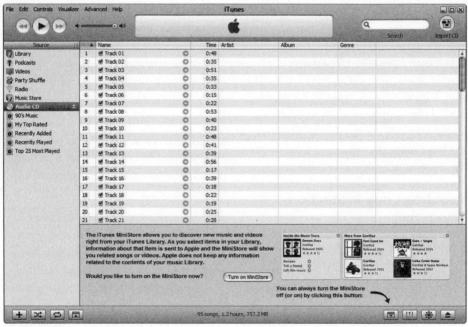

Figure 2-7
The Untitled Symphony

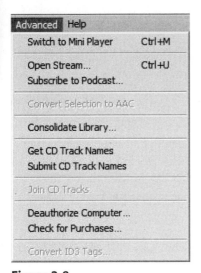

Figure 2-8
Let the CDDB's fingers do the typing.

Figure 2-9
Filling in the blanks on a new CD.

an album, artist, or track info on file yet. You'll have to add that stuff yourself. Here's how:

1. In iTunes, select the album's first track.

2. Choose File ⇨ Get Info.

3. Click the Info tab of the window. You'll be presented with the little form you see in Figure 2-9.

4. You'll need to laboriously copy all the info from the back of the CD. When you finish one track, click the Next button to move to the next track.

And this is your reward for supporting struggling independent artists. Because honestly, the only CDs that aren't in the Gracenote CDDB are coffee-shop performers who self-produce CDs in the dozens or hundreds at best. Every commercial CD is already there, no matter how bizarre. To produce Figure 2-7, I dug out my copy of *The Beatles on*

Panpipes, a gag gift I bought for a Beatles fan pal and then didn't have the courage to actually give him. "Surely this one isn't in the database," I thought. But no, a disc of panpipe-based Beatle covers had already been processed and added to the database.

After you've finished all that work, you *could* demonstrate that you're a responsible and contributing member of society by selecting the tracks and choosing Advanced ⇨ Submit CD Track Names. This will update the CDDB with the info you've just added to iTunes, and potentially the rest of the world will benefit from your labors, in perpetuity. Not the best legacy that you can leave, but it's more than some people ever contribute, I suppose.

THE FILE-FORMAT POLKA

Okey doke. Just give me a moment to prepare a damp washcloth and clean all that vitreous spittle off my screen so I can proceed.

There. That's better. We've come this far and

>TIDBIT

"But wait," you're now thinking, after fully digesting the "Beloved of the Universe" line below. "That means I really *shouldn't* go get the spaceship from *Battlestar Galactica* tattooed across my back, because although *right now* I think it's the most awesome show ever, and I believe that it sums up my outlook and philosophy of life, maybe I'll feel differently ten years from now!" Indeed it does. That's not where I was going with this line, but I'm glad that you're gleaning bits of incidental wisdom from this book.

we've only used a handful of acronyms. But they're all friendly and familiar: CD, PC, even LP, for the love of Mike.

Take a deep breath, because it's time to knock you down and pummel you with terms such as MP3, AAC, VBR, and other key players in the Obfuscation Hit Parade.

When you convert CD tracks into music files, there are a few goals you want to achieve:

> **You want the tracks to sound great.** We shall refer to this as the "Duh" imperative.

> **You want files that don't take up a whole lot of space.** You have a limited amount of space on your iPod. If iTunes creates music files that are twice as big as they need to be, then your iPod will only hold half as many tracks as it could.

> **Ripping the hundreds of CDs in your collection is a huge pain in the butt and you don't want to have to do it twice.** A subtler point, this, but nonetheless it's something you ought to consider. You are a luminous being, one of the Beloveds of

the Universe, my child; your destiny is a long one and unless you're reading this book while driving a car, it's likely that you're going to be on this planet for many years to come.

So before you rip that Strokes CD, stop. Picture yourself six months from now, when you've bought a doohickey that lets you plug your iPod into your home stereo system; or a year from now, when you have a box that can wirelessly transmit music from your computer to any set of speakers anywhere in the house; or even next week, when you upgrade your cellphone to a gee-whiz Captain Kirk–style model that also plays music.

If you make the right choices today, you can create music files that will play on your iPod (good) and in iTunes (fab), but also nearly any sort of digital audio device or accessory that you might put your hands on in the next five or ten years.

So those are your goals.

Your happiness will come down to two different decisions:

> **File format.** You can't stick an 8-track into a CD drive, and with a similar sense of injustice not all devices and software can play every conceivable kind of music file. You want iTunes to use a file format that will work on the widest range of stuff.

> **Sound quality.** "Hey, this file sounds great" is a relative term. Bruce Vilanch humming the score from *The Magnificent Seven* would sound great, too, through those crappy earbuds you got free with the iPod. iTunes will always make certain sacrifices and trade-offs when converting a CD track into a music file, and often

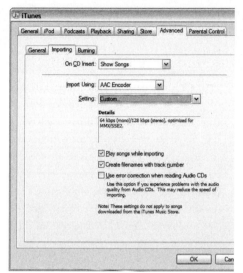

Figure 2-10
Modifying iTunes' default settings for ripping music.

Figure 2-11
iTunes' custom quality settings.

tosh). Select the Advanced tab, and then click the Importing tab (see Figure 2-10).

You set the file format through the Import Using pop-up menu. The default choice is AAC Encoder, and you ought to leave it as is.

Setting the sound quality is a slightly more complicated issue. There's a quickie menu labeled Setting but to get at the good stuff, you'll need to select Custom (see Figure 2-11).

Figure 2-11 shows three pop-up menus and two options. The only one you want to change is Stereo Bit Rate. By default, it's set at 128 Kbps. Change it to 192.

There it is: Rip all of your tracks to the AAC file format, using a sample rate of 192 kbps. I think that's the sweet spot that gives you terrific-sounding files that will play on a huge variety of devices but won't choke the capacity of your iPod.

Now let's snap on a pair of latex gloves and get into a more exhaustive explanation.

File Formats

iTunes can rip music into a buttload of formats:

> **MP3**. MP3 is the Band-Aid of digital music. It's a specific file format, but it's so popular and well-established that people often use the term "MP3 player" inter-

they're only apparent when you listen through a halfway decent set of home speakers.

And look, if you've ripped a large CD collection into iTunes, one of the first things you want to do is enjoy your music collection through your stereo. That's a bad time to discover that iTunes ripped all your tracks at the Bruce Vilanch setting.

The Settings I Think You Ought to Use

I'm betting that you're interested more in immediate gratification than technical detail. So let's cut straight to the tweaks I think you ought to make to iTunes' default music-ripping settings.

You can access these settings by choosing Preferences (found under the Edit menu in Windows, and the iTunes menu on a Macin-

changeably with "digital music player." And here you see the big advantage of MP3: practically every piece of software hardware everywhere — from a music app on a cell phone to desktop video software that lets you add music to your home videos — supports it.

> **AAC**. The Advanced Audio Coding format was what the technology industry created after digital music took off. It is the collective answer to the question "How can we make MP3 suck less?" Which is not to say that MP3 *sucks.* But it has a pretty shallow bag of tricks. AAC was developed a few years later and benefit from added knowledge and experience. As a result, AAC files sound better than MP3s and they take up less space.

> **AIFF** and **Apple Lossless**. I'm grouping these two together because they fill the same function: to create the most perfect

copy of the original CD track possible. Absolutely no sacrifices whatsoever will be made in the name of quality. This is a *good* thing if you're truly trying to archive your CDs permanently, creating a library of "masters" that you can burn duplicates from for years to come. This is a *bad* thing if you're truly trying to get more than, say, three songs to fit on your iPod at once. Sacrifices have to be made *somewhere,* and if you're not willing to sacrifice sound quality you're going to have to sacrifice file size to the max. Yes indeed, surely on this side of Jerusalem none suffer as you suffer. Just move on.

> **WAV**. The iPod supports this Windows format and so I suppose I'm begrudgingly required to report that yes, iTunes can rip to this format, too. But why on *earth* would you want to? WAV files are really big, they sound like a used coffee filter smells, and they're really only used by music producers who haven't bought new recording and mixing software in the past five years. Avoid.

It really comes down to just AAC and MP3, and MP3's sole advantage is that it's a bit more widely supported. But it's a negligible advantage and even that minor gap continues to narrow.

As a beloved industry columnist I have dozens of devices in my office that play digital music files, and the only thing I have that can play MP3's but not AAC files is a bizarre wristwatch music player that I got as a party favor.

Sound Quality

When we talk about sound quality, we're really talking about the bit rate that iTunes uses when it converts a track into a music file. A higher bit rate translates into more detail. A yellow "happy face" circle is a picture of your Uncle Sid ripped at the lowest possible bit rate. A moderate bit rate is a cartoon that looks like him. Higher, and it's a drawing that looks *exactly* like him. An image of Sid at the highest possible bit rate is a photo.

When you set the bit rate, you're telling iTunes, "Here's how much detail you can put into every second of the music file." As you might have guessed, though, when you increase the bit rate, all that extra detail amounts to a larger file. A track that was ripped with iTunes' default 128 Kbps bit rate won't sound as good as the same track ripped at 256 Kbps, but it'll take up half as much space on your iPod and leave room for more music.

Bit rates are frustrating because a drop in detail that one listener won't even notice will render a song unlistenable by another. And some songs are practically bulletproof. You can compress them down to nearly nothing without inflicting any damage on 'em.

I choose 192 Kbps because it's a good compromise. When you're using the AAC format, 128 Kbps is just fine for damned near every piece of music you throw at it. But if you rip a wide range of music styles (rock, folk, classical, progressive-house, etc.) and you listen to enough music, there will inevitably come a day when you're on the sofa, listening to (probably) a quiet piece played on acoustic instruments, and you'll realize that on *this* track and in *this* passage, a rich, thready violin sounds a bit ...well, I dunno... mushy? I'd come up with a better word for it but it didn't really last long

enough for me to focus in on it.

It's a problem of philosophy. You're going to be ripping all your music into iTunes. If you're unhappy with the sound quality later on, there's nothing you can do about it except rip it all over again at a higher setting. I have more than 500 gigabytes of storage on my Mac, and my iPod can hold more music than I can possibly listen to in a whole week. I'm willing to put up with slightly larger music files if it means that a violin always sounds like a violin.

One other Import setting that's worth mentioning: Variable Bit Rate (VBR) encoding. This is a keen idea in which instead of sticking with the same bit rate every single second, iTunes can dial it down whenever it feels that you won't be able to hear the difference. Five seconds of silence is five seconds of silence, whether it's being ripped at 256 Kbps or 60 Kbps, you know?

> **TIDBIT**
>
> Be prepared to be flexible. If you're ripping a book on tape, drop the bit rate down to 96 Kbps or lower. That drop could be the difference between a three-hour file fitting on your Nano or leaving it home. F. Murray Abraham has a fine voice, but you don't need to hear it at maximum quality to follow all the plot points of the latest Danielle Steele bodice-ripper. So before you rip that disc, open the Importing preferences and select Spoken Podcast from the Setting pop-up. Just remember to restore iTunes to its previous bit rate settings when you're done. And remember, these settings will apply to every track you rip.

Selecting this option can lead to smaller files. I leave it unchecked (which is also iTunes' default) because (a) *some* third-party music players don't like VBR encoding, and (b) although VBR encoding does indeed produce smaller files, it's not a dramatic enough improvement to risk Item A.

Consider me a member of the Sadder-but-Wiser Club. Last year, I added a humongous drive to my desktop and with it, I determined to rip every last track of every last CD I owned into iTunes — nearly 800 in all. Using that Import Songs and Eject setting I told you about earlier, I set up a laptop near the door to my office with a bin of CDs underneath. For a whole month, any time I crossed the threshold for any reason whatsoever, I would remove a "done" CD from the drive and replace it with a fresh one from the bin. At the end, the drive held a majestic 14,000 songs.

And then I had to do them all over again. Because I got this great little wireless box that streamed music files from iTunes anywhere in the house. But it didn't like the file format I chose and it gakked all over the VBR setting as well.

Which is why my personal library has been ripped even more conservatively than I've advised you guys. Maximum possible bit rate, maximum possible compatibility! I've ripped 14,000 songs twice now and if I have to do it a third time, dammit, it's going to be done by a trained monkey in a little uniform.

LPs, Tapes, and Whatnot

The Skim

Honest to God, I think the digital music industry is doing everything it can to encourage folks to try to convert their old LPs and tapes to MP3 and AAC files. It's brilliant marketing: The most foolproof way to send the average person to the iTunes store and buy their fourth — or was it the fifth? — lifetime copy of *Cheap Trick at Budokan* is to have them see what it's like to convert that 20-year-old cassette to MP3 or AAC tracks on their own.

There is confusion. There is frustration. There is probably also a certain amount of crying. And then, dear reader, there is a Moment of Clarity in which you realize that this goal is in opposition to the divine will of the Universe. From there, an expletive is uttered, a credit card is taken out of a wallet, and an online download is purchased.

Welcome to the wonderful world of analog-to-digital. It's a sketchy process, filled with trial and error and low expectations. When you convert a CD, it's a completely hands-off process and the result is a flawless digital music file. When you convert an LP, it's an intensely fiddly and interactive operation — and it's practically a creative process in and of itself.

MANAGING EXPECTATIONS

When you contemplate that stack of records, your goals should be Apollo 11 in scale. You'll get the astronauts there and you'll get them back alive. You'll emerge from the adventure with a cool box of moon rocks and some solid science and nobody can ever challenge your assertion that Yes, I Did That.

>TIDBIT

I'm not kidding about having given up on converting commercial albums to digital. All the screen images in this chapter show me converting Paul Shaffer's long-out-of-print first album *Coast to Coast* — you know, he's David Letterman's bandleader — to iTunes-studly files. By the time I was finished with this chapter, I'd probably devoted about a full week to recording, polishing, and importing all eleven tracks.

So am I now enjoying these tracks on my iPod? Nope. Because on Day Two, I used the Best Technique Ever for converting out-of-print albums: I just went to Amazon.com. If an album is out of print, the store will hook you up with an independent store that can sell you a used copy. It's nearly twenty years old but it was indeed released on CD, and inside of five minutes I'd chosen a "like new" copy from the list of 21 available sellers.

The cost: a mere $8.30, including shipping. Best of all, I have an absolutely *perfect* copy of the extended "Late Night" theme — and I ripped it in just under forty seconds.

The lesson: *Don't be a hero.* I'm a professional. I get paid to do this.

What you *won't* wind up with is a profitable, self-sustaining 800-person permanent moon colony where Will Smith, the colony's military governor, returns after two months of off-planet R&R and lands himself in the middle of a deadly conspiracy, plus two hours of action and adventure that climaxes in a ten-minute lunar buggy chase in one-sixth Earth gravity.

Nope. Instead, you'll have audio files that sound nearly as good as the original.

Even if these audio files are perfect — and, as you will see, that might not even be possible — they'll dramatically underscore the limitations of LPs and cassettes as audio formats.

You say the digital file has an annoying background hiss, and lacks a certain brightness and clarity? Well, congratulations: You've produced an MP3 that's *exactly* as good as the original tape.

To bring it up to the Apple iTunes store's quality requires not only a good tape/record player and expensive, "prosumer" recording software, but a good ear and experience in producing audio … or a $100 utility and a bit of patience. And even then, luck needs to be on your side.

Over the past few years, I've tried nearly every combination of commercial hardware and software for converting old recordings to digital.

And the experience has left me convinced that the only recordings that are truly worth all this effort are the ones that are never, ever going to be released on CD. Like tapes of family events, or conference and class lectures, or music that was simply lucky to ever win a commercial release in te first place.

WHAT TO RECORD FROM

The good news about converting those old recordings is that the basic techniques can be used with any piece of audio equipment. If it has line-level audio outputs or a headphone jack, your computer can capture the noise it squirts out.

But there are notes and gotchas for nearly everything. And there might be a few devices that you haven't thought of.

Tape Players

Any player will do. A boom box, a component deck … if you can't find one in the house, just head on over to the drugstore and plop down ten bucks for a Walkman. It's all good.

If you're converting a commercially produced tape, you'll want a player with Dolby noise reduction. It's such an immediate and dramatic improvement over a player with no noise reduction that if you have a big pile of tapes to convert, it's actually worth going out and buying one.

Whichever way you go, try to get a player with some form of variable output. The boom box and the Walkman will have some sort of volume control for its headphone jack, but not all component decks have that important knob.

Being able to control the volume on the player removes about thirty minutes' worth of fiddling with settings on the software side of things.

A player with line-level outputs is also optimal. That's a rare thing to find on a boom box and downright dodo-like on a Walkman.

Turntables

Record players are a special sort of beastie. Those of you who are old enough to remember what the first President Bush's voice sounded like will wax nostalgic about amps and tuners that had a special "Phono" input.

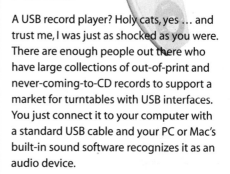

▶TIDBIT

A USB record player? Holy cats, yes … and trust me, I was just as shocked as you were. There are enough people out there who have large collections of out-of-print and never-coming-to-CD records to support a market for turntables with USB interfaces. You just connect it to your computer with a standard USB cable and your PC or Mac's built-in sound software recognizes it as an audio device.

I'm tempted to be unkind. Everyone I know who's *that* into vinyl sees digital audio as the spawn of the Cloven-Hooved One. I imagine that the only reason why such a person would want a turntable with a USB interface is to make a point of how they never, ever use it. "A cartridge needle added air and dimension around a recording; there's a certain warmth to the sound field that, sadly, no computer can reproduce" … hell, I'm sure you've been cornered by one of these types before. You know how the spiel goes.

Nonetheless: Ion Audio's iTTUSB turntable (www.ionaudio.com) is one of the three or four players pursuing this sort of divine lunacy, and it seems to deliver the goods. And I shouldn't mock. I suppose if none of my Bob Newhart albums were ever put on CD, a turntable like this would be a no-brainer. It's a question of Want.

The sound that a record player spits out is far weaker than the standard "line out" audio level, and it needs its own special pre-amp. In other words, the Phono input.

So no, it doesn't matter that your record player has standard RCA audio output connectors. In general, you can't plug it straight into your computer and expect happy results. One answer is to plug it into your home-audio amp/tuner and hook up the tuner's line-out to your PC or Mac.

Another is to rummage through the house for *any* audio device that has a pre-amp in it. I have a little microphone pre-amp box that I normally use for such things. (In the interests of brutal honesty, I'll go ahead and tell you that it is in fact a karaoke amp. I know, you're shocked.)

But many boom boxes, DJ mixers, and the like contain a pre-amp circuit. These things might not be *designed* for boosting a record player's outputs to line levels, but they get the job done.

Radio Shack also offers a bunch of pre-amps that'll fit the bill. Amongst this menagerie is a little $25 (at this writing) box that's specifically designed for record players.

CD Players

CD players? Yes: CD players. And yes, I'm aware that you can just pop a CD right into your computer and iTunes will rip the tracks toot sweet. I wrote a whole chapter on that, in fact. Have you been skipping around? You've been skipping around, clearly.

I just want you to remember that the techniques in this chapter can be used to turn any analog audio into digital files. So if some

new, harebrained scheme for copy-preventing CDs should ever turn up, and if the classic workaround (hold down the Shift key while you insert the disc) doesn't work around it, you can always rip the tracks the old-fashioned way: by connecting the audio outputs of your CD player to your computer.

This is also something to fall back on if the CD is so scratched that iTunes can't deal with it, or if it has some sort of weird formatting that prevents iTunes from recognizing it as an audio CD.

Digital Music Players

And the same sort of thing works for the music that's locked up on a digital music player. Say, for instance, that you bought a whole bunch of music downloads from Microsoft/MTV's Urge service, which is 100 percent incompatible with the iPod. One way to import those tracks into iTunes would be to burn them onto a standard audio disc and then rip the disc. But if worst comes to worst, just plug an audio cable into the player's headphone jack.

Live Music/Voice

Outputs from microphones and live instruments can be recorded "live" on your PC or Mac just as easily as anything else. But although it might *seem* like all you'll need to do is go down to Radio Shack and pick up a little adapter that can convert the porky ¼-inch cable that you normally use with your (guitar, microphone, zaftenblønflöte) into something that your computer can deal with, them's not the case. You're probably going to need a pre-amp.

Better still, you ought to buy a box that's

specifically designed for adapting musical instruments to desktop recording. Head on over to M-Audio (www.m-audio.com). The folks there have boxes for guitars, boxes for XLR microphones, boxes for that weird pogo stick-like percussion instrument from *Mary Poppins,* ... the works. These interfaces plug into your computer's USB port, which means that they're (collectively) a piece of cake to work with.

If you're interested in making a live, spoken-word recording and you're willing to settle for middlin'-quality audio, just buy any USB headset available at your local office megastore.

MAKING THE HOOKUP

Connecting an audio component to your computer isn't the black art that it used to be. Most desktops and notebooks actually come with an audio input built-in.

But you're forgetting that your computer is a colossal tease. Recall the image that the manufacturer uses in their ads: The picture shows a functional computer and a well-rested user who isn't beating the holy hell out of it with a five-iron.

Your computer's built-in audio was designed for audio chat. It's a microphone input, which means that if you plug any $8 microphone or $15 headset into it, the friend or relative at the other end of the conversation will hear you say how much you loved the pair of sensible brown slacks she sent you for Christmas. But the quality isn't high enough that she'll catch the sarcastic tone in your voice.

On top of that, it's not a line-level input, which means that at worst, your desktop

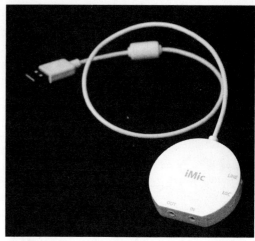

Figure 3-1
Griffin's iMic: your cheap passport to quality recording

audio software won't be able to record a thing from it and, at worst, you'll get audio that's been wracked by distortion and noise that would be unacceptable even to Yngwie Malmsteen.

Mind you, some software can try and work its way around the problem. But none of the apps I've tried have produced even mediocre results. Instead, you ought to go out and buy Griffin Technology's iMic (www.griffintech. com), as seen in Figure 3-1.

The iMic is adorably cheap at about $40 and is practically an industry standard for home recording. It just sports a microphone jack and a headphone jack, but that's all that most people really need; it interfaces a legion of old-school analog audio stuff to your computer's USB port.

The key for our purposes is the little switch that allows you to select between Microphone and Line level for the audio input. Switch it to Line level, and your computer

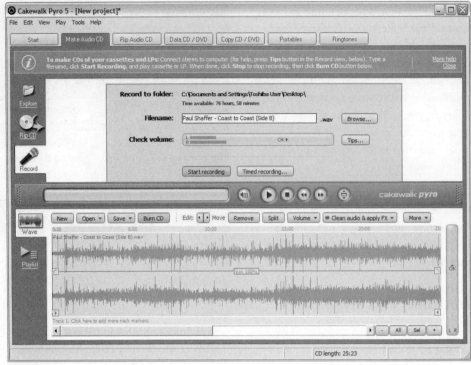

Figure 3-2
Pyro: simple, straightforward sound

and any standard audio component with line output will get along like peas and carrots.

If you don't mind spending some extra scratch, Applied Research and Technology has a $100 box dubbed the ART USB Phono Plus (check it out at www.artproaudio.com).

Like the iMic, it converts analog audio to USB, but the super-upgrade to owning this box is the wide range of connections. It has component-style RCA plugs (so you don't need any sort of converter cable, as you do with the iMic), its own gain control, its own little level LEDs so you can fine-tune the sound level before it even reaches your computer, … and even its own pre-amp to elevate phono-level audio to the proper standard.

AUDIO RECORDING SOFTWARE

Gosh, we're how many pages into this chapter already and we've yet to record diddley-squat. No, let me correct myself: That's *precisely* how much audio we've recorded.

Well, perhaps I should now stop and encourage you that *philosophically,* at least, duplicating an LP, tape, or what-have-you into a digital music file is no different from duping it from one tape deck to another. Push Play on the player. Push Record on the recording device. Push Stop when the music's over.

But it's a piece of software that'll be handling the recording chores. And from the point of view of someone who just wants their Procul Harum live concert bootleg tape on their iPod, there are way too many choices. A few highlights, among the commercial apps available:

Pyro

Pyro — a PC-only app from Cakewalk (www.cakewalk.com) — is one of my two favorite "Convert LPs and tapes to digital audio" apps. It's not designed to handle any and every sort of recording project; it's designed for one purpose only, and the result is a highly streamlined app and a simple workflow (see Figure 3-2).

It also scores points for being affordable (about $40), having sophisticated — if slightly tricky — tools for automatically removing noise and scratches from the recording, and including a feature for capturing any audio that's currently moving through your PC's speakers, from any source.

And you can tell that it was produced by the same company which makes pro-level recording software: It has some exceptionally fine editing features. None of them will be immediately useful for your tape-to-iPod project, but if you ever find yourself needing to manipulate your audio before sending it to your iTunes library, they'll be waiting for you in your toolbox.

Audio Cleaning Lab

The other swell end-to-end audio app, the PC-only Audio Cleaning Lab from Magix Entertainment (www.magix.net), costs about the same as Pyro. But it's a very different sort of app. It's far, far more aggressive in helping you create precisely the sort of recording you want; which means that whereas Pyro gives

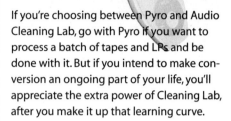

> **TIP**
>
> If you're choosing between Pyro and Audio Cleaning Lab, go with Pyro if you want to process a batch of tapes and LPs and be done with it. But if you intend to make conversion an ongoing part of your life, you'll appreciate the extra power of Cleaning Lab, after you make it up that learning curve.

you simplicity and a straightforward process, Audio Cleaning Lab was an app that I really hated for the first few days and then grew to appreciate.

One further quibble: It's not the most *stable* app in the world. When I installed it on a middle-of-the-road desktop, it tended to freeze once during every couple of sessions. But when I moved it to a fast, megamemory, up-to-date PC, it settled down.

GarageBand

Honestly, if you're using a Mac, why *wouldn't* you use the Mac-only GarageBand? Part of Apple's iLife suite, it's practically a pro-level tool, and if you bought a Mac any time in the past few years, it came free on your hard drive.

Good points, and well-made. But I don't like using GarageBand for this sort of thing. It's a real memory hog.

That's not a problem when you're recording a five-minute song or even a thirty-minute podcast, but it can't really deal with album– or lecture-length recordings without inflicting unnecessary wear and tear on your will to live — unless you're blessed with (a) an awesomely powerful Mac or (b) one of those unsinkable Doris Day–type spirits. Or

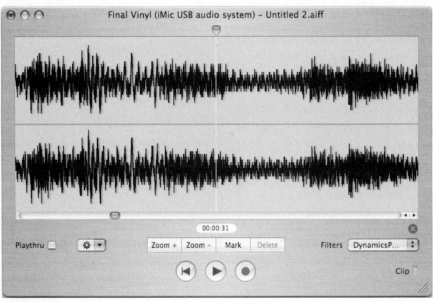

perhaps a Lindsay Lohan–type spirit from her *The Parent Trap* days. You know, before she started making the tabloids.

Even if you own a new, hyper-performance Mac, GarageBand offers no specific help for this purpose. It's much harder to transform an LP in GarageBand than it is most free and simple apps. Such as …

Final Vinyl

Griffin's iMic audio interface — you know, the one I suggested that you go out and buy — comes with a downloadable Mac-only extra: the Final Vinyl audio recording app, which will only work if there's an iMic plugged in.

For transmogrifying LPs and cassettes, it's everything that GarageBand isn't. One simple window (see Figure 3-3). Audio goes in, audio files go out. It's easy to see what sort of audio levels you're getting, and to adjust them accordingly. And it's also easy to chop up forty-seven minutes of straight recording into eleven music tracks.

The Winner: Audacity

There y'go: a whole bunch of solid, feature-packed audio apps. And now I'm going to actually *recommend* something else entirely:

Figure 3-3
Final Vinyl: free, no-frills, no-fuss sound recording for Mac

a famous and free audio app by the name of Audacity.

Download a copy from www.audacity. sourceforge.net. The same app is available for both Windows and the Mac OS.

So here's why I'm going with this app and not the others:

> **It's a wonderful app**. First and foremost, it's a powerful, yet simple, tool for recording and editing audio.

> **It's free, free, free**. Not "Free, if you buy a Mac or an iMic" or "Free as a limited demo app." Free as in "You get the whole app with all its features intact and you never have to pay a dime to anybody."

> **It's a popular standard**. Most people who have any need for recording start off with Audacity, and oftentimes they never see a need to switch to anything else. It's suited to newbies making their first podcast and it's also useful for the pros.

> **It's egalitarian**. On a selfish note … it's the only really decent audio-recording app that works on both Macs and PCs. I warily eye the little number at the lower corner of my word-processing window and can only speculate as to how big this chapter would become if I actually wound up writing two nearly identical sections detailing the proper usage of two separate apps. I am confident that you'd happily lay down $50 for a special two-volume slipcase edition of this book. But then again, today is the day when the kid comes and cuts my grass and there are a *lot* of gasoline exhaust fumes wafting through my open window at the moment.

WE ACTUALLY RECORD SOMETHING

Okay, enough stalling. Let's lay down some tracks. In this example, we'll be converting a cassette, but the principles are the same no matter what sort of audio component you're working with.

Setting up Your Gear

First, we'll have to plug everything in, assuming that you don't have an intern that handles that stuff for you. If you're using an iMic, the component goes into the In jack of the iMic, and the iMic goes into any available USB port. If you're throwing caution to the wind and using your computer's built-in audio input, run the cable straight in, after closing your eyes and commending your soul to God.

Don't be ashamed if you wind up having to race down to Radio Shack before it closes because you need to plug two ¼-inch mono whatsits into an ⅛-inch stereo thingy. It happens to the best of us.

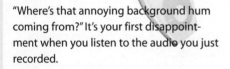

▶TIDBIT

"But wait," you're now thinking, after fully digesting the "Beloved of the Universe" line below. "That means I really *shouldn't* go get the spaceship from *Battlestar Galactica* tattooed across my back, because although *right now* I think it's the most awesome show ever, and I believe that it sums up my outlook and philosophy of life, maybe I'll feel differently ten years from now!" Indeed it does. That's not where I was going with this line, but I'm glad that you're gleaning bits of incidental wisdom from this book.

▶TIP

"Where's that annoying background hum coming from?" It's your first disappointment when you listen to the audio you just recorded.

Nine times out of ten (actually, let me hedge my bets and call it five times out of seven), the source of your misery is the AC power driving both the playback device and your computer. I've had long discussions with audio and electrical engineers about this, and I think when they explained the specifics of the problem to me they had the same motivations as a fighter pilot has when he's asked to take a celebrity or reporter up in his jet. Outwardly, you're supposed to be helping but, privately, the goal is to make your subject as ill as possible.

So I can't condense The True Reasons Why down into a paragraph. Nonetheless I happily report that you can eliminate it by making sure that the tape deck and your computer are both plugged into the same power strip.

And if you're using some form of external sound input device, check to make sure you've set its switches properly.

The iMic has a slider switch that allows you to choose between mic-level and line-level input. Make sure it's in the Line position.

Although this whole project involves applications and drivers and signal processors and whatnot, don't forget the important role that simple cleanliness plays towards getting a nice, clean recording. For many of you, this will be the first time your turntable has been out of the closet since (ironically) George Michael had a hit record.

Check the connectors at the back of the component. If the metal on the contacts is dirty or even dull, clean them until they're shiny. A "dry" cleaner like a fine-grit emory board or a rough cloth is best. Clean the heads of your tape player, put a new needle in the turntable, and stick a crowbar in your wallet and pop six bucks for a freakin' LP cleaning tool.

The Master Lesson of all this is that any noise and any distortion that *can* be removed before your computer sees it *should* be removed.

There *is* some slick software for cleaning up audio — we'll be looking at these later in the chapter — but none of them work without having to suffer some compromise. Ninety seconds with a cleaning brush beats three hours of effort with $60 worth of software.

Finally, plug a pair of headphones into your computer. Not into the playback device: into the computer. To properly set the recording levels, we're going to need to hear exactly what your computer is hearing.

▶TIP

You can avoid a lot of trouble — and the never-pleasant realization that you're an idiot — by taking the playback device and the recording out for a test-listen before you even hook it up to your computer. More than once I've been frustrated by software that kept screwing up and refused to find a correct, distortion-free sound level. There was much shouting and a little bit of spitting and then I plugged my headphones straight into the tape deck and discovered that the awfulness was the result of a screwed-up tape player, not a bad piece of software.

It's possible that you're going to have to go out and buy a new tape player or a new turntable. If noisy, muted audio is coming out of the component, no software wizardry is going to remove it.

Choosing and Preparing an Audio Source

You have the component hooked up to your PC or Mac. Both Windows and the Mac OS are slick enough to manage multiple sound inputs and outputs, so your next step is to make sure that your computer is going to be listening at the right sound hole, so to speak.

The operating system also allows you to adjust the sensitivity of the input device. By adjusting a "master" volume control downward, you can limit the loudness of the sound that all your sound apps see. You'll want to make sure that this level is set to the maximum.

Normally, when you set a volume control to the max, it's a bad thing: You introduce all sorts of distortion, and most of the highs and

Figure 3-4

Selecting an audio input device in Windows

lows of the sound are clipped off. But here, you're telling the operating system, "Please don't artificially dampen the sound levels."

Chiefly, you're removing at least one of the variables from the recording process. Here we go:

In Windows:

1. Choose Start ➪ Control Panel ➪ Sounds and Audio Devices (in the standard Windows XP interface) or Start ➪ Settings ➪ Control Panel ➪ Sounds and Audio Devices (in the classic Windows XP/2000 interface).

2. Click the Audio tab of the Sounds and Audio Devices Properties window (see Figure 3-4).

3. Select the correct input device from the pop-up list in the Sound Recording section. Your PC's built-in microphone connector — and even its built-in microphone, if it has one — probably

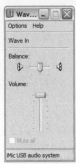

Figure 3-5
Telling Windows to keep
its mitts off your sound
input volume

won't be labeled anything obvious, like (oh, I dunno) "Built-In Microphone." Instead, Windows tends to use the name of the software driver that establishes the connection.

4. Adjust the volume of the input to 100 percent.

5. Click the Volume button under the name of your sound-input device. You'll see a little adjustment window as in Figure 3-5.

6. Move the Volume slider all the way to the top, and then click the adjustment window's Close button to return to the Sounds and Audio Devices Properties window.

7. Click OK when done. (Click Apply to make the above changes but stay in the window to make further changes.)

On a Macintosh:

1. Choose ♦ ➪ System Preferences ➪ Sound.

2. Click the Input tab of the Sound Prefer-

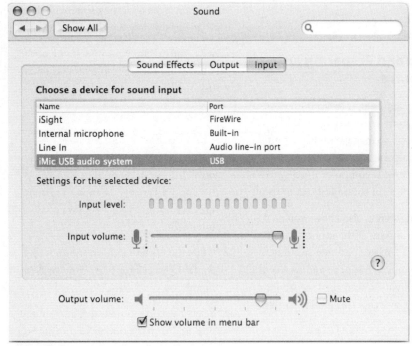

Figure 3-6
Pointing your Mac at your sound-input thingamabob

ences window (see Figure 3-6).

3. Select the correct sound input device from the list.

4. Slide the Input Volume control all the way to the right for 100 percent.

5. Close the Sound Preferences window.

Nearly all computers, both PC and Mac, automatically select the headphone jack for output when headphones are plugged in. But if at some point in the recording process you can't hear a thing, you might have to go on back to these sound-device settings and manually choose the headphone jack as the default output device.

Launch Your Recording App and Adjust Sound Levels

Launch Audacity. The apps' controls rearrange themselves to make best use of its window's real estate, but Figure 3-7 shows

you a typical arrangement.

From top to bottom, you see:

> A row of selection, playback, and recording buttons.

> A row showing you Audacity's "live" sound-out and sound-in meters. In Figure 3-7 the meters are empty, because we're not playing anything yet.

> A row with two sliders for manual control of the aforementioned levels.

> A row of tools for editing a recording

> And finally a big section showing you the waveform of the sound you've just recorded. Here it's empty, for reasons that will immediately occur to you.

You are about to engage in what is hands-down the most annoying and bothersome part of the process: getting the sound level just right. If you have it set too high, the recording will be full of distortion; the "extremes" of the sound range will be crushed against the upper and lower limits of your sound hardware's capabilities. Set it too low, and the unavoidable noise of your playback deck will start to overwhelm the audio.

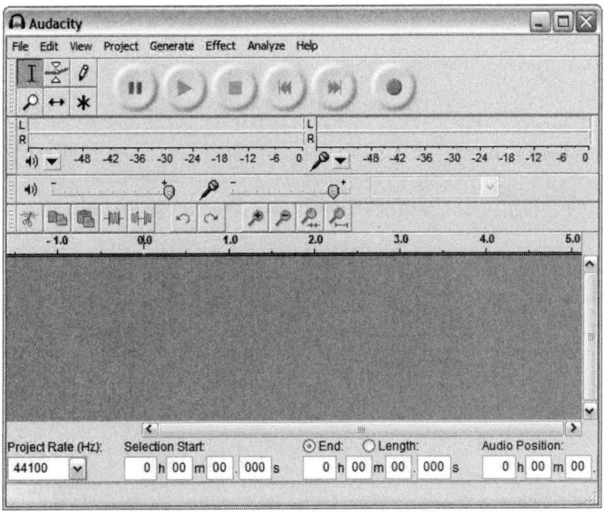

A certain amount of hard liquor is called for. You'll see the wisdom of this later. No, don't be proud: Go right ahead and get half in the bag before you even touch a single knob or move your mouse a single centimeter unless you're

Figure 3-7
Audacity, doin' nothin'

Figure 3-8
Activating the input monitor

Figure 3-9
The power meter: live and in action

underage, or otherwise have a reason why drinking would be a Bad Thing.

(Continuing.)

Start off by clicking the little pop-up menu next to the microphone icon. Choose Start Monitoring from the pop-up (see Figure 3-8). The meter will come alive, listening attentively to the incoming audio and presenting you with a dazzling animated display of Christopher Cross's mellow-gold audio fury. Clicking the empty sound-in meter will also turn on monitoring.

Start playback on the tape deck and don your headphones. *Carefully*. Be warned that the sound level might be way, way too loud.

Deep breath. Take another slug of that vodka-and-cranberry-juice. Time to start twiddling knobs.

First, we're going to adjust the Output (or Volume) knob on the playback device. Start it at zero, listen carefully, and edge the knob up, up, up. When you start to hear distortion (that grating, clipped-off mess that screams "Too Damned Loud!"), back off some.

That's where you want to keep your output device set. Where your tape deck (or boom box, or stereo receiver, or pocket audio device) is concerned, a Loud signal is a Strong signal … so long as it's not so loud that the sound quality starts to crack and fray.

Once you've set that control, forget that it exists. Forget it! It's done, in the past, like that $1,500 that you borrowed from your sister three years ago to go to St. Bart's. It's time to move on to the recording levels in Audacity.

Now, take a look at the red input level meter (see Figure 3-9). Note that it's marked in numbers. Zero represents the very loudest that a sound can be and still be recorded cleanly. Any sound that pulses off to the right beyond 0 is insignificant … which is why the meter doesn't go any higher than that.

What we want to do is play a game of chicken between that input meter and that number 0. We want to adjust Audacity's input-level slider so the red level meter pulses *as close to zero as possible* without going beyond it.

I reiterate: Loud = Strong, meaning that the maximum amount of "information" about the sound is being collected by the hardware. Loud is Good, until it gets *Too* Loud, and information is thrown away instead.

Audacity offers two handy little clues to tell us how we're doing. Notice that both the Left and the Right meter have two little extra blips at the far right.

> The blue one (farthest to the right, in Figure 3-9) shows you the loudest sound the meter has registered since you turned on the monitor.

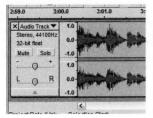

Figure 3-10
Congratulations: It's a recording.

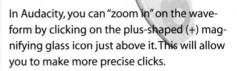

> The red one (to the left) shows you the loudest *"recent"* sound (for lack of a better word).

Remember what we've done to the playback device and your computer's master sound settings: We have the tape deck as loud as it can possibly go without distorting, and we've told the computer not to limit the sound one bit. It's likely that after a few moments, you'll spike the meter: Both blue pips will smash at the 0 mark, indicating that it's too loud for the software to record clear, useful audio.

So your mission is this: With a nervous eye but a steady hand, adjust Audacity's Input Volume slider so that the *red* pip (the "bursts" of loudness) are as close to zero as possible, without *ever* putting the blue pip in the zero position.

(Sounds like a video game — and maybe you should think of it that way. Otherwise, my advice about the alcohol doesn't seem so silly *now*, does it?)

When you have the levels where you want them, rewind the song or recording to the beginning, click Audacity's Record button, and start playback.

Keep an eye on the meters; if the blue blip hits zero, it's game over. Just like in the movie *Apollo 13*, when Gary Sinese was in the Apollo simulator trying to figure out how the marooned astronauts could restart the command module on the limited power avail-

able, and if the power meter surged past 12, that means that they'd all die? It's like that, only with weaker box-office potential.

Click Stop when the thing you're recording is done. A waveform representing your recording will appear in the window (see Figure 3-10).

Scrolling through the waveform from start to finish, I can see that I have a nice, clean recording. The gray "corridor" that each of the Left and Right waveforms are walking through represent the limits of the recording hardware; the waveform often gets very, very *close* to bumping into the walls, but it never does, and even the quiet parts of the song are nice and thick … which means that when I play this back, I'll be hearing the music, not the background hiss of the tape.

Hooray! I've recorded one of the eleven songs on this tape!

I celebrate the victory by playing it back, using Audacity's friendly and familiar audio-playback buttons.

Now I just have to do it ten more times.

Yes, each track has its own properties and idiosyncrasies. You can get away with a "set it and forget it" approach if you're transferring a lecture tape, but if its music, the only way to get consistent results is to treat each track like a separate recording project.

This is why I'm not encouraging you to play through the whole tape or LP and then chop the huge recording down into tracks. Yes, processing each song separately is more work. But the whole "convert an old recording to digital" task is a minor ordeal no matter what approach you use. Why not suffer a *little* more to get *much* better recordings?

What Software *Can't* Do For You

In X years of making my own recordings and the past few months of acquiring and testing just about every piece of hardware and software available, I have committed to some conclusions about what even the best consumer-oriented "convert LPs and tapes to digital files" apps can't do … no matter what it says on the box:

> **It can't set the proper recording level automatically**. It can give you lots of visual tools to help you set it yourself, but when you have it choose a setting on its own the results are almost always wrong. And they're *never* as good as what you'd get if you played the song through once with an eye on the input meter and a hand on the input-level control.

> **It can't automatically sense the start and end of songs to create an individual audio file for every track**. This isn't a complicated trick: You give the app a certain threshold — two seconds of silence, say — and every time the software encounters that gap, it starts a new sound file. But it almost never works properly. If it's a poor recording, even the silences won't be silent. And it's far from unheard of for a song to include a quiet bit. Even if

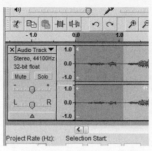

Figure 3-11
Trimming the start of a track

it *does* work properly, you're going to have to sit and listen through the entire recording to verify that there weren't any mistakes. I'd *much* rather put that time into recording it track by track, particularly since I'm going to have to adjust recording levels for each song separately anyway.

> **It absolutely can't remove all the hiss, pop, clicks, and other detritus**. There's software that can greatly *reduce* those artifacts, but it's a hands-on process and you might not truly like the results. Many people would prefer an "organic" problem with the sound than one that was imposed by software and which sounds "artificial."

But as we'll see in a little bit, "clean-up" software has its place and is worth a peek.

Cleaning and Saving

Before we import the new track into iTunes, we're going to want to clean it up a little. We can clean it up a *lot* with the help of some extra software, but let's stick to "Quick and effective and free, within Audacity" for now.

Trimming the Start and End

There's probably some noise at the start of the recording, and we let the tape roll at the end until the start of the next song. So let's fix that.

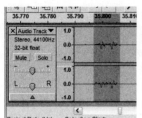

Figure 3-12
Pop: the audio
nastiness, not
the friendly
breakfast-
cereal elf

Figure 3-11 shows you the start of the track. You can see (and hear) a few "blobs" of noise before the song begins.

Don't take my word for it: Click your mouse inside that straight-line gap of silence, and then click the Play button. See? Audacity starts playback from the clicked position. That's precisely where I want my song to begin.

To cut everything that comes before that little blip of silence:

1. Drag your mouse from the start of the actual song to the start of the recording … all the way to the 0 Seconds mark in the wavelength window.

2. Hit the Delete key on your keyboard, or choose Edit ⇨ Cut.

Trimming the end of the track works the same way. You *might* want to be a little bit more careful, though; if the song fades out at the end, the cutoff might be abrupt. So consider using Audacity's built-in Fade Out effect:

1. Listen closely and try to work out the moment when the song finishes its fade out. Delete everything from that point to the end of the track.

2. Choose a point about halfway through the song's natural fade-out. Select from that point to the new end of the track.

3. Choose Effect ⇨ Fade Out.

Audacity fades the song's volume from 10 percent at the start of the selection to absolute silence at the end. This will blend the end of the track nicely.

Eliminating Pops
If the clicking and popping only occurs in a few annoying spots, you can smooth them out by targeting and eliminating them manually. Figure 3-12 show you one such nasty pop.

I've used Audacity's zoom-in magnifier so that I could select the pop, the whole pop, and nothing but the pop. Just to give you an idea of how far we've zoomed in, that's about one-hundredth of a second we've selected. *Just* enough to ruin a silent quarter-second passage of the tune.

We could simply cut the offending pop, but it's usually a better idea to just *silence* it instead.

1. Select the hated enemy of peace and smooth music.

2. Choose Generate ⇨ Silence. Audacity will toss up a little window asking how much silence you want to generate.

3. Click OK and the app will simply replace the selected sound with flat-lined deadness. The pop, he dies.

Removing Background Noise
Here's the most popular, front-of-the-box-in-big-red-letters feature of most consumer recording utilities: Automatically remove all the scratches, all the hum, all the background noise, and make this simple little track sound CD-perfect.

Lies. *Lies!!!*

Oh, wait: we're talking about user expectations.

Unrealistic user expectations. *Unrealistic user expectations!!!*

(Dang. Pointing and yelling that just isn't as satisfying.)

Algorithms that successfully and flawlessly remove unwanted noise from recordings rely on mud tainted with the blood of the impure, fingernails from a certain species of corpse, and a whole bunch of dark promises that you one day hope to worm out of. So naturally, this software is in the exclusive hands of the NSA and related agencies.

The ones that we're left with are quite decent but they have their limitations. Mathematically, digital audio is one mixed-together doughy mass of numbers, and it's simply not possible to cleanly extract one sound from the rest. At best, you can tell a piece of software "See this sound that I've selected? Please remove all sounds from this recording that sort of sound like it."

Which will do away with the original noise, mostly. But it'll

Figure 3-13

Removing noise right from within Audacity

also zap little molecules of sound from the actual music. Not enough that "Hey, Jude" sounds like "Institutionalized," but enough that it suddenly sounds like a poor recording of "Hey, Jude."

Audacity has a handy built-in tool that works

Figure 3-14

SoundSoap: the last word in clean audio

about as well as most of the others. To use it most effectively, you're going to need a section of the recording that's *supposed* to be silent, but instead is filled with hiss and humm and crackling and other evidence that the Universe doesn't really want you to replay that four-hour Jerry Garcia live guitar solo. Here's what the noise sounds like *all by itself.* Give this snippet to Audacity's Noise Removal tool and it'll try its level best to remove it from the background of the whole recording:

1. Select a passage of "noisy silence" in your track. A couple of seconds' worth should do. If you can't find that much in the track, it's probably worthwhile to rack up your tape (or LP or whatever) again and record a silent section, just to get a snippet of isolated background noise. (Audacity doesn't care if the noise sample and the track to be cleaned-up aren't part of the same file.)

2. Choose Effect ➪ Noise Removal. You'll see the Noise Removal window that looks startlingly like Figure 3-13.

3. Click the Get Noise Profile button. Audacity will load in the sample and remember it for later. Click OK to dismiss the window.

4. Once you're back in the track's editing window, select the entire track (or just the section that you'd like to have de-noise-ified) and bring up the Noise Removal window again. When it comes to eliminating noise, Audacity can be as aggressive or as timid as you want. At one extreme, you'll barely be able to tell that it's done anything at all. At the other … it's clear that Something Very, Very

▸TIDBIT

Another one of the big reasons why I chose Audacity as my recommended audio-recording app was because the biggest boasts of its commercial competitors were their abilities to take crackly tapes and LPs and turn them into clean, crisp digital sound. For one, they didn't really do a better job of that than (free, free, free) Audacity. For another, if you *really* want the best possible digital audio files, you want a fantastic single-purpose, $99 utility from Bias called SoundSoap (www.bias-inc.com). A free recording app plus a $99 cleaning utility kicks the butt of any $40 standalone all-in-one utility.

I say without exaggeration (well, just a little) that SoundSoap is the nuclear missile of its category. It's for home audio users but it's also for folks producing professional recordings, and after you've mastered its knobs, sliders, and buttons (see Figure 3-14), its improvements can be downright stunning. Just the other day, I came home with twenty minutes of live audio for which I didn't have high hopes. I recorded it on a little pocket player with a $25 Radio Shack microphone, but after just ten minutes with SoundSoap it sounded like it had been recorded poorly in a professional studio.

That's intended as a compliment, by the way. Nothing can take a casual recording made in a noisy hall on cheap equipment and make it sound like a Stephen Fry book-on-tape, but the fact that SoundSoap can take the slapdash and amateur and make it into an absolutely clean and credible recording is cause for applause.

Wrong has happened to this music.

5. Click Noise Removal's Preview button. Audacity will start to play the track with

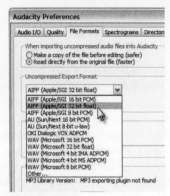

Figure 3-15
Enabling AIFF export in Audacity.

Figure 3-16
Filling in the blanks on this track

the requested clean-up in place. As you listen to the preview, keep tweaking the intensity slider until you find a happy medium between terminating noise with extreme prejudice and making sure that no innocent bystanders get swept up in the dragnet.

6. When you like what you hear, click OK. A progress bar will appear as Audacity grinds its way through the track, doing your bidding.

We appear to be done with this track. Now all we need to do is export it into a format that iTunes can handle.

The best format for an iTunes import is uncompressed AIFF. Audacity supports the format but not until you go into the app's Preferences and choose it as the default format for uncompressed audio.

1. In Windows, choose Edit ⇨ Preferences. On the Mac, choose File ⇨ Preferences.

2. Click the File Formats tab of the Preferences window (see Figure 3-15).

3. Choose AIFF (Apple/SGI 16 bit PCM) from the Uncompressed Export Format pop-up list and then click OK.

You won't have to do this again. To save the track as an AIFF file, just choose File ⇨ Export as AIFF and choose a location for the saved file.

IMPORTING INTO ITUNES

We have a bunch of AIFF files. And although we can import them into iTunes without further ado, there is still a bit to do after they've been added to the library.

Converting AIFFs to Compressed Audio Files

I think Paul Shaffer is a wonderful musician and a fantastic bandleader — honestly — but the original *Late Night with David Letterman* theme isn't worth 38.3 megabytes of my iPod's capacity. So I want to convert it into the default compressed file format that I've already chosen in iTunes Preferences.

It's a one-step thing: Once the AIFF is in the iTunes library (either by dragging it into the window or by choosing File ⇨ Add To Library), just select the track and choose Advanced ⇨ Convert Selection to AAC. If you've chosen MP3 or some other format as the default, the format's name will appear in the menu.

iTunes will percolate for a moment and you'll wind up with two copies of the same track in different formats. You're now free to delete the storage-hungry AIFF.

Adding Track Info

Cool. But you need to tell iTunes more about this track. For now, all it knows is its original filename.

One of the (many) cool things about music on an iPod is being able to rocket straight to all the songs in a specific album, or by a specific artist, or in a certain genre. When you rip tracks from a CD, iTunes gets all that information for "free," via an automatic lookup on a central database. When you transfer tracks from a tape or LP, iTunes merely taps its foot impatiently. *It's all on you.*

Select the track and choose File ⇨ Get Info. You'll see a big window of iTunes database information for the track (see Figure 3-16).

You know back in third grade, when your parents told you that you couldn't join the intramural kickball team because they'd signed you up for Laboriously Copying Track and Artist Info From The Backs of CDs lessons? "But I'll never use that skill in a million years!" you wailed. Funny how you only appreciate the wisdom of your parents when you finally become an adult.

Fill it all in, and click OK.

THE SHORT VERSION

This was such a long chapter and it covered

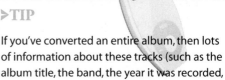

⯈TIP

If you've converted an entire album, then lots of information about these tracks (such as the album title, the band, the year it was recorded, etc.) is going to be the same. To make changes that apply to all those tracks as a group, select them all before choosing Get Info.

iTunes will give you a perfunctory warning but then the changes you make to one track will apply to them all. Then click OK, select the first track in the collection, and fill in the info for each individual song. Click the Next button to move to the next one in the list.

so much ground that I'm not going to conclude with the usual spate of (a) thoughtful wisdom, (b) wry commentary, or (c) bitchy sarcasm.

Instead, I'm going to streamline and summarize the process of converting old-school analog recordings to iPoddable digital music files.

Setting Up Your Devices

First, make sure the playback device and the computer are properly set up:

1. Check both the tape/LP and the playback device to make sure it doesn't sound like trash to begin with. Clean the device's hookup contacts and playback heads.

2. Connect the device to your computer, ideally through an iMic or another line-level audio interface. Launch Audacity and plug your headphones into your computer.

3. On your computer, open the operating

system's Preferences window and choose the correct audio input. Make sure that to set the input level to 100 percent.

4. In Audacity, turn on Input Monitoring and start playback. Adjust the output level of the playback device so that it's as loud as it can get without causing any distortion.

5. Adjust Audacity's input-level slider so that the peaks twitch as close to 0 on the level meter without ever actually hitting it.

Make and Edit the Recording

With the equipment and your OS set up right, now's the time to make the recording and get rid of any flaws or unwanted parts:

1. Rewind the recording to the beginning. Click Audacity's Record button and then start playback. Stop when you reach the end of the track or recording.

2. Trim the digital recording so that the start and end are clean. If you don't own a commercial sound cleaner such as Sound-Soap, do some simple clean-up and pop removal.

3. Save the recoding as an AIFF file.

4. If you own SoundSoap, open the AIFF in the app and clean the bejeezus out of it.

5. Import the file into iTunes and manually add all the track information.

6. Repeat steps 1 through 5 for each track. Don't try to record an entire LP or tape in one go and then cut the recording into tracks.

So yeah, it's a labor-intensive process, and acceptable results come with a lot of fiddling around and hoping for the best. But, hey, sometimes you love that Roy Clark album *so much* that you're willing to spend fifteen or twenty minutes converting each and every track.

Ripping DVDs

The Skim

A day after the first video-capable iPods shipped to stores, the entire world was so sick to death of *Desperate Housewives* that people's desire to push Teri Hatcher down some sort of shaft was even greater than usual.

It was all due to programming. The latest iPods had been nicely extended to handle video, but iTunes had been given just a cursory upgrade to support that new feature. You had a video iPod. Terrific. But if the platinum monkeys inside your head (the ones that compel you to do bizarre and wicked things) told you to actually try to *watch video* on the thing, your only course of action was to make a purchase at the iTunes store's brand-new Video department. Which initially featured just three or four TV shows, *Desperate Housewives* included.

So when I uploaded a photo of my new iPod's screen on Day Two of the Video iPod Revolution, it caused a bit of a stir and generated thousands of page views. Because incredibly, my iPod wasn't filled with a treacly retread of *Falcon Crest*: It contained two *Lord of the Rings* movies and all five *Star Wars* films then available on DVD. And that was just a handful of what I had on there.

There were those who looked upon me as some sort of modern-day Prometheus.

Well, there are millions and millions of people out there on the Internet. Let's just agree that, statistically, it's *possible* that some people looked upon me as a modern-day Prometheus and leave it at that, all right?

Copying movies and TV shows from DVDs into your iTunes library (and thence to your iPod) is something of a black art — but it really shouldn't be. iTunes will rip CDs from dawn to dusk and back again, but the app doesn't include any tools for converting DVDs. Fortunately, the idea of carrying the entire first season of *The Facts of Life* in your shirt pocket is a compelling one and whether you use a Mac or a PC, there are tools that'll easily get the job done.

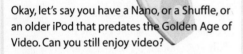

➤TIDBIT

Okay, let's say you have a Nano, or a Shuffle, or an older iPod that predates the Golden Age of Video. Can you still enjoy video?

Define "enjoy." Only video-compatible iPods can play video — that's why they call it video; it's easy to remember — but if you have QuickTime Pro (visit www.quicktime.com and purchase a registration code from Apple), lots of extra features of QuickTime Player are unlocked. Included among them: the ability to convert a video file into an audio file.

So no, I can't enjoy the video portion of *The Empire Strikes Back* on my Nano. But confidentially, I've seen this particular film many times and by now, the visuals are superfluous. A quick Export and a half-hour wait later, I have a virtual "books on tape" version of the film that I can listen to during my commute.

BUT IS IT LEGAL?

And I swear, when someone sees me watching a commercial movie on my iPod that clearly never came from the iTunes store, 25 percent of the time they assume that I downloaded the video illegally from some sort of file-sharing network.

Nuh-uh. Downloading that sort of material isn't merely illegal, it's also flat-out *wrong*. I say it without sarcasm and without winks or nudges. If you want it and the owners are selling it, then you *have* to buy it. Period. Buy me a drink sometime and we can spend an hour or two having an intellectual discussion on the topic of Information Wanting to Be Free and whatnot, but that doesn't change the fact that theft is theft and wrong is wrong.

But is it illegal to duplicate a DVD?

Again: *Nuh*-uh.

Probably.

At this point I'll turn my Sarcasm Sequencer back on and say that copyright law is in a rather adorable state at the moment. One section of the law states in crystal-clear language that if a consumer has purchased a legitimate copy of a copyrighted work, then he or she has the right to duplicate it for their own personal purposes, such as (and this is spelled right out) making a backup copy or transmogrifying the content from one format to another. At the time, the courts were thinking, "Copy an LP onto a cassette so you can listen to that album in your car," but the principle is the same here in the Push-Button World of Tomorrow.

In the Nineties, Congress complicated things

Figure 4-1
CloneDVD converts DVDs to files that'll play on dang-near anything.

by creating the Digital Millennium Copyright Act. This legislation threw some new mojo into copyright law, stating that if the copyright holder has sold you content that's wrapped in encryption to prevent copying, then breaking that anti-copy technology is agin' the law. Commercial DVDs are usually encrypted — that's why you can't just stick one in your DVD-ROM drive and duplicate it with a disk utility.

So you see where that leaves us: Copying the DVD is clearly legal, but you can't *make* that copy without using tools that could be illegal. It's like having a huge, lush, green public park in the middle of town, with all citizens given the right to enjoy it as they see fit … and then allowing a company to erect a forty-foot concrete wall around it punctuated by gatehouses that charge $20 to get in.

Fortunately, the question's largely a moot one. A law hasn't received its formal bar mitzvah until it's been challenged in court, and the movie industry has no interest in suing a consumer who paid for a DVD of *Beyond the Valley of the Dolls* and then copied it to their portable player.

Or, more to the point, they don't want to risk losing — and having a precedent on the books that emphasizes the consumers' right to duplicate what they purchase.

But this hasn't stopped the movie industry from going after the companies that *make* DVD-copying tools.

Any time a commercial DVD-ripping app gets so popular that it's about to become a household word, the industry tries to get it taken off the market … usually by threatening to file so many lawsuits against the pub-

Figure 4-2
Opening a DVD

lisher that their *ancestors* will have to file for Chapter 11.

So a quick word of warning: It's possible that some day, the apps I'm about to show you won't be around any more. But the basic technology for breaking DVD encryption is an open secret, and there are always alterna-

tives available.

I've chosen these two apps not only because of their value, but because of their credibility and longevity.

THE WINDOWS WAY

The star of our show is a terrific app by the name of CloneDVD Mobile. You can download a 21-day trial copy from www.slysoft.com. CloneDVD Mobile is a slick, start-to-finish solution for ripping DVDs. DVDs go in, iPod-compatible QuickTime MP4 files go out.

As you can see in Figure 4-1, part of the überginchiness of CloneDVD is the huge range of mobile devices that it supports.

Yes, you're reading a book about loading up an iPod, but as you buckle yourself into an aisle seat on a 757, nothing fills you with

Figure 4-3
Showing CloneDVD where to find the disc's table of contents

a greater feeling of peace and well-being than the knowledge that you have playable episodes of *The Simpsons* on your iPod, your phone, *and* your PlayStation Portable.

To convert a DVD with CloneDVD Mobile:

1. Select Apple iPod Video from the CloneDVD's device list and click Next.

   This will take you to the Title Configuration screen. Figure 4-2 shows you CloneDVD's view of the DVD and the titles that have been recorded on it. It can only collect this info after you've pointed the app at the folder that contains the disc's table of contents.

2. Click the pop-up file menu next to DVD Video Files and use the standard Windows file browser to point CloneDVD at the disc's VIDEO_TS directory (see Fig-

ure 4-3). The app fills the Title Configuration screen with a list of the disc's contents, and a preview image. The table of contents was meant to be accessed by software on the disc and not viewed by a human. You can't figure out what title refers to what sort of content unless you select an item from the list and then scroll through the video on the left side of the window.

3. Select a title from the list and click the Next button to take you to the Audio and Subtitle Settings screen (see Figure 4-4).

Each title on the DVD can have multiple soundtracks and multiple subtitle tracks. The disc in Figure 4-4 is in three different languages, encoded for two different kinds of home-theater surround sound systems. Often you'll encounter multiple English tracks. The first one is the conventional

Figure 4-4
Telling CloneDVD what you want to read and hear

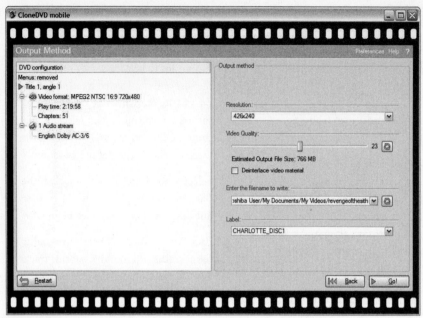

Figure 4-5
The petty details of the movie file you're about to create

soundtrack and the others are the director's and actors' commentary tracks.

Subtitles are actually generated electronically by your DVD player. So if you're converting *La Dolce Vita* and you want to have a halfway decent shot at making sense of it, make sure to click the English option in the subtitles. As CloneDVD copies the DVD into a video file, it'll "burn" the text right into each frame.

Click Next to head onward to the Output screen (see Figure 4-5).

4. Give the movie file a name and tell CloneDVD where to save it. You can type a path and filename directly into the Enter the Filename to Write text box, or you can click the orange button next to the box and use a file browser.

> **TIDBIT**

The title list can really get absurdly complicated. The movie, the trailer, and the 12-minute "behind the scenes" video are all separate titles. Another title is a special track with added scenes. If it's a DVD of TV shows, each title will be a different episode, and then there'll be one humongous title that contains them all together one after the other for the Play All feature. And another dozen titles are thirty seconds to three minutes long: these are the little clips that play in the DVD's animated menus.

As Cole Porter composed, and Kevin Kline sang as Cole Porter in *De-Lovely*, ... experiment. You'll find the content you want eventually.

Figure 4-6
Onward to conversion

This window also gives you options for controlling the size of the movie file. You can control the size of the file itself through the Video Quality slider. Slide it to the left and the app will create smaller, lower-quality movie files. Move it to the right, and the file will be take up more space on your iPod, but it'll feature smoother, cleaner images.

There's also a Resolution pop-up menu that lets you define how large the movie file should be in terms of actual screen resolution. By default, CloneDVD automatically matches the movie's vertical dimension to the vertical dimension of a typical iPod (240 dots). Making the image larger or smaller will also make the file's size larger and smaller.

5. Click Go and the fun begins. I say "fun"

because CloneDVD will start puzzling out your DVD, and it's going to take anywhere from thirty minutes to an hour for it to finish converting a feature-length film. A perfect amount of time to spend harassing linebackers through the miracle of home console gaming.

As you impatiently glance back at your PC, you'll be looking at the screen shown in Figure 4-6. The image on the left is the bit that the app is currently working on. The green progress bar on the lower right gives you an idea of how many minutes remain in the rip. As for the orange graph above it, it's the cousin of SlySoft's CEO. Ignore it. It's dead weight on the payroll.

Eventually, CloneDVD will trill in a self-satisfied manner, signaling that the file is complete. Drag it into your iTunes library

➤TIP

SlySoft's apps are worth every penny, truly. And I mean that from a selfish point of view, as an author who wants to explain something in a few pages instead of a few freakin' chapters. Google for "Windows DVD ripper" and you'll get a huge, wobbly pile of links. The pile is wobbling because 90 percent of those links are structurally unsound. They either lead you to spyware apps that do more harm to you than to the movie industry, or to half-baked apps and procedures that would seem simple and efficient only to someone who's ever attempted to assemble a motorcycle using only his feet.

and you're good to go.

As swell as this app is, it's only 5 percent of an answer for converting DVDs.

Remember when I mentioned that the movie industry would be very, very pleased if DVD-cracking software didn't exist? Well, this lack of community spirit has forced SlySoft to split its product into two pieces. On its own, CloneDVD Mobile can only rip unprotected, unencrypted discs (such as the ones that come out of your home DVD burner) so in theory, it should be safe from the slings and arrows of outrageous MPAA attorneys.

But naturally, SlySoft offers a solution to DVD copy protection via an additional piece of software. AnyDVD is a background app that transparently acts as a go-between for encrypted DVDs and any Windows app that might want to work with them. There's nothing to set up or tweak. If AnyDVD is running, the disc will appear to CloneDVD Mobile (or a backup utility or a DVD burner) as just a plain old disc with nothing special about it at all. The steps for converting a disc are the same whether the disc is protected or not.

It's a nice utility. On top of everything else, it also blocks region encoding (so you can enjoy those Japanese cartoons that haven't been released in the U.S. yet) and all kinds of other malarkey.

At this writing, AnyDVD costs about $24 from www.slysoft.com. But it's well worth the dough, and SlySoft offers a package discount when you order it with CloneDVD Mobile.

THE MACINTOSH WAY

There's only one really good DVD-ripping tool for the Mac ... but that's because with this thing out and about and readily available, there's really no need for an alternative.

Download Instant HandBrake from http://handbrake.m0k.org. It's free software, so keep your wallet where it is. Instant Hand-Brake contains everything you need to rip DVDs, whether they're copy-protected blockbuster disappointments or just a disc of old Letterman shows that you burned on the DVD recorder in your living room.

Rippage commences thusly:

1. Launch Instant HandBrake (see Figure 4-7). The app will automatically select your DVD drive as the source of incoming video.

2. Click Continue to proceed to Hand-Brake's features and settings window (see Figure 4-8). Each of the titles available on the disc appear in a list at the top of the window.

3. Click the checkbox for each title you'd like to convert.

The rest of the doo-dads in this window are for tweaking the conversion settings. But the idea of Instant HandBrake is to deliver an iPod-studly video file with a minimum of mouse clicks, so ignore them.

4. Click Convert to start converting video.

Ah, ruthless efficiency. Like a cool glass of lemonade during a day of extreme heat, or when the living dead rise from their graves roam the earth to feast upon the hearts of the wicked. Still, it can be useful to adjust those settings from time to time, and we do seem to have some space here in the chapter for some more detail:

▷ The first pop-up menu lets you choose where the video files will be saved. Instant HandBrake chooses your Movies folder by default.

▷ File Format will, naturally, be iPod. But you're given a choice between H.264 and MP4. H.264 generally results in higher-

quality video that takes up less space than MP4. But at this writing, MP4 conversion takes a lot less time. Leave it at H.264 unless you're in an ungodly hurry.

▷ Widescreen video is swell, and your iPod is savvy enough to blow up a widescreen movie to fill the whole screen during play-back if you ask it to, cutting off the sides to make the image fill the whole screen. By default, Instant HandBrake chooses the Fullscreen option, meaning the converter includes only an iPod-sized middle chunk of the frame. This results in a video file that takes up a lot less space.

▷ Finally, you can choose an audio track and a subtitle track. Just as with CloneDVD, these options allow you to create a special copy of the DVD in which you're listening to the director commentary audio, instead of hearing all the noise that all those damned actors were making as they did

Figure 4-7
Instant HandBrake: free and easy DVD ripping for Macs

Figure 4-8
A handful of options, each of which you can safely leave alone

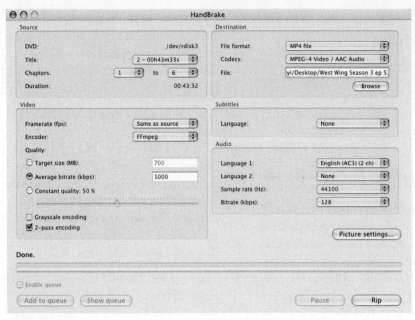

Figure 4-9
HandBrake: Instant HandBrake's more powerful big brother

their so-called "acting."

> And watching *Rashomon* without English subtitles is a lot more trouble than any movie could ever be worth.

Once you let Instant HandBrake do its thing, it starts depositing QuickTime files in the designated folder. You then have to go in and change the filenames to something sensible. The app simply starts with the name of the DVD and appends "Title 1," "Title 2," etc. as it munches its way forward through the disc.

Instant HandBrake is the little brother to HandBrake, a more venerable, more powerful, and certainly more *complicated* Macintosh DVD-ripper. As you can guess by Figure 4-9, the full edition is for people with special needs. Or annoying control freaks. A

fine line, there.

Whereas the Instant edition is designed to efficiently transmogrify DVD content into iPod-studly files, HandBrake can generate video files to suit nearly any purpose.

You have only 64 megs of storage on your cellphone, and you want to watch *Kill Bill* on it? No prob; HandBrake will do whatever it has to do to make the video file fit in a user-specified space, and can resize the video all the way down to the phone's puny 160-by-120-pixel screen.

I rely on it all the time to convert all my DVDs into full-resolution video files. All 200 or so of my DVDs now sit on a big hard drive in my office, which means that I can watch any movie or TV show I want from any PC or Mac in the house.

A MONUMENTAL EXPERIENCE

When you start ripping DVDs and adding them to your iTunes library, it's another one of those monumental First Step into a Larger World moments. You had one when you started ripping CDs, and you learned how much more flexible and enjoyable your music collection could be when it wasn't locked down onto plastic discs. Ripping movies has the same effect.

As I write this, I spy the 10-disc carrying case that I used to fill with CD and DVDs, and then later on, exclusively with DVDs, everywhere I traveled. Now, before I head off the airport, I take a minute to copy some movie files to my laptop and to my iPod. I don't have to be terribly choosy; everything is available and neatly sorted, and I'm not limited to just ten slots in a pouch. Just yesterday, riding on a train into the city, I had an impulse to watch *The Stunt Man* and so I *watched The Stunt Man*.

It's great. It's all working out so that I don't have to spend even as little as ten minutes in quiet contemplation of my surroundings any more.

Videotape, DVRs, and Other Video

The Skim

Quick! Get everybody into the lifeboats! No time to discuss it! *Now now now!!!*

The camcorder cassette from your trip to Kauai in 1998! The wedding video that you paid $3,000 for but never watched! That 1993 VHS tape of David Letterman's last show on NBC!!! All of it!!! Magnetic tape is *sinking,* and if we don't get these poor souls into digital files, the tape will deteriorate and there won't be anything to play 'em on, anyway!!!

It's *fun* to pretend that you're a person of infinite command and bravery in a crisis situation, isn't it?

Nonetheless, it'd be a dashed shame if you never got to see *The Far Side Halloween Special* ever again. And what about the great shows on your TiVo? In four days, your PVR will need to make room for new recordings. Say goodbye to last Tuesday's evening newscast, where a visibly inebriated weatherman made some inappropriate speculations about the weekend hobbies of the sports guy, and then after a slurry shout of "I'm Bart Conner! I'm Mary Lou Benneton!" tried and failed to vault Camera 4. *That's* a keeper, for sure. And who's going to believe the extended crimes against humanity that you performed last night on your Playstation with the latest edition of *Grand Theft Auto*? Not me … unless you recorded it all.

Just about any video component can be hooked up to a Mac or a PC, where free software that you already own can capture a show and record it as digital video. All you need is a little box that can transmogrify your VHS deck (or laserdisc player, or PVR)'s output to a digital signal that your computer can grok. And if you have the right sort of camcorder and the right sort of computer, you don't even need *that*.

THE HARDWARE

To plug a video player into your computer, you'll need an analog-to-digital video bridge, which from here on out will be referred to as a doohickey. My personal doohickey for such

>TIP

While we're discussing the hardware you ought to buy to convert your old video to iPod-studly digital files, I probably ought to point out that you can buy a DVD recorder pretty cheaply these days. A hundred or two hundred bucks will get you a box that plugs right into the VCR or TiVo and that can copy the content onto a DVD with no greater difficulty than pressing Play on the player and Record on the recorder.

Then you take the burned DVD to your computer and use the same desktop software we discussed in Chapter 4 to rip the disc into video files. In many ways it's a less-complicated way of going about it. Plus, hey … you get to slide a DVD recorder under your TV set!

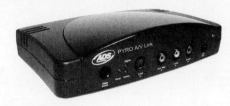

Figure 5-1
From NBC's broadcast tower to your iPod, through a video bridge

things is ADSTech's Pyro A/V Link box (see Figure 5-1).

You can check it out at www.adstech.com. At $150 (including Adobe's very wonderful $80 Premiere Elements video editing software), it's somewhere between a rudimentary, dirt-cheap consumer device and something that a professional videographer would use to justify the fact that he's charging you $700 to edit an hour of your Great-Aunt Mimsy's anniversary video down to a more humane twenty minutes.

You can buy similar doohickeys for as little as $60, but usually these bargain boxes can only capture video at minimal resolution (barely iPod-screen quality) and might lack S-Video and component-video connectors. Often, $80 is the difference between a box that creates very credible desktop video and video files that look like tenth-generation analog bootlegs no matter how clean the source video was.

The most important consideration (for our purposes, anyway) is that the device outputs DV video. That is, it squirts out a video stream that Windows and Mac OS' built-in video software can instantly recognize and handle. If you see the words "Works with Windows Movie Maker and iMovie," you're good.

Camcorders

If your camcorder is a modern digital model and it has a FireWire (aka iLink aka 1394) output jack, you might not need to buy anything at all. Many desktops and laptops come with FireWire jacks built-in; all you'll need to buy is a simple cable to get things going.

On the Desktop Side

You have the right doohickey. Do you have the right connectors on your Mac or PC to plug the doohickey *in?*

It depends on what *type* of doohickey you bought. Most of the more expensive ones talk to your computer via FireWire. If your computer doesn't have one … it's time to go out and buy a $50 card for your desktop. The cheaper doohickeys usually work via USB 2.0, which can be found on nearly every PC and Mac notebook and desktop that doesn't boot up with some sort of hand-crank.

Making Connections

Hooking up all the hardware is straightforward and shouldn't involve any undue wear and tear on your élan or sense of well-being. Plug the video component into the box, using the best-quality video connector supported by both the video device and your interface box. In decreasing order of video quality, it's component video (where the video is split into separate red, green, and blue plugs), S-Video (where it's all ganged into one round connector with lots of pins inside it), and then plain-Jane composite video (the lowly Single Yellow RCA Plug).

Natcherly, you can only use one of these at

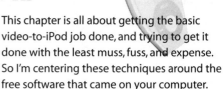

> **>TIP**
>
> This chapter is all about getting the basic video-to-iPod job done, and trying to get it done with the least muss, fuss, and expense. So I'm centering these techniques around the free software that came on your computer.
>
> But a quick trip to the local electronics superstore reveals that there's no shortage of "package" solutions … a cheap interface box and a special piece of software that knows how to work with it. It's a good idea to browse around a bit before committing to any purchase of hardware.

a time. But if your PVR has component-out and so does your video doohickey, it'd be a shame not to run down to Radio Shack and spend $25 on the cables that'll give you the highest-quality video possible.

From there, you just plug the doohickey into any available USB or FireWire port. If it does indeed comply with industry video standards, your PC or Mac should recognize and configure it automatically.

Now it's time to start assaulting your video with software.

RECORDING VIDEO WITH MICROSOFT WINDOWS MOVIE MAKER

Windows Movie Maker is the basic, grit-your-teeth-and-get-it-done app that Microsoft provides for simple acquisition and editing of digital video. If your edition of Windows XP is up-to-date (meaning that you're running at least Service Pack 2), it should be available under the Start menu

Figure 5-2
You plug in the video device;
Windows thinks, "Launch
Movie Maker." That's class.

or maybe in the Start menu's Programs submenu. If not, you can download it from Microsoft. Just head to www.microsoft.com, search for "Windows Movie Maker" to get to the main product page, and then click the download link.

On most PCs, the moment you plug in a DV video device, Windows will ask if you'd like to launch an app that can capture video (see Figure 5-2). Choose Capture Video Using Windows Movie Maker to launch the app. This will take you into a helpful wizard that walks you through the capture process step by step.

1. The Video Capture Wizard will ask you for a name for the new video project. Think of something catchy. I mean *Snakes on a Plane* catchy. Click the Next button.

2. Next, you're confronted with the Video Setting window. The app wants to know if it should capture video at ultra-high-quality

(as though you were going to be spitting the video back onto a tape later on) or if desktop-video quality will suffice. For the moment, we're just putting video on an iPod, so click Best Quality for Playback on My Computer and click Next.

3. The next step in the wizard is the capture method. If you're using a digital camcorder, your PC can control the device on its own. Capture the Entire Tape Automatically will tell Windows to play the whole tape through to the very end and then rewind it. Otherwise, select Capture Parts of the Tape Automatically.

With this method, the capture process is like copying from one tape deck to another. Push Play on the playback deck and start and stop the recording on the PC manually. Make sure that the Show Preview During Capture option is checked. That way, you can see what your PC is seeing and exercise some greater

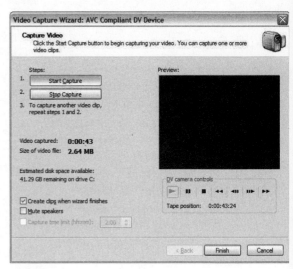

Figure 5-3
Capturing video, one clip at a time

control over what's being captured.

4. Finally! You get to capture some video (see Figure 5-3). On your playback device, cue up the recording to where you'd like the capture to begin. With a digital camcorder, you can use the wizard's Play/Fast Forward/etc. buttons to cue things up through the window. Otherwise, click the Play button to activate the windows' live preview of the video, and operate the buttons on your VCR or TiVo or whatever.

5. Click Start Capture to begin capture. If your recording is full of undesirable elements — commercials, bits where your Uncle Anzio got up and sang "The French Mistake" in front of 200 horrified wedding guests — click Stop to pause the capture while the tape continues onward. Then click the Start Capture button again when the horror show is over. Note that every time you click the Start Capture button, Movie Maker creates another new clip.

6. When you're done grabbing video, click the Finish button to see all the clips you've gathered (see Figure 5-4).

Windows Movie Maker gives you an easy

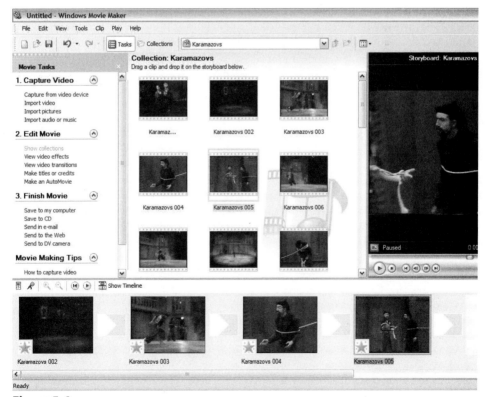

Figure 5-4

Clips ahoy! All of your video clips, awaiting assembly

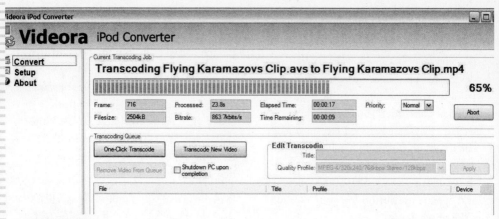

Figure 5-5
Nearly there: converting a Windows Media video to iPod-friendly QuickTime for free, with Videora

drag-and-drop interface to string all these individual clips together into one sequence. Just drag each clip in to the Storyboard strip at the bottom of the window, in their proper sequence.

>TIDBIT

I like Videora because it's free, and my personal corporate policy is that things that are free! free! free! and that work are always worth recommending. But it's certainly not the clean, consistent, and reliable solution that QuickTime Pro and Total Video Converter are. Many times I've used Videora and discovered that the converted file's sound and video slip out of synch halfway through.

But this is a fine solution to start off with. If you start to really get into video conversion in any sort of a serious way, though, you should spend $30 on QuickTime or even a little more on TVC. No question.

You can also trim the beginning and ends of individual clips:

1. Select the thumbnail of the clip you'd like to trim.

2. Click the Show Timeline button, just above the Storyboard. The clips will expand. You can also click the magnifying glass icon to zoom in on the clip and make it easier to trim with precision.

3. Grab the handle at the start or the end of the click and drag it. The preview window will show you the new start or end frame of the clip. Release when you have it where you want it to be.

When you're finished assembling and trimming clips, save the finished movie as a video file:

1. Choose File ➪ Save Movie File.

2. Choose My Computer/Save Your Movie for Playback on Your Computer as the destination and click Next.

3. Give the file a name and choose a location. Click Next.

4. Finally, the Save Movie Wizard will ask you what sort of video quality you'd like. You could save it as a postage-stamp thing appropriate for a Web site, for example. But we'll be converting this file to iPod format in a future step, so just select Best Quality For Playback on My Computer and click Next.

5. Windows Movie Maker will grind on the file for a little while. When it's done, click Finish to exit the wizard.

The end result of all this is a Windows Media–compatible file. Which your iPod won't touch with a ninety-meter pike. We'll need to convert it to an iTunes-friendly QuickTime file instead. There are a few ways to do this:

> Chapter 10 discusses a really nifty Windows utility from www.effectmatrix.com called Total Video Converter. As the name implies, it can transmogrify a video file from damned-near any format to any (damned-near) other, and if you're already planning on buying it for converting videos that you've downloaded from the Internet, well, there's no need to buy it twice.

> The chapter also gives a well-earned plug to QuickTime Pro. The basic QuickTime player is a free download from www. quicktime.com, but if you pay thirty bucks, Apple will unlock a host of ginchy features ... including converting Windows Media files to an iPod-compatible Quick-Time format.

> Here in the cozy confines of Chapter 5, we're just talking about this one Windows

>TIDBIT

I don't get too weepy about Windows Movie Maker because it is what it is: a basic video capture utility. But iMovie is a magnificent toy that allows even the most bored and disinterested user to create some rather remarkable narrative videos.

So I'm encouraging you — nay, ordering you, though please don't ask me how I might go about enforcing that — to spend some time exploring the app. *It's fun.* To me, the success of an app is measured by its power to totally kneecap office productivity. I can't tell you how many times a simple "Take this videotape of a never-coming-to-DVD-ever TV show and preserve it as a QuickTime file" task has turned into a day-long project. Not for the usual reason when computers are involved (the machine and the software kept locking up and forcing me to start again) but because I was having so much fun and exploring so many different ways of cutting together the footage.

And this is as good a place as any to boast about my most magnificent achievement as an editor: I took the absolutely disgusting, unwatchable, and indefensible 90-minute *Star Wars Holiday Special* — produced in the Seventies by the same people who did those awful Saturday-morning foam-rubber costume shows; it actually starred Harvey Kroman in drag — and cut it into a brand-new 42-minute narrative that was actually sort of entertaining.

God may now take me whenever He, She, or It wants to. I die knowing that I've left this planet in better shape then it was when I arrived.

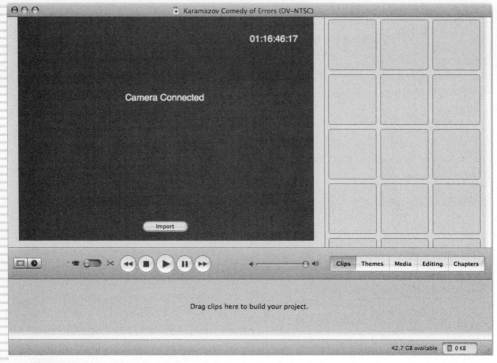

Figure 5-6
iMovie, awaiting input

Media format, so I'll also give a shout-out to a free (free! free!) utility from Videora called Videora iPod Converter (see Figure 5-5). The URL for the download is www.videora.com/en-us/Converter/iPod/.

It converts the Windows Media video that you've just created thusly:

1. Click the Convert button on the left side of the Videora window.

2. Click the One-Click Transcode button.

3. Select the video file.

Videora will grind for a while and spit out a proper .MP4-formatted video file, which you can import into your iTunes library (and thence to your iPod) without any further ado.

By default, the new file will be saved to the VideoraiPodConverter folder inside your Program Files folder, but you can change this by clicking on the app's Setup button.

RECORDING VIDEO WITH IMOVIE

Apple's iMovie software remains a bit of a marvel. It's almost a bold affront to the iMovie gods to use it for something as simple as capturing video and then spitting it out into iTunes, but part of its glorious perfection is that iMovie is endlessly patient and indulgent.

Figure 5-7
A tray of clips, ready to be strung together

iMovie doesn't use wizards (like Windows Movie Maker) to walk you through its procedures ... but then again, it doesn't have to, particularly when you throw such a simple task at it. Let's get cracking and make us a video file.

Capturing Video

1. Plug in your camcorder or your video doohickey, make sure it's cued up vaguely to the start of the video that you'd like to import, and launch iMovie.

   iMovie will ask if you'd like to create a new movie project or open an old one. Make a new project and give it a name.

   iMovie will open on its single master Editing window (see Figure 5-6). Nothin' there yet, but we'll soon fix *that*.

2. Click the User mode switch below the big Video Viewer pane of the window so that the slider is in the "camera" position. The Video pane will turn blue and if your camcorder or video doohickey is powered up and working, the pane will say Camera Connected and it'll sport an Import button.

3. Click the Import button to start capturing video. Even if you're not using a camcorder, you can use the Pause and Play buttons to pause and resume video cap-

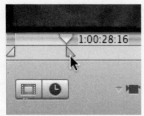

Figure 5-8
A bit of video, marked for a quick and emotionless death

Figure 5-9
Exporting an iMovie to iPod the iEasy iWay

ture. This is handy if you want to zap out big areas of unwanted video, though for clean edits you're better off cutting them using iMovie's editing tools. iMovie will capture all the inbound video into clips, thoughtfully organized in the Clips pane to the right of the Viewer pane. Every time you click the Stop button and then the Import button, a new clip will be created. It'll also create a new clip automatically every hour or so.

4. When you're done importing video, click the Stop or the Import button again and then click the Mode slider switch to put it back to the Editing position. You know, the position marked by the little pair of scissors.

Editing Video

You build an iMovie by dragging clips

together into the Clips viewer at the bottom of the window (see Figure 5-7). Just pick 'em up from the Clips pane and drop 'em into place.

You can also make trims to the clips, to further eradicate the moments of Unwatchable-fulness, such as commercials or a relative's Flavor Flav impression:

1. Click the clip containing the bit you'd like to remove. The first frame of the clip will appear in the Viewer pane. There's a blue bar below the viewer. The pointing-down triangle at the top is the playhead; it marks your current position in the clip. The pointing-up triangle at the bottom is used to select the start and the end of a selection. It's split in half.

2. Drag the left half of the selection marker to the start of the bit that you'd like to delete. Slide the right half to the end. The selected run of video will be colored gold in the playhead bar (see Figure 5-8).

3. In iMovie's menu bar, choose Edit ⇨ Clear. The offending video will be eradicated as though it had never happened. If only you could do the same to your *memories* of your Aunt Mimsy and Cousin Stall singing "Lady Marmalade." (If you want to clear away everything *but* the selected video — the start and the end are garbage but the middle is pure milk-chocolate goodness — choose Edit ⇨ Crop instead.)

Exporting an iMovie to iTunes

Boy, how would you react if you discovered that taking a video created with an Apple video app on an Apple computer and putting it on an Apple iPod was a complicated, soul-crushing ideal?

Sleep well, Virginia. Saving an iMovie project as an iPod-compatible QuickTime is no more difficult than saving it as an iMovie.

I hate to even break out the Numbered List thing for this, but hell, I paid for it so I might as well use it:

1. Go to the iMovie menu bar and click Share ⇨ iPod. (Figure 5-9)

Yeah, y'see, that's it. You'll see a little message pop down that merely confirms that iMovie is about to convert the entire movie to iPod format and that because it *likes* you and it *wants* you to be happy and it thinks you *deserve* good things to happen to you, it's going to take the converted file and put it in your iTunes library.

Again, I feel like I need to keep explaining things. I've been using a tape of one of the Flying Karamazov Brothers' most wonderful stage performances in my examples, so in keeping with that spirit I'll tell you that the secret to juggling is to train yourself *not* to look at the things your juggling or even your hands.

Instead, you should keep your eyes focused on an invisible little spot about a foot in front of your forehead, and concentrate on throwing the balls *through* that spot. With very little practice, they'll just sort of land in your hands on your own.

O SWEET MEMORIES!

When it came time to write this chapter, I didn't have to go digging around for a VHS tape to use as an example. I have a

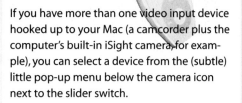

> **TIP**
>
> If you have more than one video input device hooked up to your Mac (a camcorder plus the computer's built-in iSight camera, for example), you can select a device from the (subtle) little pop-up menu below the camera icon next to the slider switch.

little editing setup to the right of my main computer table, here. Little by little, I've been going through the hundreds of old tapes I have in storage and converting them to video files.

It'll sound silly, but I actually take a little bit of pride in doing this. It's a damned shame that so much entertainment is allowed to die forgotten, because it was broadcast once and then never again.

One of the greatest hours of television I've ever watched was when David Letterman devoted an entire hour-long show to Warren Zevon, who then had less than a year to live before dying of cancer. Dave, Zevon, and the audience all knew this would be his last appearance anywhere, and it was as good a send-off as anybody could ever hope for.

But stupidly, I imagined that CBS would re-run the show as a tribute when the sad day finally came … and of course, they didn't. So I just have to *remember* Zevon's dry wisecracking and his advice to "enjoy every sandwich."

That won't happen to the Flying Karamazov Brother's incredible Lincoln Center interpretation of *The Comedy of Errors*, which aired once twenty years ago and never again. And if I feel this way about TV shows, imagine how I feel about videos of friends and family.

A hundred bucks for a video interface doo-

hickey is pretty bloody cheap, when you think about it.

Radio

The Skim

I didn't realize just how completely I'd weaned myself off traditional broadcast radio until one day last year, when I drove home from an auto-body shop in a loaner vehicle. I had an iPod packed with entertainment as usual, but I'd left my cassette adapter in my car. Or maybe it had been ejected from both the tape player and the window when I hit that moose. Regardless, I was forced to turn on the radio and listen to whatever The Man insisted was worth hearing.

And actually, I hit upon a great discussion on a talk radio station. It was so engrossing that I stayed in the car for five minutes after I pulled into the driveway, waiting for a commercial break so I could dash inside, turn on another radio, and not miss anything.

Um … yeah. It turned out that I didn't have a single working radio anywhere in the house. I've got a vintage shortwave in the office, but it's just decoration — and I've never bothered to connect an antenna to my home stereo.

Truly, podcasting and digital music players have kicked radio's butt straight to the curb, *Serpico*-style, without notice or apology. But when your iPod becomes the hub of all your audio, it's easy to forget that any metro area features at least a dozen channels of free streaming

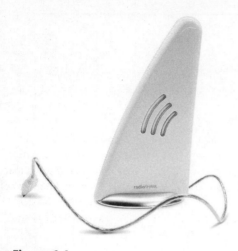

Figure 6-1
The RadioShark: instant awesome

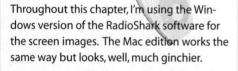

audio, usually with high-quality content that includes the same national news and talk that costs you $2 an episode on the iTunes store. And the biggest trouble with those Morning Zoo radio shows is that they broadcast in the morning. Who's awake at 9 a.m.? I mean, really?

Buying a bit of hardware that allows your computer to receive and record broadcast radio lets you morph an ancient analog medium into the 20th or even the 21st century. If it helps a local broadcaster sell a few snow tires and stay on the air, I'm all for it.

THE RADIOSHARK

There are a bunch of PC and Mac radio receivers on the market, but I believe that all discussion of What To Buy begins and ends with the RadioShark, by Griffin Technology (www.griffintech.com). My case, which I promise you is quite ironclad:

> It's an external USB device, and installs as easily as a mouse whether you're using a desktop or a notebook.

> It lives up to its marketing tagline as "TiVo for radio." The software makes it dead-simple to schedule regular recordings, and save those programs as files that can slurp straight into iTunes without any further ado.

> It's both PC- and Mac-compatible, which means you can move it from system to system, cackling with glee.

And that's all very, very true. But the trump card, the feature that closed down the competition before it ever really started is this: It's shaped like a shark fin, and is studded with colored lights (see Figure 6-1). Game, set, and match. There is no piece of office equipment that cannot be immeasurably improved by having a light-up electronic shark fin placed atop it or on a nearby shelf. I mean, come *on*.

To be honest, I might have recommended it even if it didn't actually do anything. Conveniently, it works exactly as advertised. Installation takes less than five minutes and leaves you with a radio tuner window on your desktop (see Figure 6-2).

You spin the dial (or just use the Seek button for auto-tuning), you enjoy the sounds as they float down through the air. If you like what you're hearing, you punch the Record button.

Simple, but not simple enough: We want to make every episode of NPR's *All Things Considered* or just next Thursday's Red Sox game as easy to iPod as a podcast. RadioShark has a full compliment of scheduled-recording features (see Figure 6-3).

You can schedule an event days or even months in advance, and if it's a regular show you can specify that it's a "repeating" show that should be recorded every Sunday, or every weekday, or on whatever schedule you specify. And there's no limit to how many items you can add to the schedule.

IMPORTING RECORDED AUDIO INTO ITUNES

Whether you punch Record manually or allow RadioShark to record shows for you automatically, the app will stash the recording inside your default music folder. That's My Music if you're using Windows, Music if

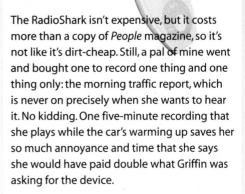

>TIP

The RadioShark isn't expensive, but it costs more than a copy of *People* magazine, so it's not like it's dirt-cheap. Still, a pal of mine went and bought one to record one thing and one thing only: the morning traffic report, which is never on precisely when she wants to hear it. No kidding. One five-minute recording that she plays while the car's warming up saves her so much annoyance and time that she says she would have paid double what Griffin was asking for the device.

As for a custom little script that automatically creates a brand-new iTunes playlist of podcasts and music, with the traffic report always inserted into the #1 position ... *that,* she was more than happy to let me write for free. Yes, it still stings.

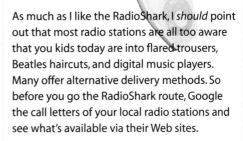

>TIDBIT

As much as I like the RadioShark, I *should* point out that most radio stations are all too aware that you kids today are into flared trousers, Beatles haircuts, and digital music players. Many offer alternative delivery methods. So before you go the RadioShark route, Google the call letters of your local radio stations and see what's available via their Web sites.

Oftentimes, their most popular shows are posted as podcasts shortly after transmission. Or, maybe they simulcast all their programming via streaming audio; in Chapter 9, you can read about software that will allow you to schedule and automatically capture these feeds to audio files. Either way, you might get a cleaner reception through a download than from over the air.

you're on a Mac.

Windows

By default, the Windows edition chooses Windows Media as the audio format, with conservative settings that result in tight, compact files. You can downgrade the quality (and get smaller files) by selecting a lower bit rate in the Format pop-up menu when you schedule the recording.

To use these files in iTunes, just drag them into your iTunes Library window. iTunes will automatically convert them to the AAC format.

Macintosh

RadioShark's Mac app has a nifty little bonus feature: By clicking the Add Recordings to iTunes checkbox in the app's Record & Playback preferences pane, RadioShark will automatically send the recordings it creates straight into your iTunes Library … and right into the playlist you specify (see Figure 6-4).

By telling iTunes to keep this playlist synched to your iPod, your device will always contain the local morning news and traffic when you plug it into your car stereo and begin that brutal, soul-wrenching commute morning after morning.

Otherwise, just locate the files inside your Music folder and drag 'em into your iTunes Library window.

REDISCOVERING LOCAL RADIO

I'm grateful to RadioShark for one thing: by allowing me to listen to programming

whenever I wanted, it's caused me to rediscover local radio. These days, radio is typically represented by nationally syndicated political blowhards and Wacky Morning Zoo

Figure 6-2
The main tuner window (in Windows)

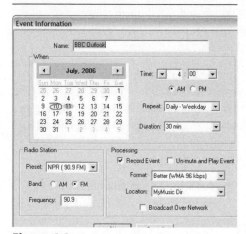

Figure 6-3
Setting up a scheduled recording (in Windows)

Figure 6-4
Putting the morning news onto your iPod automagically

teams that are about as edgy and entertaining as emptying out the lint catcher on your washer/dryer.

But there's a huge wealth of local programming zipping over (hell, *through*) your head at all times. It's really the last refuge of extended and thoughtful discussion of local issues, and I'm glad that this stuff is waiting for me on my iPod when I unplug it from my dock.

Radio is still doomed to die a deathly death, methinks, but I'll get my money's worth out of my RadioShark while the medium is still kicking. And even afterwards: That fin will continue to look *awesome* on top of my CPU.

> > >

Glorious Television

The Skim

I'm glad you haven't skipped over this chapter. Your friends and I have been wanting to speak to you about this for a long time, now: *You're simply not watching nearly enough television.*

Seriously, man. I know you've been trying your hardest, but spending nine hours a day on your Xbox is simply no substitute. There's a lot of toothpaste and shady credit services that need to be sold, and a lot of desperately down-on-their-luck actors and actresses who need to sell them. Robert Vaughn is a *good man,* dammit, and now that both *Diagnosis: Murder* and *Walker, Texas Ranger* are off the air, the only thing keeping him from having to eBay all his remaining *Man from U.N.C.L.E.* wardrobe to keep the lights on in his apartment is people like *you* making a commitment to pick up the remote and watch TV on an early midday afternoon.

There's also a selfish reason — if you have a PC or Mac with TV-tuner hardware, you have a hundred channels of free iPod content streaming into your house 24/7, just waiting to be captured and imported into iTunes — but I'm sure you're not interested. The mental image of Napoleon Solo in his kitchenette rubbing his hands over a toaster oven for warmth is already spurring your humanitarian impulses.

It's unlikely that your computer came with any TV-tuning hardware, so

— sure — you're probably going to have to buy some. But hey, you can afford it. What if Robert sells the really sharp blue suit he wore as President Harry Truman in *The Man from Independence*? That's the suit he wears to *job interviews!*

TV TO PC TO IPOD

On the Mac, there's really only one choice for TV-recording hardware and software. But on a PC, there's … let's see …

(Ihnatko shoves the edge of his desk and propels self and his chair to the other side of the office; retrieves a big plastic tub full of hardware; crab-walks chair back to desk.)

… At least nine. Three of 'em are worthy of a shout-out and a recommendation:

Hauppage WinTV

I like Hauppage's gear (www. hauppage.com) because there's such a wide variety of consistently high-quality hardware to select from. You can buy a dirt-cheap, $55 card that installs inside your desktop PC, $100 USB boxes that can plug into any notebook, or even $200 cards that can record digital satellite

TV and feature dual tuners so that they can record more than one show at a time. They all use Hauppage's WinTV 2000 tuner/PVR software, which is a treat to use. WinTV is available in both conventional analog and bleeding-edge digital TV editions.

The WinTV PVR software doesn't support iTunes and the iPod directly. But the company offers Wing, a $25 add-on app that can record TV shows directly to your iPod by simply clicking a checkbox (see Figure 7-1).

Pinnacle PCTV Pro

Pinnacle's hardware (www.pinnaclesys.com) — available as an $80 desktop PCI card or as a $100 USB device for your notebook or desktop — isn't as ambitious as Hauppage's. But it has a clear goal of being as easy to

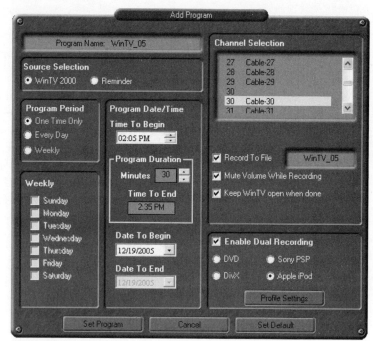

Figure 7-1

Recording WinTV shows to your iPod on a Wing

set up and use as a TV set itself. And given that *Serenity* got cancelled before its entire first season had aired and yet *Big Brother* continues to get renewed year after year, you *know* that this translates into a goal to be functional even if the user is as dumb as a jar of asphalt.

The other great advantage (from our perspective) is that PCTV Pro's software supports the iPod right out of the box. You can record shows directly to your iPod, using the included Pinnacle MediaCenter software. I don't think it's as slick as using Wing with WinTV, but it's simple enough, and it saves your having to buy and install another app. Plus you can easily edit recorded shows with Pinnacle's companion Pinnacle Studio software.

ATI All-in-Wonder

ATI's (soon to be AMD's) All-in-Wonder cards (www.ati.com) aren't cheap — they start at about $130 and go all the way to $350 for the top-drawer model — but they offer more than just a TV tuner. ATI's bread-and-butter industry is designing video hardware. Chances are that you already have an ATI card (or its chips) inside your computer right now.

But when you throw a Visa card at the company directly, it can sell you the sort of high-performance graphics card that professionals in the video industry rely on for fast response and true color.

Or the sort which gamers rely on for 60-frame-per-second hyperfragging of petulant hellspawn, on a game field that's three screens wide at 1920 by1,200 pixels. (Translation: megahypersuperawesome video.)

The All-in-Wonder cards were designed to pack as many features as possible into a single PCI card. So if you're going to be spending some money on a new video card *anyway,* and you're into gaming, an All-in-Wonder can save you some dough and some space inside your desktop. And like Hauppage's WinTV, ATI's cards are also available in HDTV/DTV flavors.

ATI's PVR software doesn't support the iPod directly. However, the cards typically come bundled with video-editing software (such as Adobe Premiere Elements or Pinnacle Studio), which can be used to open the recorded video files directly and save them in an iPod-studly format (MPEG-4 or H.264), usually through a pop-up menu with the iPod listed as a pre-set.

Converting Shows from Windows Media Center Edition

We're not even halfway through this book and I think you've already twigged to the fact that I tend to prefer Macs over PCs. But good heavens, Windows Media Center Edition gives me a consistent case of Windows-envy. You don't see those two words placed side by side very often, but this is one of those times.

You have a conventional Windows PC or notebook. But pick up a remote and push a green button and — whoosh! — the entire Windows interface goes away (maybe that's why I like WMC so much) and is replaced by a clean and efficient screen of big buttons and menus that can be operated with the remote's four directional arrows and an OK button.

And unlike Apple's *vaguely* similar FrontRow

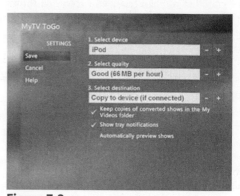

> **>TIP**
>
> I honestly don't get why *all* the TV tuner cards available for PCs don't directly support iPod export. I *understand* it — they're wimping out to pressure from TV networks, who would rather that everybody *purchased* their shows in digital format, rather than transcoding them for free as is their right — but still, I don't get it.
>
> Nonetheless, every PC tuner card I've seen records your TV shows in either MPEG-1 or MPEG-2 format. And both formats can be converted to an iPoddable MP4 file easily with iSoft's $45 Total Video Converter (www.effectmatrix.com). Just locate the file (it might be buried inside the app's Program directory), choose the app's pre-set iPod configuration, and click. Turn to Chapter 9 for the whole rundown.

app, Windows Media Center is extensible. It can't export recorded programs to your iPod by itself, but with the $30 MyTV to Go plug-in from Roxio (www.mytvtogo.com), Media Center and the iPod are a perfect match (see Figure 7-2).

After a few minutes of pointing and clicking, the shows you record will be transcoded into the correct format and deposited on your iPod automagically.

TV TO MAC TO IPOD

In the grand tradition that's been kept alive by everyone who's ever gotten a Tasmanian Devil tattoo on an impulse — and truly, apart from getting drunk with the wrong sort of friends, is there any other way? — I'm going to pretend that something bad is actually exactly the perfect thing. Watch me:

"Hey, isn't it *terrific* that there's pretty much only *one* solution for recording TV on a Mac?"

Okay, well, it's not like there's *really* only one piece of tuner hardware and PVR software available. There are as many as … um … two. Maybe three.

But the only one I'll tell you about is the EyeTV from Elgato. The hardware and software are head-and-shoulders above anything else. They offer a whole line of external boxes that work on nearly all Macs, including conventional and HDTV options. Check out products and prices at www.elgato.com.

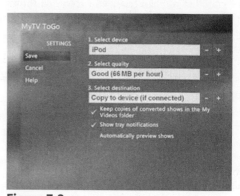

Figure 7-2
Adding iPod support to Windows Media Center Edition with MyTV to Go

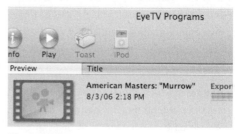

Figure 7-3
TeeVee to iPod PDQ with EyeTV

As a Mac-only product, the EyeTV software was upgraded to support iPods weeks after the release of the first video iPod. Any recorded show can be transcoded to iPod specs and added to your iTunes library, with just one click (see Figure 7-3).

Yes indeed: It's the big button that looks like an iPod and says "iPod."

As with almost any transcoding process, it'll take a while before the file's finished (even on an Intel-based Mac, it can take two times the running length of the show). But if you've set EyeTV to record your favorite shows, you can have the app start converting the programs the moment recording is finished. Just select the Export to iPod checkbox in either the show's schedule detail view (see Figure 7-4) or in the schedule list itself.

With the iPod option enabled, by the time you wake up in the morning, all the evening's recordings will be waiting for you on your iPod.

Just don't watch them while you drive. It's *very* rude to the person you're talking to on the phone in your other hand.

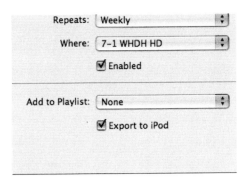

Figure 7-4
iPod Conversion ... the zero-click method

> **>TIDBIT**
>
> I have sort of a genetic attraction toward the "Record TV on a computer, have the computer transcode the show to the iPod" solution. When the computer handles everything from start to finish, you feel as secure and at peace as you do when you see the lady at Dunkin' Donuts box your half-dozen with a set of tongs.
>
> But if you're going to go around buying hardware, you probably ought to at least *consider* the option of just buying a standalone DVD recorder. It can make a timed recording from the output of your cable box just like a VCR, and after you've burned the disc, you can pop it into your PC or Mac and use any DVD-ripper software to convert the shows therein to video files. (Read all about that in Chapter 4.)
>
> And because that DVD isn't copy-protected, you won't even need any of the extra decoding software that the PC apps usually require. Sure, this scheme is more complicated than recording shows directly to your hard drive, but maybe you *wanted* to buy a DVD recorder anyway. It's up to you, all right? I'm just a man, here.

THE DIGITAL DILEMMA

The fundamental coolness of turning TV broadcasts into iPod content is the price. A TV card costs so little, compared to the constant influx of variably awesome shows that just start to appear on your iPod as though the elves from that old fairy tale got sick and tired of making shoes for the cobbler night after night and have decided to switch to video production.

But there's a wrench that's about to be thrown into the works, and it's the media industry that's about to throw it. In 2009, the U.S. government wants all transmission of old-fashioned analog broadcast TV to end. Well, that's only a problem if you bought an analog card instead of a digital one, right?

Mmm … maybe. One of the so-called "features" of digital television is the "broadcast flag." A network can encode a signal right into the transmission that tells any and all hardware, "Don't allow the viewer to record this show." Today, we don't even *wonder* if we can save a show to watch later on, or to keep forever. There are actual laws on the books stating that we're perfectly free to do so. But if the networks choose to flip this switch for anything that's worth watching — or any-thing that they hope to sell you on DVD or on the iTunes store — that's the ball game.

As far as I'm concerned, it's just another one of those reasons why viewership is going to decline and the networks are going to claim that the drop in viewership is due to piracy. I dunno. I suppose the networks ought to be applauded for sending people away from awful sitcoms and reality shows and towards the Martin Scorsese movie that just opened a month earlier … or the 120-year-old novel that the movie was based upon.

➤ ➤ ➤

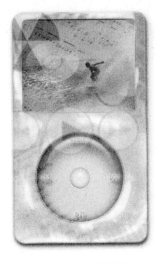

PART II

Where iPod Meets the Internet

Podcasts

The Skim

I'm sitting here trying to think of a reason *not* to say that podcasts are the best thing about owning an iPod. An extreme position, yes, and it overlooks the fact that while you're trying to get through a workout on the treadmill or a 90-minute interview with the author of a book on global hunger, a podcast really doesn't get your feet moving like a Curtis Mayfield track does.

But what a compelling sell. Podcasts combine all the best technologies and infrastructures of the Internet in ways that you, the user, can safely ignore:

> Someone in the world sits down behind a microphone and records a show. They upload it to a server somewhere on the Internet.

> The server also contains a file that keeps track of each episode. A *TV Guide*-type description, a list of contributors, and most importantly for your purposes, a record of the date and time the show was first posted to the server.

> You've told iTunes that you like this show, so iTunes periodically checks the show's file. It automatically downloads new episodes as they appear, and adds them to your iTunes library.

> And because you've also told iTunes to automatically copy new podcasts to your iPod, each morning when you snatch your iPod from

your desktop dock, your morning commute is filled with fresh content that (a) appeared from thin air without your having done anything at all, and most thrillingly, (b) didn't cost you a penny.

Behind the "it doesn't cost you a penny" thing, the second-most-thrilling thing about podcasts is that the content is controlled by the same fundamental principle that guides *all* the content you encounter on the Internet: On the Internet, nobody can hear you say 'But what's the point of this, really?'

Which means that there's a truly dizzying array of content available. Any jerk with a $10 microphone and a two-bit opinion has the ability to put his words in your ears as

easily as any of the Big Four networks. So during that morning commute, it's entirely possible that you'll be listening to last night's professional and highly illuminating broadcast edition of *ABC News: Nightline*, followed by a heavy-metal show by Jason from Salt Lake City, who's complaining about his *awesome* Motorhead tattoo on his back but feels cheated because he's the only person who never gets to *see* it.

When iTunes started supporting podcasts, it totally changed the way I used my iPod, and it completely killed any remaining interest I had in traditional, broadcast radio. I get the best programming from all over the world, and it's available any time I want to hear it. Think about your least-favorite national radio personality. I mean, come on: do you *really* think they'd have a career if listeners had any choice in the matter?

There's a three-pronged approach to filling your iPod with podcasts:

1. Locate a podcast that you're actually interested in hearing.

2. Tell iTunes to subscribe to that podcast.

3. Configure your iPod to automatically load new episodes as they land in your iTunes library.

WHERE PODCASTS LIVE

Apple maintains a huge and fairly ginchy searchable directory of podcasts, and you can access it from iTunes. But Apple is highly ecumenical, embracing podcasts from all sources; it's happy to subscribe you to a podcast that the iTunes Podcast Directory has never heard of before.

Figure 8-1
Your first step into a larger world

Figure 8-2
A link to the iTunes Podcast Directory.

The iTunes Podcast Directory

To visit the iTunes Podcast Directory, click Podcasts in the iTunes window's Sources list.

iTunes will tell you what you've just clicked on and explain why clicking it was such a good idea (see Figure 8-1).

Click the Go to Podcast Directory button to proceed. If iTunes doesn't display the Helpful Explanation, you can access the directory by clicking the Podcast Directory link that appears at the bottom of the iTunes window after you

Figure 8-3
The front door of the iTunes Podcast Directory

≻TIDBIT

The iTunes Podcast Directory lives on an Apple server on the Internet, not on your hard drive. So you'll need a live connection to the Internet to access the directory.

Figure 8-4
iTunes'
Top Pod-
casts:
It's a
popularity
contest.

click the Podcasts source (see Figure 8-2).

Either way, you'll wind up at the directory's front door, in all its majesty (as shown in Figure 8-3). At this point you should regard yourself as not unlike young Charlie Bucket in *Willy Wonka & the Chocolate Factory* — no, not the Johnny Depp movie, the

good one, the one where the kids get to run through a park made entirely of candy and sample to their hearts' delight.

Obviously there's lots of eye-candy at the front door. Individual podcasts get front-row attention, usually because they're new or suddenly hot, but your first clicks should

Figure 8-5
Featured news podcasts

Figure 8-6
Podcast categories on the Directory's front page

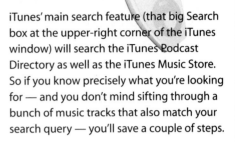

>TIP

iTunes' main search feature (that big Search box at the upper-right corner of the iTunes window) will search the iTunes Podcast Directory as well as the iTunes Music Store. So if you know precisely what you're looking for — and you don't mind sifting through a bunch of music tracks that also match your search query — you'll save a couple of steps.

probably go to the Top Podcasts list (see Figure 8-4). It's a ranking based on popularity, which almost always means that they're well-produced shows with terrific content and that they are updated regularly.

In the center of the directory window are big, colorful category buttons … your next focus of attention. Click one of these, and

iTunes will take you to a selected assortment of "featured" podcasts related to the category (see Figure 8-5).

Why *these* podcasts and not others? Because

Figure 8-7
All the news that fits. … on your iPod

Figure 8-8
The iTunes directory's Search box

they're all produced with a professional attitude (even if they weren't necessarily produced by professional broadcasters), plus they are popular and regularly updated.

But there are plenty more podcasts where these came from. To see the entire list, return to the main directory (just click the Back button at the top of the Directory window; it works just like a Web browser) and feast your eyes on the Categories list (see Figure 8-6).

Click any category name and you'll see every podcast that iTunes knows about, with no filtering whatsoever. Figure 8-7 shows you part of the News directory.

Gone are the eye-grabbing colors and cozy graphics: it's a basic directory list. But boy, what a list: nearly 2,500 podcasts in the News category alone.

Again I cite the Fundamental Principle of the Internet: Apple allows *anybody* to submit their podcast to the directory. Unless there are legal issues involved, it'll be added to the directory without any further ado. So you'll find lots and lots and *lots* of noise, with a few gems in the mix. So the directory's Search box is far more useful than scanning through

Figure 8-9
Searching for WBZ podcasts

➤TIDBIT

Okay, but how much is this going to cost? Nothing. Podcasts are, by their cultural definition, free. On those rare occasions when a podcast has become so popular (and thus so expensive to distribute) that its producers decided to start charging for the thing, it's left the iTunes Podcast Directory and moved into the main iTunes Music Store. That's what happened to the *Ricky Gervais Show* podcast (you know, the funny dude from *The Office* and *Extras*.) Of course, things could change in the future. But if Apple ever mixes "pay" podcasts with free ones, it won't charge you for the shows until you explicitly acknowledge and approve the fee.

thousands and thousands of individual podcasts (see Figure 8-8).

I mentioned earlier that I don't listen to the radio any more. I listen to radio *shows*, however. I wonder if any of my local radio stations here in Boston have podcasts? It's easy enough to find out. iTunes can search on any word that appears in the podcast listing: people, topics, places, anything. I'll just pop the call letters of WBZ into a search. Witness the result in Figure 8-9.

Learning More about a Podcast

No matter how you hit upon a Podcast of Interest, you can find out more about the show by clicking its name or its thumbnail icon. iTunes will take you to the podcast's

Figure 8-10
Looking at a podcast

Figure 8-11
The Subscribe button

main directory listing (see Figure 8-10)

The main directory listing describes the podcast, provides a list of all the shows available at the moment, and possibly some user comments. Clicking the Web site link will open the show's official Web site in your Web browser. Double-click an individual episode to listen to it in iTunes.

Subscribing to Podcasts through the iTunes Directory

If you've spent some time noodling through the directory, you've spotted Subscribe buttons here and there (see Figure 8-11). Yes indeed, this button does precisely what you think it does: Click it, and iTunes will subscribe to that podcast.

It starts off by downloading the latest episode and adding it to your personal iTunes library. And from that point onward, iTunes will download new episodes automatically.

Other Podcast Directories

As neat as the iTunes Podcast Directory is, Apple didn't invent the concept of podcasting and it doesn't own it, either. Nobody does. So there are plenty of podcasts available that don't appear in the iTunes directory.

But honestly, if you eagerly download a show that doesn't appear in the iTunes Podcast Directory, be prepared to have your heart broken — there are some really, *really* terrible podcasts out there.

I find that the biggest advantage of the alternative directories is that they highlight shows and organize their content a little differently. There's a good chance a terrific podcast is buried deep inside iTunes where I'll never find it, but that I might trip over on another directory by accident.

So now you're salivating for some swell podcast directories, right? Well, dude, here are some great places to start your search for the tastiest or most exotic podcasts — it's your menu:

> **Odeo.com**. Probably the prettiest — and therefore the easiest-to-navigate — directory. It's very iTunes-like in that it's well organized by categories and makes Odeo. com the place to easily spot the popular and most heavily updated podcasts.

> **Podcast.net**. A good'un, chiefly because it's so exhaustive. Which is also its weakness. I'm not particularly interested in learning about *every* technology podcast that's ever been published. I just want to find a couple of *good* ones. But Podcast.net is great for casting a wide net.

> **Podcastalley.com** A strong front page. No directory provides an "I don't know what I'm really looking for; what do you have that's going to catch my eye?" search, but the front page of Podcastalley.com is the next best thing.

> **Podnova.com** Like Google for podcasts. Other directories offer search features but Podnova.com returns the results in a way that makes it easy to spot the good'uns from the duds.

> **PodcastingNews.com** offers yet another directory of podcasts, which is fine and

dandy, but what keeps me coming back is its news and information about podcasting in general. When a podcast creator lands an interview with J.D. Salinger, she sends a new item to PodcastingNews. When a terrific new directory or service launches, you can read about it on PodcastingNews.

Subscribing to a Podcast Manually

Naturally, subscribing to a podcast that you discovered without the help of the iTunes Podcast Directory, or just by browsing around on the Web, isn't as simple as clicking a friendly Subscribe button.

Umm, unless the podcast has a friendly Subscribe to this Podcast in iTune button or link, that is. It might incorporate the icon in Figure 8-12, which is Apple's special "this is a link to a podcast" button. But it might not. The thing is, the people who create Web pages are all mavericks. They're wild stallions, unbroken, untamed; they may bend your precious rules but dammit, they get the job done.

But it isn't terribly complicated. Remember when I told you that every podcast is represented by a simple file somewhere on the Internet? All you need to do is give iTunes the address of that file.

I apologize in advance, but I am forced to introduce a technical three-letter-acronym into the proceedings: RSS. It's the simple, worldwide standard that powers podcasts (and Web logs and all sorts of Internet services). Technically, the address you're hunting for is known as an RSS feed.

For instance, Figure 8-13 shows the Web

Figure 8-12
Apple's little podcast icon; clicking this icon on a Web page will subscribe you to a podcast.

page for ITConversations. It's a podcast intended for geeks, so needless to say the site has included its podcast links in the geekiest way possible. And why not? Its audience groks that sort of thing.

In this case, the colored buttons that read RSS 2.0 attracts our full and immediate attention. Each button represents a link to an RSS feed we can give to iTunes.

To copy the link:

1. Right-click the link. If you're using a Macintosh with a one-button mouse, press the Control key on your keyboard while clicking.

2. Select Copy Link or Copy Link Location (depending on which Web browser you're using).

And that's it. I deliberately chose a pretty awful example.

But not to worry: Most podcast Web pages put the RSS feed out in the open. Figure 8-14 shows you the podcast page for a National Public Radio show. I mean, *now* we're talkin'. The URL is explicitly pointed out to you *and* there's a direct iTunes button. Your tax and pledge dollars, working for *you*.

After you've copied the link to the podcast's RSS feed, just hand it off to iTunes:

1. In iTunes, choose Advanced ⇨ Subscribe to Podcast.

2. Paste the URL into the text box and click OK (see Figure 8-15).

And from that point onward, iTunes treats the podcast the same as it would if you'd found it in the iTunes directory: It'll add the podcast to your list of subscriptions, download the most recent episode, and then download future shows as they're published.

MANAGING PODCASTS

You can see all the podcasts you've subscribed to by clicking Podcasts in the Source list of iTunes' main window (see Figure 8-16).

If iTunes knows there are episodes that it hasn't downloaded — for instance, it's a new subscription, which would mean that iTunes

has only downloaded the latest show — you can manually download the new episode by clicking the Get button next to its title.

Updating a Podcast Manually

By default, iTunes will automatically look for new episodes on a regular basis. If you want iTunes to look *right freaking now* — just click the Update button in the upper-right corner of the iTunes window.

Just make sure you're looking at your list of podcasts first; since if you're looking at your music library, that button will say and do something else entirely.

iTunes will update all your subscriptions immediately, automatically downloading any new episodes that you don't already have. If

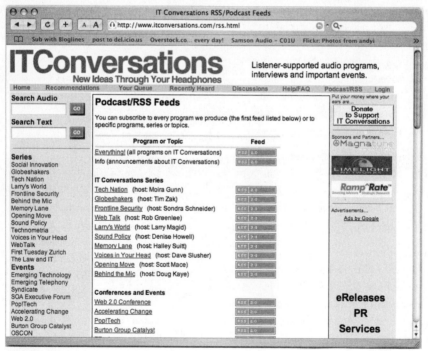

Figure 8-13
Hunting for a podcast's RSS feed à la geek

Movie Podcast is neither weekly, nor is it consistently about movies, let alone super-awesome, you can unsubscribe to the podcast by clicking its title and then selecting the Unsubscribe button at the lower-right corner of the iTunes window. It's that easy!

Changing Podcast Settings

The lower-right corner also sports a Settings button, where you tell iTunes how it should manage all your podcasts as a group (see Figure 8-17). Here, you can tell iTunes how frequently to update your podcasts, and what it should do with them once you have 'em. Through the Check for New Episodes pop-up menu, you can tell iTunes to check hourly, daily, weekly, or manually. That last

you'd like to update just one show, select it in the podcast list before you click Update. Only the shows you've highlighted will be updated.

Unsubscribing

If at some point in life you discover that *Shawn and Kyle's Super-Awesome Weekly*

Figure 8-14
A less-cruel display of a podcast's RSS feed

Figure 8-15
Manually subscribing to a podcast

option means that it's entirely up to you to remember to click the iTunes' Update button and check for new episodes.

And what should iTunes do when it finds new content? When New Episodes Are Available offers three choices:

> **Download All** grabs every episode you don't have. If *The Jeff Boring McDullsworth Show* has 230 half-hour episodes available, then iTunes will download all 230.

> **Download the most recent one** does what it says. It assumes that you're not obsessive-compulsive and you just want whatever's newest. But iTunes will kindly grab all the information about the shows it didn't download, and add the info to the podcast's program listings so you can peruse them at your leisure.

> **Do nothing** seems like a waste of a good resource. But at least it's fairly easy to understand. Instead of downloading any new episodes, iTunes will simply add information about those episodes to your subscription listing.

After iTunes updates your podcast subscriptions, the new content will be snug and secure in your iTunes library, and any info about episodes that it didn't download will appear in the listing. Just click the Get button next to

Figure 8-16
A glorious cornucopia of free content

Figure 8-17
Podcast settings let you tell iTunes how it should update your podcasts.

the show description to have iTunes download it immediately (see Figure 8-18).

The final thing in iTunes' Podcast settings window is iPod Preferences. This button takes you straight to the Podcast settings panel of your iPod's preferences page (see Figure 8-19). Your iPod must be plugged into your computer before you can see this.

By default, iTunes selects Automatically Update All Podcasts. Every podcast that appears in iTunes will automatically be copied into your iPod, where they'll appear in its built-in Podcasts playlist. Fabulous. This works peachy-keen if (a) you've just started getting into podcasts and don't have many subscriptions, (b) you have an iPod with *ginormous* capacity, or (c) you have a modicum of self-control.

Figure 8-18
Manually downloading an episode you missed

Otherwise, you're quickly going to run of space on your iPod.

Picture yourself in the car, laughing merrily at the bumper-to-bumper traffic. It's not a stomach-knotting delay; it's an opportunity to spend three hours listening to a mega-podcast interview with the creators of *The Matrix*, in which they admit that the first movie was sort of okay but the final two were self-indulgent, pretentious nonsense. And then you discover that none of it got copied to your iPod because everything you've downloaded over the past month is choking its capacity.

So clearly, it's a Good Thing to allow iTunes to be a bit selective about the content it sends to your iPod. Automatically Update Selected Podcasts Only allows you to point-and-shoot a handful of podcasts that should always be automatically updated, leaving the rest behind.

As for the Manually Manage Podcasts option, well, that's no fun, obviously. iTunes won't automatically copy any shows to your iPod at all. It'll leave that task completely up to you. Bummer.

Figure 8-19
Deciding how podcasts wind up on your iPod

Truth be told, though, that's what I've selected in *my* iTunes library. Those automatic features are terrific because they don't require any heavy lifting, but the cost is that you cede a lot of control.

If you become even slightly adept at iTunes and how to manage playlists, you can easily set up iTunes to copy podcasts precisely the way you like 'em, by organizing them into Smart Playlists. (See Chapter 1 for the first step on that journey.)

For example, Figure 8-20 shows a Smart Playlist I set up for one of my favorite podcasts. The first line specifies the title of the podcast. The second line says, "Make sure that it's a podcast," not a song from an album that happens to be named *Martini Shot*.

And here's where I get into the good stuff: The *third* line says, "Only include episodes that I haven't heard yet." So if I get home from a long drive, plug my iPod into my computer, and iTunes learns that I've already heard last week's episode, it'll be removed and replaced with an episode I haven't listened to yet.

Finally, I've specified that this playlist should always contain the most recent two shows that meet all the above criteria. *Martini Shot* episodes are brief — about five minutes a throw — and so I can afford to have several on my iPod. That right there is a big advantage over having iTunes update podcasts on your iPod automatically.

Yes, iTunes' automatic features let you select some podcasts for iPod listening and not

Figure 8-20
Fine-tuning your iPod content with Smart Playlists

others, and yes, through the podcast settings you can tell iTunes to update only *X* number of episodes, but those changes are applied to every single freakin' podcast you have.

Through Smart Playlists, I can produce *exactly* the mix of content I want: many episodes of some, few episodes of others, and no episodes that I've already heard. And iTunes will synch them to my iPod automatically. These Smart Playlists are full of podcasts, but they're just playlists, after all, and all you need to do is add 'em to the iPod's collection of automatically-updated playlists. Period.

Podcasts, believe it or not, make me very, very happy that I chose a career in technology instead of accepting that contract to catch for the Red Sox's AAA-team in Pawtucket. As soon as I finish writing this chapter, I'm going to grab my iPod from its dock and go run some errands. And holy cats: Elves have installed seven hours of new programming onto the thing while I slept. Er … wrote. Well, you have this book in your hands: You be the judge.

Podcasting is a standard that belongs to the entire world, that any company or individual is free to support. Apple ought to be applauded for supporting podcasts so aggressively. It jumped right in, baking a podcast directory right into its own iTunes store even though thousands of free, high-quality podcasts can steal revenue from it. It's easy to set up and it just plain works.

There are only two costs: One, I'm driving a lot more than I used to, putting at least eight percent of my odometer miles on endless circling of my neighborhood as I kill time waiting for the end of an episode. And secondly, roving bands of radio executives, thrown out of business by their inability to compete with a free solution that listeners can tailor to their specific needs, are slowly turning feral through fear and a desperate need for food.

But hey, they're radio executives. They were going to feast upon the flesh of the living no matter *how* the industry went.

➢   ➢   ➢

Audio Streams

The Skim

In fairness, not everybody gets that important memo … the one that announces to the whole world that Progress has once again had its way with a beloved Tradition. Yes, you laugh at these poor idiots, but let's be fair. I'm sure that many of you are still cooking steaks and chicken on an old-fashioned George Foreman grill instead of using that cheap and efficient aerosol spray that cooks and seasons meat, fish, and poultry in a single five-second application. And do I make fun of *you?* I do not. I just think that maybe you should get out to a Target store more often, that's all.

Nor do I get all snarky when I learn that you're still listening to Internet radio shows and other Netcasts while sitting behind your desk. The big lesson learned in the past decade of delivering content over the Internet is that spending an hour sitting in an uncomfortable office chair in front of a $2,000 PC isn't exactly an upgrade to sitting anywhere you want and listening to a $12 AM/FM radio. No. But instead of tuning in at a certain time, you can download an hour's worth of audio and listen to it whenever you like, on practically any device you happen to have on you. Streaming is *out.* Podcasts and audio downloads are in.

And yet, some of the best programming on the Internet is still trapped behind streaming-media URLs. The (radio show, conference keynote,

As a guy who creates stuff for a living, I ought to acknowledge a question: is it *right* to capture audio to a file? Shouldn't we consider the possibility that the content creators didn't make a podcast (for example) of this show available because they don't *want* people listening on their iPods?

I gotta admit that I don't have an aggressive and arrogant answer to that one. It's certainly wrong to use this software to steal a copy of someone else's locked, purchased music, for example. But when the audio is on a CD that you own, using an audio-capture utility to get around the record company's copy-prevention scheme is almost *righteous*.

Unfortunately, most examples fall in the middle. I suppose it comes down to the advice your parents gave you (if they were good parents, I mean): Would you feel awkward justifying your actions to someone? I continue to record BBC programming because it's free, and they publish the URLs to their streams openly, and (unlike many radio sites) they don't even use Web ads to subsidize the broadcasts.

But your mileage will vary. Please — I say, sincerely — don't be naughty. One day you're going to wonder why nobody creates any *decent* content any more, and the answer is because nobody could make any money doing it.

live convert) streams when it airs, and once the sound squirts out of your speakers, it's gone forever.

It's such a bizarre and unfortunate turn of events that energetic programmers have developed software that can "capture" all the sound coming out of your speaker and

write it to a file, where you can listen at your leisure. And although naturally it's this "But why doesn't the BBC podcast *I'm Sorry I Haven't a Clue*?!?" insanity that's gotten me the most worked up, there are lots of ways to use a capture app to enhance your general lifestyle and improve your overall sense of well-being.

THE BIG IDEA

The function of these utilities is so basic and fundamental that I need to break it out of that preceding paragraph and let it stand all by itself in its glory:

It can capture any audio playing through your PC to a file that you can then import into iTunes and put on an iPod.

Well, that's game, set, and match, isn't it? It's a solution to any and all permutations of the question "How do I get this audio onto my iPod?" Examples:

> The BBC streams enough brain-mincingly great content that the sheer awesomeness of it all can affect the tides and confuse migrating birds. But I can only hear this great stuff on a computer with an Internet connection.

> Plus, they're like five hours ahead of us. I can't be listening to a 9:15 a.m. airing of *The Archers* … that's 4:15 a.m. our time and I'm just getting to bed!

> Just like … um … well, I think a Biblical reference would work well in this example, but I'm not really all that religious. Wasn't there a dude who went down The Wrong Path before seeing The Light? Let's call him Reggie. Yes, just like the biblical Reggie, you strayed before you finally accepted

the wisdom and perfection of Apple and the iPod. You'd bought hundreds of dollars' worth of music from a competing online music service, and it's all locked up with a digital rights-management system that prevents those tracks from working in any music software but Windows Media Player. You've seen the error of your ways … so *must* you purchase *all* these tracks all over again in the iTunes store to get them to work on your iPod?

➤ Evil lizard scum at a music company have corrupted the CD you paid $19 for, to prevent you from exercising your legal right to rip the tracks into music files. The disc will play fine in the desktop player that came on the CD, but iTunes doesn't even recognize it as an audio disc.

➤ Through the magic of audio chat, you and four or five people are having an online meeting. You'd like to, you know, *record* all this so that when the whole project inevitably fails and takes the whole company down with it, you can have a swift and conclusive rebuttal to the charge that it was *you* who suggested a buddy-cop movie starring the grown-up cute little kid from *The Sixth Sense* and a wise-cracking cartoon Vespa scooter voiced by Jimmy Fallon.

➤ You think that Hunter S. Thompson's stream-of-consciousness rantings in one of the commentary tracks to the *Fear and Loathing in Las Vegas* DVD is exactly what you need to motivate you through your morning run. But you're not terribly interested in ripping the movie with one piece of software and then using a second piece of software to strip the audio portion into a separate file.

On and on. This is the sort of tool where you put it on your hard drive … and then just wait. You can be certain that eventually, it's going to be the solution to *some* sort of problem.

RECORDING A SHOW IN WINDOWS

Applian Technologies' Replay A/V is an absolute marvel. It kind of serves to remind me how low my expectations are for apps, after so many years of writing about this stuff.

"In a perfect world," I pronounce as I launch the app for the first time, "if you wanted a piece of software to record *Car Talk* on NPR, you'd search for 'Car Talk,' the app would find the show automatically, and all the settings would be made for you without any intervention on your part whatsoever."

Glorying in the sound of my voice, I continue, "Alas, no. This world is but a vale of tears and I'm sure that by the time I hear Click and Clack talking about what sort of noise a duck would make if one were trapped inside an air filter, I'll have a new, violent, PC-shaped hole in my window and a new commitment to pursue a new career in agriculture."

But gorblimey. Yes, it really is *that* simple to record a radio show in Replay A/V. You can download a trial copy from www.applian.com, or buy it online for about fifty bucks.

Figure 9-1

Replay A/V: sticky fingers for PC audio

Recording a Show by Name: 100 Percent Automagically

Let me do the fancy numbered-lists-and-screenshots thing and formally explain how to record a show:

1. Launch Replay A/V. The main window is shown in Figure 9-1.

2. Click Replay's Media Guide button. This will open a new window containing the Replay Media Guide. It's not incorrect to compare this to the iTunes store; it's an online entity that helps you search for all manner of online content.

3. Click the Media Guide's Shows button, seen at the top of the Guide window (see Figure 9-2). You'll be taken to a search page.

4. Type the name of the show that you'd like to record in the Show Name box, and then click the Find Show button. If

Figure 9-2

The Replay Media Guide's search buttons

the show's listed anywhere in the Guide, you'll then see a list of matches (see Figure 9-3). In many cases, the same show will be available from many different online radio stations, airing at different times. Pick your poison.

5. Click the Add button next to the show description you'd like to schedule. Next, you'll see a window where you can tell Replay how you'd like the show to be recorded. Here's the Stuff We Care About:

   ➤ The Schedule tabbed pane lets you

Figure 9-3
Advice about a Miata transmission is now close at hand.

set up this show as a recurring recording. By default, Replay will record the show every time it airs (the Media Guide database knows that this station streams it every Sunday at 6 p.m.). But this is where you can make it a one-

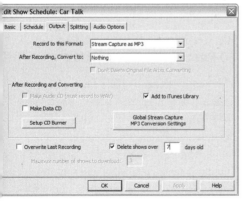

Figure 9-4
Sending the recording straight to iTunes

off, for example, or pad the recording by having it start a little early or end a little late.

> Output is the most important pane in this whole window (see Figure 9-4). Here's where I set up this recording so that the output always lands directly in the iTunes library, in a format that the iPod can handle.

> Click the Record to this Format pop-up and select Stream capture as MP3. That's the only iPod-compatible format in the list. Click the Add to iTunes Library checkbox, for obvious reasons, and for good measure, click the Delete Shows over [X] Days Old box as well. Replay will keep its own copy indefinitely unless you check this box (and put in a time limit) or delete the shows manually. You don't need

>TIDBIT

Replay is double-plus clever. The Media Guide knows everything it needs to know about every show and every radio station that streams it. And if the station simply leaves the streaming-media file on its servers where any app is free to download it … then Replay will simply download this file in one big blast instead of letting the show slowly stream its way in.

these copies, because they're all going to be copied into iTunes automatically.

6. Click OK.

Replay will add the show to its to-do list.

The rest is elfin magic: At the right day and time, Replay will contact the streaming-media server that hosts the show and start recording the data "live." You won't hear anything coming out of your PC's speakers but that's okay; it's turning the raw data straight into audio without bothering to clutter your eardrums with it. You can even have other things going on with your PC; if your e-mail client chirps, "You've Got Mail!" it *won't* show up in the recording.

Recording a Show by Radio Station or Server: 80 Percent Automagically

If the Media Guide has never heard of the *SuperMegaHyper Checker Ultra-Ska Nutty Hour* at your local 1,000-watt college radio station, you can still record the show and get Replay to do nearly all the work for you:

1. Open the Media Guide and click the Stations button to search for the station.

2. Enter the station's name or call letters in the Station Name field and click the Find Station button.

3. Click the Add button next to the name of the station you'd like to record. Replay will take you to the same Edit Show window you saw in Figure 9-4. But the information that the Media Guide provided automatically for *Car Talk* will have to be provided manually … by, you know, *you*.

4. In the Basic pane, give the show a name. Click the Schedule tab and tell Replay what time to start and stop the recording, whether it should just be recorded once on a certain date, or if it should be recorded on a recurring schedule on certain days of the week.

5. Click the Output tab and use the same iPod and iTunes-friendly settings as in the previous example.

6. Click OK to add the new show to the to-do list.

Recording a Show by URL: 50 Percent Automagically

The Replay Media Guide is filled with miracles, have no doubt, but it doesn't know *everything*. It probably doesn't know that the little coffee shop you found in that city you visited on business — the one with the Tuesday Night Open Mike that was absolutely filled with the most breathtakingly bad but vastly entertaining musicians you'd ever heard — streams the parade of confessional catastrophe and free-form lute-jazz live every week.

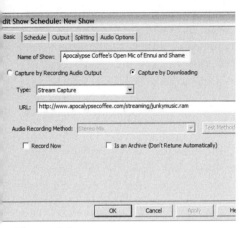

Figure 9-5
Doing it the hard way: adding all the
show's details yourself

Still (unlike many people), Replay can be
taught. All you need is the URL of the audio
stream. You can usually find it by visiting
the site that promotes or lists the show. Look
for a button or a link that says Listen Now
or Open in RealPlayer or somesuch. Right-
click the link and copy it to the Windows
Clipboard.

Then:

1. Click Replay's Manual Add button. You'll
   be taken straight to Replay's (now-famil-
   iar) Edit Show Schedule window (see
   Figure 9-5)

2. Give the show a name and paste the
   stream URL in the URL field.

3. Input the settings for Schedule and Output as before.

Recording Whatever's Coming from Your Speakers Right Now: 0% Automagically

It is yet another testament to Replay's awe-

> **>TIP**
>
> If you're having no luck locating the elusive
> URL of a streaming broadcast, Replay can help.
> Just start the stream playing with Real Player,
> QuickTime Player, Windows Media Player,
> or the player that's embedded in your Web
> browser. Then switch over to Replay and click
> the Stream Capture button.
>
> Replay will sniff around and compile a list
> of all the URLs that are delivering streaming
> media to all the software on your PC at that
> moment. Click on the likeliest candidate, click
> the Add Selection as New Recording button,
> and Replay will take it from there, acting as
> though the URL had been delivered from the
> Media Guide.

someness that only *now* am I getting to
the "Record Whatever Audio Happens to
Be Coming Through Your PC's Speakers"
motive that I cited at the beginning of the
chapter.

Replay offers so many features for recording streaming audio that, honestly, the only
times you'd ever really *need* this feature is if
the sound you want to capture isn't coming
from the Internet. You'd use this feature to
capture DVD or chat audio, for example.

Replay A/V is to be commended for not
being a total control freak when it comes
to this whole recording business. Phil Spec-
tor could have learned a thing from Replay.
There, I said it.

Yes, although the app gives you bales of
resources for recording shows and streams
automatically, it'll also go into Idiot Man-
Child mode. Click a button and anything
that's playing on your PC will be captured to

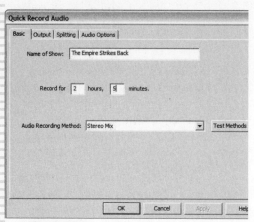

Figure 9-6
Click-and-record any PC audio in a jiffy

an audio file:

1. Set up whatever app will be making all that noise — your desktop DVD player software, your audio chat app, Windows Media Player, the Real streaming client — and get it ready so you can start the audio with a minimum of clicking

Figure 9-7
Your remote control to WireTap's features.

around.

2. In Replay, click the Quick Audio Record button. You'll see the Quick Record Audio window (see Figure 9-6).

3. Give the recording a name.

4. In this specific example, I'm recording the audio from my DVD of *The Empire Strikes Back*. So I'm also telling Replay to stop recording after 2 hours and 5 minutes, the running time of the flick. Plus a little wiggle room.

5. Click the Output tab and make all those iTunes-ish and iPod-ish settings that I'm so keen about.

6. Click OK.

Recording begins immediately, and the Quick Audio Record button turns into the Stop Recording button. You're ahead of me on what that does. I can sense it.

RECORDING ON A MAC

Well, I'm just a little bit depressed now, fellow sensation-seekers. The Mac OS "capture any audio to a file" app I'm about to recommend is a fine, fine program. I just wish it were more like Replay A/V, that's all.

Ambrosia Software's $20 WireTap Pro (www.ambrosiasw.com) doesn't offer any of Replay's spectacular goodities and niceties. It's just a straightforward "capture sound" utility.

(Sigh.)

No, no. It's a terrific program. I've just been spoiled, that's all.

Onward, onward.

Recording Whatever's Coming from Your Speakers Right Now

WireTap has a very clean and dare I say *pretty* little controller (see Figure 9-7). Capturing "live" audio to a file (from a media player like RealPlayer, the DVD Player app, iChat, etc.) couldn't be simpler:

1. Click the Record button to start recording. The LCD-ish numbers at the bottom of the controller tell you how long the recording has been running, and how big the file is so far.

2. Click the Stop button to stop. WireTap will prompt you for a filename and location.

3. If you fold down the two sealed corners of a FedEx overnight envelope, you've got an instant pope hat.

Number Three has nothing to do with sound recording but the steps for this are so easy that I felt that I needed to beef up the list a little. ... Oh, wait! I can complicate things by explaining how to tell WireTap where to save the resulting file, and in what format! Wonderful, wonderful:

1. Choose File ⇨ Preferences.

2. Click the Saving tab of WireTap's Preferences to specify a default destination for the audio (see Figure 9-8).

3. Choose iTunes as the Save Files To destination. All recordings will automatically be sent to your iTunes library. If you check the Automatically Save Recordings option, it'll be automatically saved to iTunes as soon as recording stops. You can also tell WireTap to add the recording to a specific playlist. The only drawback

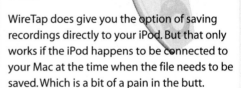

of automatic saving is that WireTap will give the recording a fairly generic name. Later on, you might not know what the recording is until you give it a listen.

4. Click the Format tab to choose a default audio format. Select your favorite format from the list. If you know that you're chiefly going to be recording spoken audio instead of glorious stereophonical music, you can also click the Settings but-

ton to choose a configuration that'll result in smaller files. Mono instead of stereo, 22K bit rate instead of 44K … that sort of thing.

5. Click OK to accept the new settings.

Recording a Streaming Broadcast

WireTap has quick and clean features for scheduling recordings. It's a pity that you can't just tell it the name of a program and have it fill in the blanks for your automatically, but I suppose I should knock off the Replay references. If I keep going, I'm liable to give WireTap one of those "middle child" syndromes. Or complexes. Well, I'll stop, either way.

1. Go to WireTap's Recording Sessions window and click the New button. You'll see a window with lots of tabbed panes (see Figure 9-9).

2. Give the recording a title (via the Description box). The Saving and Format panes will be pre-set to the defaults you created in the app's Preferences window.

3. Click the Processing tab to provide WireTap with the URL of the audio stream. Remember: WireTap records *all* the audio spilling through your Mac. If you leave the RealPlayer app (or QuickTime, or the audio stream's live Web page) open and playing, you don't need to provide a URL; at the specified time, WireTap will leap into action and start recording. But

Figure 9-8
Choosing the "where" of WireTap's sound saving

it can be pretty dashed annoying to have the local spite-rock station blaring 24 hours just to get the Heavy Metal Traffic Report at 6:50 a.m. So, …

4. Paste the URL for the stream into the first text field of the Processing pane. It contains grayed-out text reading "AppleScript, URL or File" before you replace it. As in the PC example, you can get the URL for the stream by looking for a direct link on the broadcast's Web page — usually it's marked with a Listen or Open in RealPlayer label or somesuch.

5. Choose the app that you'll be using to tune in to the stream. By default, WireTap chooses your Safari browser. It's a safe thing for WireTap to choose because every streaming media player comes with a Safari plugin; Safari is the one app that's sure to be able to play anything. But for convenience, you'll want WireTap to open the URL in a standalone media

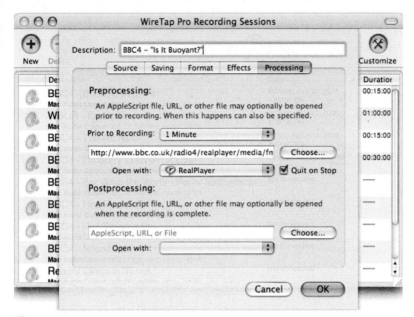

Figure 9-9
Setting up a new automatic recording

player (RealPlayer or QuickTime Player). That way, you can tell WireTap to Quit the player app when the recording's finished.

Why would you want to do that? Because if the URL is the radio station's constant "live" feed, then the URL will remain open even after the recording is complete. So the first recording of the evening will be the 30-minute BBC4 quiz show you wanted. The second recording, made two hours later, will be the NPR report on the woman who makes quilts from used driver-side airbags … and it'll be overlaid on the audio of whatever's on BBC4 at the moment.

6. Click Quit on Stop to terminate the sound from the streaming radio station after the recording is complete. Click OK.

The recording info will be saved to WireTap's Recording Sessions list. As is, whenever you select this item in the list and then click the Record Now button, WireTap will record the audio from that URL, starting immediately.

But you can turn this into a scheduled recording that starts and ends automatically. Here's how:

1. Select the item and click the Schedule button. WireTap will open the Mac OS's built-in iCal calendar application, and will create a brand-new appointment for this show (see Figure 9-10).

WireTap takes advantage of some of the keen features of iCal and the Mac OS. WireTap creates its own iCal calendar that contains all its scheduled recordings. Just fill in the date, time, and duration details just as you would for any other appoint-

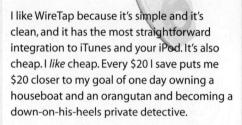

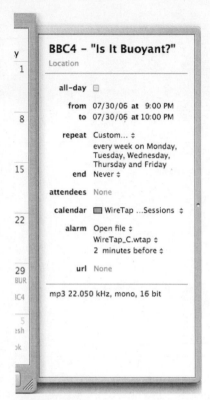

BBC4 – "Is It Buoyant?"
Location

all-day	☐
from	07/30/06 at 9:00 PM
to	07/30/06 at 10:00 PM
repeat	Custom... ⬍
	every week on Monday, Tuesday, Wednesday, Thursday and Friday
end	Never ⬍
attendees	None
calendar	▨ WireTap ...Sessions ⬍
alarm	Open file ⬍
	WireTap_C.wtap ⬍
	2 minutes before ⬍
url	None

mp3 22.050 kHz, mono, 16 bit

Figure 9-10
Setting up a hot date with the BBC

ment. When you return to WireTap, you'll find that the particulars have been added to the item in the Sessions list.

And that's it. You just trust things to work, and they do … unless, again, other Mac apps start making noise while WireTap is recording.

But until the rest of the world arrives here in the warm, indulgent embrace of the 21st century, WireTap is indispensable. You and I are probably the last generation to grow up with media that we can't access whenever and however we want. Our grandkids will mock us as we spoke of barbaric practices where we

arranged to be listening to a device at a specific pre-arranged time so we could hear our favorite programming.

Well, what do we care? We shall unscrew our heads from our Friendly Grandparent bodies and plug them into scary, Akira-style robomech battle intimido-armor, specially designed for teaching bratty young kids to respect their damned elders.

10

Internet Videos

The Skim

It's a vicious cycle from which the corporate world cannot hope to break free with any semblance of victory or dignity. The Internet provides a new sort of service that catches on; workplace productivity slows to a crawl; however, traffic is being generated and money is being made, so other companies bankroll the development of *further* and far more viral iterations of that idea, leading to an even lesser likelihood of anything getting finished before 11 a.m. on a Tuesday.

Meanwhile, the companies who are profiting from this Internet service are raking in record profits — and they're under tighter scrutiny to keep the gravy train rolling, so they put more pressure on their developers to enhance and expand the idea. The programmers respond by goofing off on their own, creating a *new* diversionary technology that the original company can't profit from but that sends the Wheel of Distraction spinning anew.

What I'm getting at is that the fact that Internet video is becoming more sophisticated can only indicate that yet another crack has formed in the foundations of the world economy. Clearly we're all one step closer to reverting to a purely agrarian existence. If you've loaned your shovel to a neighbor … go and get it back. I'm serious. Go. Now.

But while we await the glorious nihilistic post-apocalyptic, post-crash

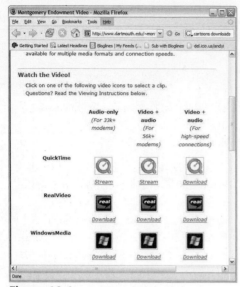

Figure 10-1
The Easy Button: Click to download.

future, let us gaily splash around in the trough of free video entertainment available for online viewing. Thousands of hours of video are available online and by applying a little mojo, most of it can be enjoyed on your iPod.

In broad strokes, there are two steps:

1. Pull the video off the Web and into a video file on your computer. Which can be a problem, as many videos are

>**TIP**

Sometimes, a Web page will describe the format of the file by its filename extension instead of something more human-friendly. The file extensions .AVI or .WMV denote Windows Video/Windows Media files. Extensions .QT and .MOV indicate QuickTime files.

intended solely to be played through a Web site.

2. Convert that file into a format that your video-studly iPod can play.

GRABBING VIDEO FROM THE WEB

Gifted with the power of free will, the folks who publish content on the Web have done so with their own selfish needs in mind. "But what about those of us who want to watch that [movie trailer, music video, viral video — you fill in the blank] from the comfort of our iPods?" you ask. But your lament falls on deaf ears.

Techniques for saving videos onto your computer range from the Violently Simple to the Somewhat Tricky, depending on how it's being served and how it was prepared.

Just Save It

If you're lucky, there's a big fat button right next to the video that lets you download the file without using any special tricks or tools.

Figure 10-1 shows a Web page of videos available from Dartmouth University's site. It is such a flawless and easy-to-read example of this sort of thing that I really ought to send them twenty bucks or something:

Not all Web pages are this easy to grok. Figure 10-2 shows a more or less worst-case scenario: itsy-bitsy little QuickTime and Windows Media logos.

Videos are often available in multiple formats and can be either streamed or downloaded. "Streaming" means that the video is squirted into your viewing window and

Figure 10-2
Stalking the wily Download button

every second of it disappears forever as soon as you've seen it. You want a Download link, which will transmit the whole file to your computer.

You'll be leaning about video file formats later on in this chapter. Whether you're using a PC or a Mac, the format that iTunes is happiest to work with is, naturally, Apple's own QuickTime format.

But if the video isn't available as QuickTime, Windows Media is a fine second choice no matter what sort of computer you're using. And if you can't get either, then just take what you can get.

Click on the button to download the video. If your Web browser knows how to handle the file's type of video, it'll open the video file within the browser itself, as shown in Figure 10-3. Choose Save or Save As from your browser menu to save the file to your hard drive. If your browser hasn't the foggiest clue how to play a Windows Media file or a QuickTime, it'll save the file directly to your drive.

To save a little time and some possible aggravation, you can download the file directly by clicking the link with your right mouse but-

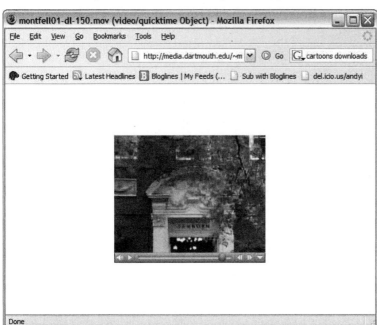

Figure 10-3
A video file that opens right in its own browser window.

Figure 10-4
Embedded Web video: one click, no waiting

ton, and selecting Save File As (in Windows) or Download to Disk (on the Mac) from the pop-up menu. If you're a Mac user and have a one-button mouse, you can do the same thing by holding down the Control key on your keyboard while clicking. The possible aggravation you'll avoid is the possibility that the file will be handed off to Windows Media Player or another app automatically.

You can save from the browser, you can save from a contextual menu, you can save from a media player — there are many roads to Saving This Video File to Disk, depending on what operating system and browser you're using. These are but a few.

Yeah, you can safely guess that Windows is already set up to handle Windows Media files, and that Mac OS is set up to handle QuickTime files. But Microsoft and Apple both offer cross-platform solutions. Visit

www.quicktime.com to download a free QuickTime player and plug-in for Windows. The player's a Very Useful Thing and I'll be talking about it later on, when I get to the part that tells you how to convert some of these files for iPod use.

Microsoft doesn't *directly* offer a Windows Media player for Mac users, but it's extremely pleased that a company by the name of Telestream jumped in and did the dirty work for it. Visit www.flip4mac.com to download Flip4Mac, a bit of software that adds Windows Media to the Mac's usual bag of QuickTime tricks.

Embedded Video

Sometimes, the Web designer gets a bit fancy. Instead of direct download links, a QuickTime or Windows Media video player is embedded into the Web page itself (see

Figure 10-5
QuickTime Pro allows you to save many embedded videos directly from the player.

Figure 10-4). And while embedded video is a real peach if you're just interested in watching it and then moving on with your life; it can complicate things if you want to save the video and watch it on your iPod later.

Of course, *if* the video is in a format that QuickTime understands *and* you've paid Apple $30 to upgrade your free QuickTime software to the QuickTime Pro edition, it's entirely possible that downloading the video will be a piece of pie. Easy as cake. Whatever,

because one of the Pro features you get for the thirty bucks is a Save item in the little pop-up menu in the lower-right corner of the movie viewer (see Figure 10-5). Just select Save As QuickTime Movie from the pop-up and you're good to go. The Big Win of the QuickTime Pro player is that it can convert video files from one format to the other, which will figure heavily in the last section of this book.

If you *haven't* bought the QuickTime Pro upgrade, the Save menu item will numbly refuse to respond to your mouse clicks. Mockingly. Head on over to www.quicktime.com and after some mojo with your credit card, you'll receive a 20-digit code that will unlock all the hidden features of the Quick-Time browser plug-in as well as the stand-alone QuickTime player.

Now that we've established some dramatic tension in our narrative, we press on to the always-uncomfortable reminder that life is a vale of tears and that our daily struggles serve to build Character.

Alas, many embedded videos don't have any

>TIDBIT

When saving video files in QuickTime Pro, you'll see a Save As Source option in addition to the Save option. Save as Source saves the video in its original file format. It's possible the original format is some freaky thing that neither iTunes nor the iPod wants any part of. So saving it as a QuickTime will save you an extra step down the road — and that's why just choosing Save is the best option, since it saves the video in QuickTime format no matter what format it started life in.

located at this address," you ought to be able to download it directly without any muss or fuss.

Finding the video's address is often very easy. With the Web page open in front of you:

1. View the page source in your browser. In Internet Explorer, choose View ➪ Source. In Firefox, choose View ➪ Page Source, In Safari, choose View ➪ View Source.

   This will open the HTML file that defines the contents of the Web page, and it includes the addresses of all the files that appear on it. Please do not look *directly* at the text you see in Figure 10-6. Years of watching *Star Trek* and reading bad sci-fi have largely desensitized geeks and nerds like me to this sort of gobbledygook. Fortunately, you don't really need to understand everything that's going on in this window.

2. Press Ctrl+F in Windows or ⌘+F on a Macintosh to search the contents of this HTML file.

   The video file *usually* has a very predictable marker near it, such as the filename extension at the end of the file. If it's a QuickTime file, search for the filename extension ".mov." If it's a Windows Media file, try ".avi" or ".wmv." For Flash video, try ".flv." You can also try looking for "embed." Embed is the page-description code often used to actually embed the video file into the page. In Figure 10-7, Firefox has found an embed in the file and has highlighted it for us. Here's the entire line:

```
<embed type="application/
x-mplayer2" pluginspage=
"http://www.microsoft.
com/Windows/MediaPlayer/"
```

pop-up menu at all. Particularly Windows Media files. Or maybe they don't even *have* a visible player. "I have been foiled," you may mutter. "Thwarted, indeed," your compatriot might add, because he, like you, has recently taken to speaking like an eighteenth-century English nobleman whose plans have been upset by a lowly-but-handsome young stableboy with a keen sense of Right and Wrong.

If the Web site's designer has failed to provide you with any tools for downloading the video from the Web site, you might be able to download it anyway. Like the Web page itself and like all the pictures on it, the video is (most likely) just a file on a Web server. If you can figure out the address of that file, and tell your browser, "Please load the file

> ➤**TIP**
>
> Sometimes, you'll find just a partial URL like "movies/funny/applepiehubbub.mov." You can usually convert this to a full URL by just tacking the Web site's URL to the front. If you're visiting www.larrysdumbvideo.com, try http://www.larrysdumbvideo.com/movies/funny/applepiehubbub.mov as the download address.

```
name="mediaplayer1"
showstatusbar="1"
EnableContextMenu=
"false" autostart="true"
width="480" height="430"
transparentstart="1" loop="0"
controller="true" src="http://
f6.putfile.com/videos/a1-
13720364138.wmv"> </embed>
```

3. Copy the URL of the video file. And here you'll have to use your eyes. The URL of a video file starts with "http://" and usually ends with the file's filename extension (such as .wmv). In this example, the URL leaps straight out at you:

```
http://f6.putfile.com/videos/a1-
13720364138.wmv
```

But sometimes it can get a little tricky.

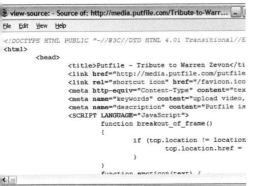

Figure 10-6
The DNA of a Web page

src= means "this is a file address," so you typically should just copy everything that sits between the first and the final quotes. But sometimes, the URL is buried elsewhere; the Web site logs file transfers through a customized system so that it can track which files are the most popular, what time of day folks like to watch 'em, etc. Fortunately, trial-and-error costs you nothing.

4. With the URL in hand, paste the URL of the video file into the Address line of your browser and either press the Enter key (in Windows) or Return key (on the Macintosh) or click the Go button.

If you guessed, right … bingo! Everything proceeds smoothly.

Depending on how your browser is configured, the video will download directly to a file on your computer or it'll open all by itself inside its own player — in that latter case, you can save it using the browser's Save command.

When All Else Fails

The basic techniques I've already given you will work for most video pages you'll come across. But there are always those occasional Tough Nuts to Crack, and when confronted with these things one must turn to a higher power: KeepVid.com (see Figure 10-8).

The folks behind KeepVid maintain a list of all the places and methods video sites use to store their video files. You provide them with the URL of the Web page and they'll generate a link from which you can download the video.

1. Copy the URL of the content.

Figure 10-7
Stalking the wily video file

And here I don't mean the URL from your browser's address bar. I also don't mean the URL of the video file (if you had *that,* you wouldn't need KeepVid!). No, I mean that you should hunt for what the Web site calls a "permalink," which is a link to this content that doesn't change from user to user. Figure 10-9 shows a permalink on the YouTube. com site: http://www.youtube.com/watch?v+z965UU3mdB8

2. Paste the URL into KeepVid's Download field.

3. Click Download.

KeepVid will generate a Download link to the video file (see Figure 10-10). Right-click this link and choose Save to start downloading the file to your computer. (If you have a Macintosh with a one-button mouse, holding down the Control key while clicking your mouse button is the same thing as a right-click.) If KeepVid tells you to rename the file so that the name ends in ".flv" do what it says. Most of the content on Google Video and YouTube arrives in the Flash

Video format.

KeepVid has no way of knowing what to call this file so you're free to name it something sensible, such as "AwesomeRollerbladeWipe-outWhereTheDudeGetsHitInTheGroin-WithLikeAMillionTrafficSigns.flv."

But *do* examine the download page closely before using YouTube. Google Video often has the friendliest direct-download button you could ever hope for (see Figure 10-11):

Just choose Video iPod from the pop-up menu, click Download, and you're done. The result is a video file that will synch directly onto your iPod without any trans-mogrification necessary. Would that you could say the same for *every* video you download from the Net.

CONVERTING VIDEO TO AN IPOD-FRIENDLY FORMAT

In life, there are hardships and then there are *hardships.* Not being able to watch a 52-min-ute *Star Wars* fanfilm on your iPod the min-ute it finishes downloading isn't on the same level as being two months behind on the rent and having seventeen dollars to your name. Still: Man, that stinks.

But once again I say that these challenges in life lead to a stronger being. "Steel is hard-ened through fire," etc. Plus, there are utili-ties that do a fine job transmogrifying video files into an iPod-studly format.

Oh, you want technical details? Here's what a video iPod wants by way of video format:

H.264 video: up to 768 Kbps, 320 x 240, 30 frames per sec., Baseline Profile up to Level 1.3 with AAC-LC up to 160 Kbps, 48 Khz, stereo

Figure 10-8
KeepVid can snag video from most of the popular video sites.

---

audio in .m4v, .mp4 and .mov file formats. MPEG-4 video: up to 2.5 mbps, 480 x 480, 30 frames per sec., Simple Profile with AAC-LC up to 160 Kbps, 48 KHz, stereo audio in .m4v, .mp4 and .mov file formats. That's copied directly from Apple's Web site, and is current as of this writing.

The upshot is that it's not as simple as dragging a video file into iTunes and then letting the software sort it all out.

At least not right now, and, yes, I was as disappointed as you are when I first found out. When I got my first video iPod, I figured that I'd just drag QuickTime files into iTunes and bang, I was good to go. In truth, iTunes copied some of my videos to the iPod but not others. Some files just happened to be

formatted correctly; it was the luck of the draw.

So even if you're sporting a drawer full of Apple QuickTime files, steel yourself — you might have some more work to do. But you're not alone in Wanting to Put Video Files on an iPod — one would be so bold as to declare that this is the whole point of having a video iPod in the first place — so there are plenty of utilities to help you.

QuickTime Pro

I mentioned QuickTime Pro earlier. Quick-Time is free, but when you give Apple some dough, it'll send you a special code that'll unlock added features that converts plain old QuickTime to the super-duper QuickTime

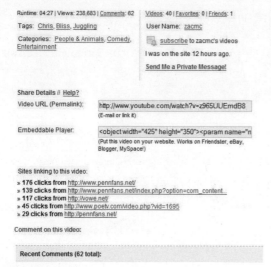

Figure 10-9

A permalink to a video on YouTube.com

Pro. One of these features is the ability to download video straight from an embedded online video. Another one is the ability to convert video from one format to another — and there's an explicit option for converting a video for use on an iPod.

To convert using the QuickTime Pro player:

1. Open the video in the Player.

> **TIP**

Even if you never avail yourself of KeepVid's download service, the site's a fantastic place to visit for its utterly exhaustive list of Places on the Internet Where You Can Watch Online Videos, accessible through its Sites pop-up list. Most people are aware of Google Video and YouTube, but there are hundreds of smaller sites out there with content that's free for the taking.

2. Choose File ⇨ Export (see Figure 10-12).

3. Select the Movie to iPod (320x240) option next to Export.

4. Click Save.

QuickTime will begin saving your video. If the video is of any real length, this is a good opportunity to refinish the antique dining-room table that your grandmother left you a few years ago.

QuickTime Pro has many fine features and characteristics, but let us also be mature enough to note that sometimes, as you wait for it to finish converting a file, you can hear the grim hoofbeats of Death's horse approaching, and as time ticks by you begin to look forward to his icy embrace. ("Format conversions can take a while" is what I'm saying.)

Using Apple's QuickTime Pro to convert a video file is a good way to make absolutely

Download

>> Download Link << (Right-click -> "Save Target As" OR copy and paste the lin
extension to .flv)

History (clear)
http://www.youtube.com/watch?v=z965UUEmdB8

Figure 10-10
Downloading a
video via KeepVid

Amazing Juggling Finale
Chris Bliss
4 min 27 sec - Mar 3, 2006
chrisbliss.com

Download for [Video iPod ▼]
                Windows/Mac
Chris Bliss perforr Video iPod
juggling routine.   Sony PSP

« Prev - Next video »

Playlist - Details - ☒ Send - Embed

Figure 10-11
Downloading directly from Google
Video … sometimes!

sure that the file is being converted to an
iPod format. But QuickTime Pro has its
drawbacks. Chief among them: It can't
handle all the file formats that you'll encounter on the Web. For Pete's sake — note that
I am toning down my language to reach a
mass-audience — the Windows version can't
even convert Windows Media files. The Mac
version can't either, without a third-party
plug-in that you need to purchase at added
expense.

Which is why if your chief goal is just to
convert videos so you can use 'em on your
iPod, you're better off using a third-party
conversion utility.

Windows:
iSoft's Total Video Converter

Total Video Converter (TVC) is a bit of a

marvel. It's a bit pricey, compared to some
of the other apps ($45 at the moment; about
50 percent more than the competition) but
it's so totally worth it for the bucketload of
features that it delivers. Download it from
www.effectmatrix.com; you can use it for
free for up to 15 days before you have to
make with the credit card and purchase an
activation code.

But the app's user interface isn't as *clean* as
QuickTime Pro's, as you can see in Figure
10-13. Nonetheless, converting video is fairly
1-2-3-ish:

1. Click the New Task pop-up button, and
choose Import Files. You can select more
than one file to convert.

2. Select the destination file format by clicking
the iPod MPEG4 pop-up button, found in
the Mobile section (see Figure 10-14).

TVC offers a few different options.
All three formats work on your iPod.
H.264 will produce smaller files than
the two MPEG-4 options, but H.264
takes a notoriously long time to encode.
Don't use it if you're in a hurry. The two
MPEG-4 flavors are essentially identical.
One creates a .MOV file, the other uses
the .MP4 extension. Both will work just
fine and produce files of the same size
and quality. It's the same data in two different wrappers. I use .MP4 because it's
more widely understood by non-Apple

Figure 10-12

Exporting a video from the QuickTime Pro Player.

video players, like the players you might find on a PDA or a cell phone.

3. If you've selected more than one video file to convert, check the boxes for all the files that you'd like to convert using the settings you've just created.

4. Click the Convert Now button.

TVC will percolate for a while, processing all the files you've selected. Go on about your business; the app is perfectly happy to run in the background. When it's done, your files will appear in TVC's Converted directory, a folder that it's kind enough to open for you when the job is done.

I can't say enough about Total Video Converter. I tried a pile of different video converters before TVC, many of which involved lots of steps and lots of different apps working in unison and even then, it was a partial solution, good for some problems but not others.

TVC is the only tool you'll ever need. It handles every format and exports to just about everything. Whenever I need to demo a new phone or some other gadget on the morning news, part of my preparation always involves running one of my feature-length Quick-Time files through TVC. No matter what sort of device I'm using and what sort of file format it needs, TVC can handle it.

Macintosh: iSquint

iSquint isn't the same sort of app-of-all trades as Total Video Converter.

But it does have one feature that TVC lacks, and it's something that every consumer is looking for in a product: It's free for the downloading. Head on over to www.isquint.org and snag yourself a copy.

The other, lesser advantage is that it works just as well for converting videos to the iPod and it's a lot simpler.

1. Add files to iSquint's conversion queue (see Figure 10-15).

You can add files by either clicking the plus (+) button at the top of the file list, or you can simply drag the file icons into the list directly from the Finder. By default, iSquint is set up to create files that are sized and optimized for your iPod; why waste file space by creating a video image with more pixels than your iPod can actually display? Well, maybe you'd like to watch that video through your TV sometime. And then there's that H.264 thing again.

The advice here is the same as it was with TVC: Converting a video to H.264 will take *way* longer than plain-vanilla MP4. Enable this checkbox only if you want the absolute smallest file possible (without sacrificing quality) and if you're willing to wait for results. Are you good at crochet? No? Well, the time you spend waiting for H.264 to finish its business is ample time to develop some mad skills in that area.

2. Choose a destination for the converted files by clicking the button next to the Saving In field.

3. Click Start.

All the files you've added to the queue will be converted, one after the other. And if you enabled the Add to iTunes option, they'll automatically be added to your iTunes library.

What a wonderfully useful app. And it's free!

I am routinely amazed by the fact that hugely useful and effective software is written and just plain *given away*. Nothing against the Total Video Converter folks, of course, but there are a lot of folks who barely scraped together enough discretionary income just for the iPod. They don't have any cash left over for a utility that could allow them to take full advantage of all the free video content that's available on the Internet.

In early 2006, this chapter would have been a pretty stupid idea. Internet video was on the same level as motion pictures were in 1902: there were plenty of videos available,

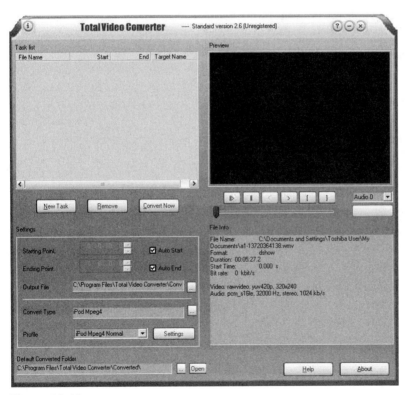

Figure 10-13
iTinySoft's TotalVideoConverter

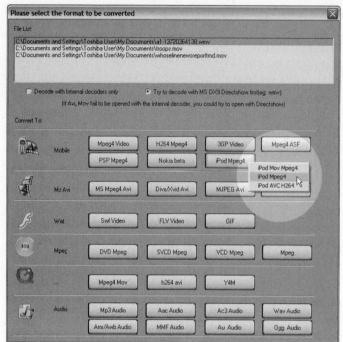

Figure 10-14

Three iPod-studly file formats

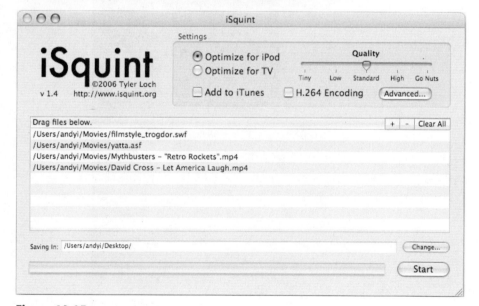

Figure 10-15

Loading videos into iSquint's conversion hopper

but they were all just short clips of trivial things. Your entertainment chiefly came from the novelty of watching somebody sneeze, as a group experience.

But the world is full of frustrated filmmakers, and with the proliferation of (a) high-bandwidth Internet connections, (b) whoppingly huge hard drives that cost about the same as a novelty pencil, and (c) sites like YouTube and Google Video, there's no shortage of valuable material. Recently, I downloaded an hourlong *Star Wars* fan movie and blast me if it isn't a professional-quality production.

The acting's a little ... well, variable, but the sounds and the effects are spot on, and I'd stack it against the very worst of what Lucasfilm has released.

And when you parse that last sentence, please consider that I'm a big *Star Wars* fan and that while *Attack of the Clones* caused me to still taste metal for three hours after I left the theater, I still considered it ten bucks well-spent. I mean, it wasn't meant as a veiled insult about *Star Wars: Revelations*.

Download Free Music (and Get Away with It)

The Skim

You're not a cop, are you?

Seriously, dude, could you lift up your shirt or something so I can see if you're wearing a wire? Because if you are, I wanna say that I have no intention of illegally trafficking in pirated music, and if there's any evidence or anything that I did, then it was entrapment and stuff.

No, no, I hope I didn't offend you or nothin'. But I had to ask. We've been gettin' hassled a lot, y'know. Can't be too careful. Particularly *now*. Because The Man's been coming down hard on downloading unprotected music off the Internet. And I've got this *awesome* plan that lets us all download truckloads of music every day … and there ain't a *thing* the recording industry or the Feds can do about it.

The secret — you gotta swear you won't tell nobody else — is simple: *Make sure you don't do anything that's actually illegal.*

Yeah, I know. I was pretty proud of that scheme myself, after I shook the final few bugs out of it. You should have seen the look on the dude from the Recording Industry Association of America's face after he confronted me on my doorstep with network logs proving that I'd down-

>TROUBLE

Keep in mind that the music-file URLs in blogs and search results, as well as in many sites that take public contributions, are unmarshalled, unpoliced bookmarks. So it's possible that you'll find links to illegal downloads. And remember: Downloading music illegally is just plain wrong, and can result in some serious consequences.

Figure 11-1
Beats for deadbeats: free music from the iTunes Music Store

loaded hundreds of megabytes of MP3s. He was all smug and triumphant-like, and then he learned that I'd done so completely legally, with the encouragement and permission of the files' original copyright holders.

Mind you, he still sucker-punched me in a delicate area and then poured the rest of his take-out coffee on me as I writhed in pain on my porch, before he stormed off to his car and backed over my novelty mailbox. But let's be clear: My moral and legal victories were absolute.

THE CASE FOR GOING LEGAL

Lots of people make fun of the recording industry's copyright watchdogs, and for good reason: Their excesses are, well, so *excessive*. I suppose you could praise them for having an unusual dedication and determination to see their tasks through to the end, even when it's been demonstrably proven that the person they're prosecuting into bankruptcy is an octogenarian retiree who doesn't even own a computer.

You could also suggest that they're a separate branch of the evolutionary tree and have

seven webbed toes on each foot.

Nonetheless, that wouldn't change the fact that piracy is wrong. You want it? The copyrightholder isn't giving it away? Then you gotta pay for it. Period.

And if the moral angle doesn't work for you, do keep in mind that at this stage in the game, detecting illegal music downloads is a routine and fairly automated process.

Rest assured that the recording industry's copyright goons became aware of that illegal file-sharing site well before *you* did.

Also be aware that even if you never typed in a name and address, your computer left behind a sequence of digits that can rewind the download all the way back to your house, and that the aforementioned goons can exchange these digits for a name and address with one e-mail to your Internet service provider.

So piracy is wrong, and it's dangerous.

And most of that music sucks, anyway. Do you really want to risk a $3,000 fine over a song from a band that, twenty years from now, you're going to swear to your kids you never ever liked or listened to?

BECOMING A PAWN IN A MARKETING PLAN

Yes indeed, it's possible to (1) download music, (2) copyrighted music, by name-brand artists, (3) not pay a dime for it, and — most bizarre of all — (4) do so with the encouragement of the recording industry.

It all comes down to merchandising, promotion, and the companies' desire to Go Viral. Record companies regularly seed the major commercial music stores with tracks that you can download for free.

iTunes Music Store

And naturally, the iTunes Music Store is your first and simplest click. The store's front door always contains a few links to free downloads. Usually you'll find these links at the bottom of the page, as in Figure 11-1.

Naturally, you won't exactly be spending hours and hours poring through the cornucopia of free selections. Usually there are only a handful of freebies available at any given time, and they're only available for a limited time.

But iTunes shoppers are such a huge and important part of the music market that music publishers are often willing to give away tracks by chart-topping acts instead of the factory-floor sweepings you'd expect to see.

Amazon Music

Amazon.com's free music page isn't remarkably easy to find, but if you plug music.amazon.com into your browser, you'll find a new navigation tab for Free Downloads right at the top of the page (see Figure 11-2).

Figure 11-2
Navigating the Amazon to reach untapped riches.

Of all the commercial online music services, Amazon usually offers the greatest quantity and quality of free music. If you scroll to the very bottom of the Free Music page, you'll discover a list of Top Downloads in the category of free music; click the More Top Downloads link and you'll be presented with hundreds.

AOL Music

AOL follows the iTunes model of hiding its freebies at the bottom of the page (at music.aol.com). In this case, the AOLites are hoping that you'll sign up for their subscription music service. The selections usually aren't as sweet as what you'll find on iTunes, but AOL is worth a regular peek: The service often snags some real gems.

HELPING PRESERVE OUR CULTURAL HERITAGE

… Or at least that's how you feel when you visit the Internet Archive (www.archive.org). It's no mere repository of audio files; as a nonprofit member of the American Library Association, the Internet Archive's goal is to protect and preserve content and make it available to current and future generations.

It's an ambitious agenda. Archive.org will show you Web pages stretching back to the very start of the World Wide Web. Classic books and essays are available as electronic texts. Movies, television shows, old software, and, yes, music — all from artists who support Archive.org's cause (see Figure 11-3).

You might think that this audio archive contains, I dunno, public-domain jug-band music transferred off wax Edison cylinders. You would be correct.

But it also contains modern tunes, speeches, conferences, and the largest and best-indexed collection of legal concert recordings available anywhere … many from major, currently touring groups. With tens of thousands of music files available, it's easy to fill an iPod from Archive.org alone.

FINDING FREE MUSIC

Of course, the sites I've mentioned aren't the only spots where you can find free music. Ninety-nine percent of the other free music sites fall into a couple of predictable categories:

Figure 11-3

Archive.org: free music with a higher calling.

> They offer free music, but you can't actually download any of it. It's like a radio station where you can be your own DJ. Which is fine if you're trying to kill some time at work, but not so good if you want to fill an iPod.

> They offer free music, but chiefly as a way to sneak spyware, adware, keystroke loggers, and other nasty Trojan horses onto your system. Which is why you should be careful about Googling for "free music downloads." It's up there with "free ringtones" "free wallpaper," and "Do you have the same credit-card or Social Security number as a famous celebrity? Take our free online quiz and find out!" — it's something of a Red Flag Word for fraud.

> They offer free, downloadable music, no fooling, but it's just a few specific bands. Which is terrific from my point of view, as I have hundreds of pages to fill here, but what help would that be to you, the consumer?

Figure 11-4
Holy Zarquon! Look at all the free music Singing Fish found!

No, instead I must press on and talk about ways to locate free music via search engines.

A Music-Specific Search Engine

Singing Fish (www.singingfish.com) has two things to recommend it. First, its name is a subtle in-joke from *The Hitchhiker's Guide to the Galaxy*; and second, you can use it to search specifically for unlocked music files. It'll steer you straight to files that you can load straight onto your iPod without having to chase down false leads or do any file conversions (see Figure 11-4).

Checkboxes allow you to limit your search to just MP3 or QuickTime formats, and if you're more interested in thrash-metal music than the president's most recent radio address, another checkbox allows you to limit the search further.

Freebies from Music Blogs

The Web is a powerful tool for a band that wants to promote itself and its music.

And thousands of lower-tier bands offer their MP3s on their personal sites as a way to entice you to maybe drive thirty miles to a hole-in-the-wall venue just outside of Pittsburgh and pay a $5 cover charge to see 'em play live. But how to *find* these sites?

Well, you can try a straight-up Google search for the sort of music you like ("Bluegrass MP3 download") and keep clicking around until you get lucky. Or, you could subscribe to any of a number of music-oriented blogs.

Or, you could visit one blog that keeps tabs on all the music being linked from all the *other* music blogs. The Hype Machine (hype. non-standard.net) is a Web log in which

➤TIDBIT

Oh, yes. MySpace.com, the community-building, social-network Web site that took off in 2005. Well, okay, it's hugely popular among unsigned bands and performers. But music that you can actually download to your desktop and load on your iPod is about as hard to find as, well, a band on MySpace that doesn't suck. Either way, it's not a terrific resource.

side benefit is that it doesn't take long before the Machine has introduced you to a bunch of music sites that, to your delight, regularly feature the music that the parents of today and the kids of tomorrow can't abide.

Googling for Tunes

Eventually, it comes down to rummaging through dumpsters and trashcans for scraps of entertainment.

At least that's what it feels like when you start using Google to locate music files. It's a hopelessly random tool for this sort of thing.

It works a treat if you click on the search box armed with the name of a fantastic band that you heard playing in Harvard Square on your way to buy comic books at Million-Year Picnic, but a search for "music I'm not already sick and tired of" doesn't return the

every posting is simply a link to a track that's recently become available through another music blog or podcast (see Figure 11-5).

Results can be a bit scattershot. Hype Machine gives you the fire-hose treatment, as opposed to giving you one nice friendly clickable button marked "Music you'd be likely to show half an interest in." But the

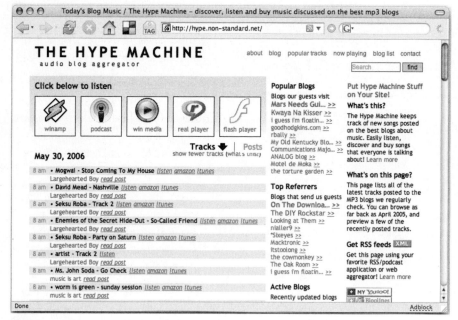

Figure 11-5
Hype Machine: All the music in the blogosphere, at a glance.

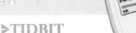

results that it ought to.

Google *could* become a monster tool for finding and downloading free music. But as of this writing, the Googlers don't appear to be interested in giving us that sort of tool. Google does have a Music Search feature, but all it means is that if you search for "Janis Joplin" it'll begin its list of search results with a list of albums and links to music services where you can purchase them.

The next best thing is to exploit one of Google's advanced search features. I'll cut to the chase and give you a sample Google search string:

`awesome bluegrass link:*.mp3`

"Awesome" and "bluegrass" are straightforward search terms. "Please find me some bluegrass, and I only want stuff that's Awesome."

The meat of the string is at the end: link means "return Web pages that link to the following Web address." Any downloadable MP3 file will have a Web address that ends in the .mp3 filename extension.

Natcherly, we can't possibly know what that address will be, but Google will interpret the asterisk (*) as a wildcard. Non-techie meaning: It'll look for anything that ends in .mp3.

In total, the search string means "Find me Web pages that contain the words 'awesome' and 'bluegrass' and that contain at least one link to an MP3 file." Plug this into Google and it's all over but the endless wading through dozens and dozens of pages of results.

Delicious Music

There's a similar trick that uses del.icio.us, the (hypermegasuperawesome) community-

> **TIDBIT**
>
> You *know* that the instant I typed the words "a search for 'music I'm not already sick and tired of'" doesn't return the results that it ought to," I had to click over to Google to see what would come up if I actually performed that search. And I must duly report that the third link was to a page of lyrics to one of my favorite albums. I would caution, however, that this was probably due to the fact that it's a popular album that contains a lyric with "sick and tired" in it.
>
> It's extremely unlikely that a shadowy-financed government agency intercepted the search request and specifically chose a result that would have personal meaning. Still, for our mutual safety, let's just pretend this conversation never happened.

based Web directory. Del.icio.us — yes, that's a URL — is a valuable tool for navigating the Web. Its users can "publish" bookmarks to the del.icio.us Web site, tagged with keywords that make it simple to find pages that fit certain categories.

Search Google for "poker tips" and Google will return every Web page everywhere that contains those two words. No discretion, no stamp of approval.

But if you search del.icio.us with those words, it only returns Web pages that del.icio.us's legions of users have personally tagged with those two descriptive words, and (hooray!) were considered valuable enough to actually bookmark. So nearly every page it returns is pure Tabasco.

You can indeed search for "free music" and get lots of productive hits. But del.icio.us

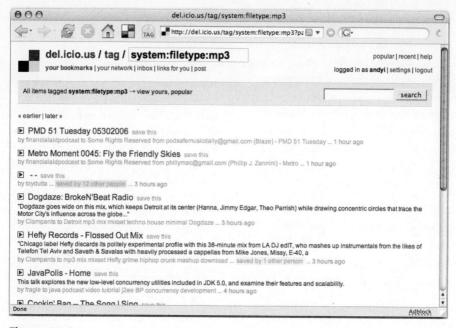

Figure 11-6

Del.icio.us MP3 bookmarks: like *American Idol* voting, only not quite so dippy.

will search specifically for music files if you know how to ask. Bookmark this URL:

http://del.icio.us/tag/system:filetype:mp3

The result is a list of recently bookmarked MP3 files that del.icio.us's users have located and saved all over the Web (see Figure 11-6). It's way more valuable than searching through Google because, by definition, these are all music tracks that del.icio.us's millions of users have bookmarked. Each bookmark is an implicit statement that "this track is worth remembering."

There are two potential misconceptions that I want to dispel before we move on. First, when I say that downloading music illegally is just plain wrong, I'm not winking furi-

ously as I do so. The recording industry is guilty of a great many sins, but that doesn't make piracy right. Just don't do it.

I'd also like to state that just because I happened to use bluegrass music for most of my search examples, it doesn't mean that I'm, you know, not all hip and stuff. Remember when I mentioned plugging "sick and tired of" into Google and getting one of my favorite albums? That album is *Suicidal Tendencies*, not a cast album from *The Lawrence Welk Show*.

(Please don't ask when that album was released. ... 1983. Bastard.)

12

Take the Web Page and Run

The Skim

I'm suggesting that you move Web pages and Web sites onto your iPod, and I acknowledge from the get-go that this topic betrays a fundamental lack of understanding of the Web's true purpose: as an unbeatable tool for goofing off at work while still giving a credible impression of getting actual work done. When you're using your iPod, you're driving home, relaxing on the sofa, walking through a downtown park watching, judging, and mocking all you see. It's *your* time. Why on *earth* would you need the Web *then?*

This is the point where I urge you to consider the Web's many incidental advantages. Such as delivering unto you vast acres of free, readable entertainment and information. It's worth investigating even when you're *not* being paid to do something else. I'm surprised that the Web's marketing people don't put that on the brochure somewhere.

And while words aren't all that exciting compared with music or video, when you put Web pages on an iPod they become cool by implication. The Web is Good when you're sitting at home with a wired PC. It's Great when you're in a coffee shop with a Wi-Fi–studly notebook.

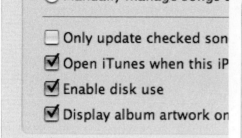

Figure 12-1
The Enable Disk Use feature allows
your iPod to act as a storage drive.

Figure 12-2
Behold! Your iPod's built-in folders!

But neither of these incarnations are any help to you when you're waiting in line at the post office and it becomes depressingly clear to you that neither the patron ahead of you nor the clerk assisting him has any idea whatsoever whether or not it's legal to ship a tuba to Kyzyl and, if so, how to arrange for delivery confirmation in a country where signatures are considered vulgar and impersonal and people just spit on each other as a way of identification.

These are the moments when having an iPod with fresh, interesting stuff to read isn't merely Convenient or Entertaining. It becomes a way to distract you from committing some form of misdemeanor.

TEXT ON AN IPOD

Many people live out their entire lives unaware that the iPod can also serve as a text reader.

That's because text is the only form of media that you copy onto the iPod without any help whatsoever from iTunes. When you load pictures, iTunes doesn't manage or organize your photo content but it at least acts as a conduit.

Not with text. There's almost something illicit about it. Just go into Windows Explorer or the Mac OS Finder, copy a plain, text file into the device and it'll appear under the iPod's Notes menu, where you can peep the contents in all its scrolly, unformatted goodness.

Go ahead and try it. I'll wait.

Aha. "But the iPod doesn't even show up in Windows Explorer or the Mac OS Finder, Andy!" you cry. "I curse you and all those who begat you!"

You're right to lash out. Truth be told, I'm having sort of a tough Thursday here. I was in an uncharitable mood when I wrote the preceding third paragraph and I apologize for having knowingly wasted your time.

But that *does* illustrate the need to turn on a special and somewhat hidden iPod feature: the ability to use the iPod as a storage device.

The magic happens when you check Enable Disk Use in the iPod's Options window (see Figure 12-1).

Enable Disk Use is near the bottom of the

>TIP

You can bring up the Options window by clicking the iPod's button at the bottom of the iTunes window. Or you can select iPod Options from the pop-up contextual menu that appears when you right-click the iPod's name in iTunes' Source list. If you're a Mac user with a one-button mouse, click the name while holding down the Control key to activate the contextual menu.

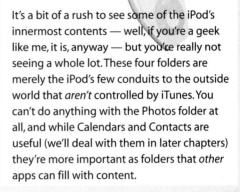

>TIDBIT

It's a bit of a rush to see some of the iPod's innermost contents — well, if you're a geek like me, it is, anyway — but you're really not seeing a whole lot. These four folders are merely the iPod's few conduits to the outside world that *aren't* controlled by iTunes. You can't do anything with the Photos folder at all, and while Calendars and Contacts are useful (we'll deal with them in later chapters) they're more important as folders that *other* apps can fill with content.

window. Select the checkbox, click OK, and in a moment, your computer will mount your iPod as a USB storage device (see Figure 12-2).

Yes, it's your iPod … stuffed and mounted, with a bunch of standard folders ready and waiting for you to paw all over 'em.

The Basic Gist of Things

Once you've activated Enable Disk Use, putting text on your iPod is thrillingly simple: Just drag a plain, text-only–formatted file into the Notes folder (in Windows, these have the filename extension .txt). When you undock the iPod and navigate to the Notes menu, presto: you can click the filename and

read the file.

There's a downside to the iPod's Enable Disk Use mode, but it's a tiny one: Normally, it's safe to unplug your iPod at any time without ceremony, unless iTunes is in the middle of an update.

But with Enable Disk Use mode activated, you have to manually eject (or "unmount") the iPod before you can disconnect it. If you don't, you might damage all the stuff stored on it. You'll have to erase the iPod and start all over again.

You can unmount your iPod by either select-

Figure 12-3
Organizing notes, folder by folder

Figure 12-4
A Web page, chained to a massive computer

ing the iPod in iTunes and then clicking the Eject button at the bottom of the window, or you can click the tiny Eject button that appears to the right of its name in iTunes' Sources list.

I'm going to talk about text documents and iPod notes in greater depth in Chapter 15. For now: onward to the task of converting a Web page to a file that notes can deal with.

CONVERTING A WEB PAGE TO TEXT

Figure 12-4 show you a typical Web page from a great metropolitan newspaper.

Microsoft Internet Explorer for Windows has a built-in feature for turning a Web page into a plain text file.

Windows Convertsion

To export a Web page to test In Windows:

1. Choose File ⇨ Save As.

2. Choose Text File (*.txt) from the Save As Type pop-up menu (see Figure 12-5).

3. Select My Computer and click the name of your iPod. Navigate to your iPod's Notes folder.

4. Enter a name for the file. Make it short — say, under 18 letters. Remember that

this name will appear on your iPod's narrow screen.

5. Click the Save button.

Macintosh Conversion

On a Macintosh, you have to convert the page to text manually. So there are a couple more steps involved:

1. With the Web page open, choose Edit ➪ Select All.

2. Launch the TextEdit application.

3. Create a new, empty document and choose Edit ➪ Paste (see Figure 12-6). The contents of the Web page splatter into the window, including all its graphics, which the iPod's Notes menu can't handle. So we need to convert this to plain text.

4. Choose Format ➪ Make Plain Text.

5. Choose File ➪ Save. Navigate to your iPod's Notes folder in the file browser and save the file, using a short name that you can easily read on the iPod's narrow screen (see Figure 12-7).

A Better Page

Let's take another look at the text file that we've just created. In Figure 12-8, I've opened the text file in Windows' plain-Jane text editor, Notepad.

Hmm. Okay, well, when you scroll down a bit, the formatting settles down and you can read the article. Except for the bit where there was an ad in the middle of the column.

Yeah, there's a basic weakness to an exported Web page. Your browser has no way of telling which text is actually important to you and which bits are ads and navigational links and other flotsam.

You *could* get around this by manually selecting just the text you want to read and pasting it into Notepad or TextEdit. But that sounds very similar to "work."

Instead, look around on the original Web page for a button or a link marked Printer-Friendly or Print This Article. If the designers of the site are true friends to the user, they've also set up an alternative layout in which everything flows in one column and interruptions (and formatting) are kept to a bare minimum (see Figure 12-9).

Export *this* page and you'll spend far less time scrolling through text-versions of ads for zero-credit home mortgages.

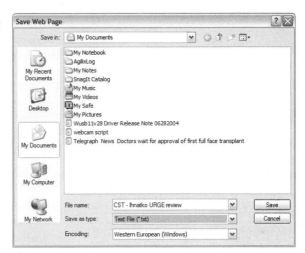

Figure 12-5

Exporting a Web page to your iPod in Internet Explorer.

Figure 12-6
Pasting the Web page's contents into TextEdit

IPODDING THE WEB WITH SOFTWARE

Doing it yourself is a fine solution in a rustic, log-cabin-y sort of way. But there are tools that can do the job for you automatically.

The Windows Answer

Snagging a single Web page is a simple enough task that few commercial apps really bother with. The best utilities will go ahead and *subscribe* you to your favorite Web sites and blogs, so that all the new content is tracked, harvested, and loaded onto your iPod automatically.

Just as when we were working with e-mail, contacts, and calendars, our best friend here is iPodSync (www.ipod-sync.com). Beware

that Apple tends to go after companies that put the word "iPod" in a product name … by the time you read this, they might have changed the name and you'll have to Google for the new name and Web site address.

iPodSync can synch any Web site or blog that has a syndication feed. You can tell by looking at the page: usually, there's either an orange XML or RSS badge or an explicit link that says Syndication Feed. This is a link to the address of The Magic File on the Web Site that a newsreader app (like iPodSync) examines to learn what's on the site and when it was posted.

To keep a Web site or blog synched to your iPod via iPodSync:

1. Launch iPodSync and click the Web but-

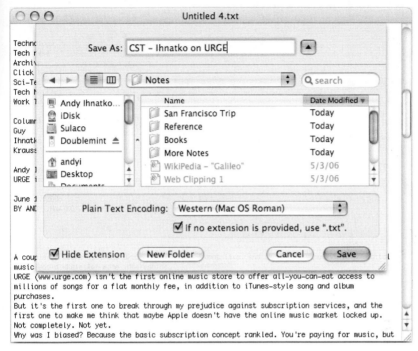

Figure 12-7
Saving the plain text to the iPod's Notes folder

ton. It's the one that looks like a planet. iPodSync will open its Newsfeeds pane (see Figure 12-10).

2. Click the Synchronize News checkbox if it hasn't been checked already. iPodSync comes pre-configured with the addresses of many popular news and entertainment feeds. Check the ones that you like.

3. Go to your browser and open the Web page you'd like to synch. Look for an XML or RSS or Syndication link.

4. Right-click the link to bring up the browser's contextual menu.

5. Select Copy if you're using Internet Explorer, or Copy Link Location if you're using Firefox (see Figure 12-11).

6. Go back to iPodSync's News Feeds pane and click the Add button.

7. Paste the feed URL into the URL box and click OK.

The next time iPodSync synchs your iPod, all the latest news from your subscribed Web sites will be downloaded and copied to your iPod as notes, under a new Web submenu.

The Macintosh Answer

On the Mac, the $24 NewsMac Pro (www.thinkmac.co.uk) app is the solution you want. It's a full-featured newsreader app, not just an iPod utility. But the operation is pretty much the same:

1. Launch NewsMac Pro. NewsMac comes

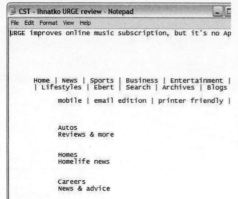

Figure 12-8

Our export. Starts off badly, huh?

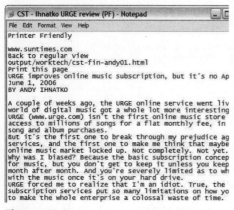

Figure 12-9

A printer-friendly Web page is also an iPod-friendly one.

Figure 12-10

The news, via iPodSync

Figure 12-11

Getting the link to the Web page's syndication feed

with several blogs and Web sites already configured. To add one of your own, copy the URL of the newsfeed: Look for an XML, RSS, or Syndication link somewhere on the Web page, and right-click (or hold down the control key while clicking, if you have a one-button mouse) to choose the Copy Link command from Safari's contextual menu. In Internet Explorer, choose Copy; in Firefox, choose Copy Link Location.

2. Choose Channel ⇨ New from News-Mac's menu bar.

3. Paste the URL into the Add a New Channel dialog box (see Figure 12-12).

4. Click OK.

>TROUBLE

Unless you have one of the absolute latest iPods — so new that they haven't even been announced — you'll also have to deal with the iPod's stingy limits on the length of notes. A text file can be no larger than 4K, or (roughly) less than two printed pages.

But there are two solutions. You can use a utility that chops a long text file into iPod-friendly chunks. It'll even include links from note to note, so it still "feels" like one document. You can learn about these utilities in Chapter 15. Or, you can buy a new, wide-screen iPod that (again, going from rumors) will have a built-in e-book reader.

With luck, Apple will also release an update to the software of *all* iPods that will allow them to read long files. But here in 2006, none of those products have been released yet ... and Apple doesn't comment on unannounced products. (Uh-oh! Is that Apple knocking at my door? I better stop talking about products that may or may not exist.)

To synchronize all NewsMac's unread articles to your iPod:

1. Make sure the iPod is connected to your Mac and you have Enable Disk Use turned on in iTunes. The iPod should appear as a storage device icon in the Finder.

2. In NewsMac, choose File ⇨ Synchronize (see Figure 12-13).

3. Choose your iPod from the Destination pop-up list.

4. Click the Include Headlines checkbox.

5. Click the Synchronize button.

Figure 12-12
Adding a newsfeed to NewsMac Pro

Figure 12-13
Sending headlines and articles to your iPod via NewsMac

And after a moment's percolation, the articles and headlines will be copied onto your iPod.

A BETTER WAY: AUDIO

Now let's go for broke: Instead of *reading* the news like cavemen or trombone players, we can use some utilities to convert Web pages and syndication feeds to *audio files* that import straight into iTunes — and thence into the iPod.

Audio Text in Windows

My favorite Windows text-to-speech utility is TextAloud from NextUp.com. It has a metric buttload of features ... so many that Appendix B contains a detailed rundown of what the app is and what it can do.

>TIP

To be *completely* honest, I actually prefer to cut-and-paste pages into text files by hand. You get the Text and Nothing But the Text, without any garbage sidebars. You shouldn't be afraid to roll up your sleeves from time to time, son. It builds, I say, it builds *character*, boy. Y'ain't gonna get *nowhere* unless y'got some *character*.

For our immediate purposes, we'll focus on its Web-to-speech feature. TextAloud installs a few new buttons into your Web browser that take this whole brilliant "listen to the Web as you drive, ride, or jog" idea and reduces it to just a couple of mouse clicks:

1. Navigate to the page you'd like to speech-ify.

2. Click the Add Article button from TextAloud's bank of browser buttons (see Figure 12-14).

3. Switch to the TextAloud app (or launch it if you haven't already). The text of the Web page appears in TextAloud's speech window (see Figure 12-15).

4. Click the Speak to File button, choose a place to save the audio file, and then click OK.

>TIDBIT

Some syndication feeds don't include the full text of every new article; many simply include a summary.

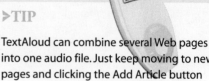

>TIP

TextAloud can combine several Web pages into one audio file. Just keep moving to new pages and clicking the Add Article button in your browser; the new Web text will be pasted onto the end of what you have in there already.

TextAloud will create an audio file with the same title as the Web page. Just drag the file into iTunes and it's ready for your iPod.

NextUp has a companion product called NewsAloud. This app goes beyond point-and-shoot Web-page capture and automatically grabs all the new items from a syndication-studly blog or Web page and converts them to text while you sleep. Even if you sleep during work.

By now you know the drill for locating syndication feed URLs, so I'll cut to the chase:

1. Launch NewsAloud.

2. Choose Options ⇨ RSS Feeds.

3. Paste the syndication feed URL into the text box and then click the Add URL button.

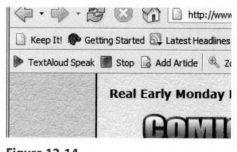

Figure 12-14
TextAloud's built-in browser buttons

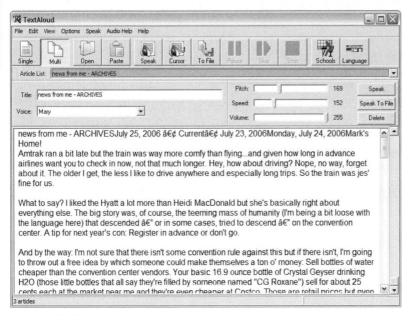

Figure 12-15
Web text, locked, loaded, and ready to process

4. NewsAloud will ask you to provide a name for the new feed. The default is the name that God (in the guise of the man or woman who created that Web site) gave it.

5. Click OK to name the new feed, and then Done to dispose of the new feed's window.

By choosing Options ➪ NewsAloud Preferences, you can specify how frequently you'd like all your feeds to be updated, and if you'd like 'em to be transmogrified into text in the background while you do other things.

Audio Text in Macintosh

On the Mac side, we don't need any external utilities to convert Web pages to speech. Mac OS X 10.4 and later come with a fairly awesome tool called Automator. You (yes, you, normal user who has no interest in

learning how to write software) can snap together a stack of pre-configured "actions" into a repeatable step-by-step process called a *workflow*.

Appendix A tells you all about Automator. And it even includes a detailed example of a workflow that takes whatever Web page you're peeping in Safari and turns it into an audio file on your iPod. No steps, no conversions, no nothin'.

NOTES: THE GOOD, THE BAD, AND THE UGLY

Notes is a feature that elevates an iPod into the big leagues, and I'm certainly not finished talking about it yet. We'll be using it in nearly every chapter that deals with loading office-type data.

It's a feature with a thousand uses. And in

many ways it's far, far easier to put a text file on your iPod than it is to install a music or a video file. "Oh how I wish all data could be as easy to manage as text!" you say, grabbing a nearby monkey's paw.

Silly human. If *all* data were this easy to install, it'd be a huge mess. We'd have a music player that was as difficult to navigate as Windows Media Player often is, because nothing's properly organized. Didn't you read the original short story? Or at least the really bad horror movie with Joan Collins that did a ripoff of the Monkey's Paw tale?

The "Treehouse of Horror" episode of *The Simpsons*?

There you go. Enjoy the notes capability for what it is, and be careful what you wish for. The moral is that you get what you asked for but never what you actually *want*.

➤　➤　➤

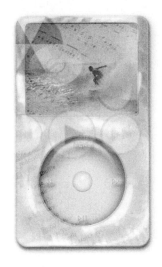

PART III

iPod Goes to the Office

13

Contacts, Appointments, and To-Dos

The Skim

This is probably not the best time for me to be writing an introduction to this chapter, sensation-seekers. The subject: keeping people's contact info on your iPod, along with calendars of the exact dates, times, and places in which you've agreed to go out and mingle with them.

Leave the house? *Socialize?* Well, I suppose it takes all sorts of people to make up a society. Do these people *know* that when they go outside, there's nothing between them and a 4.3-billion-year ongoing nuclear fusion reaction but a weakened ozone layer and a whole lot of wishful thinking?

And if you've made it this far in your life without learning that humans are deceitful and flawed creatures, well, I suppose there's nothing I can do to teach you. You're just going to have to go out there and figure it out for yourself.

I grudgingly suppose that if you do indeed keep your contacts and addresses on your iPod, there's every chance that you'll learn these valuable lessons far more quickly. "You were right, Andy," you will e-mail me late one night. "I just went out to eat with seven people. Three of them said they were low on cash and would make it up to me later. Two of them insisted that I should pay for a third of the $40 bottle of wine that they ordered, because they asked if I'd like to try it and I took a sip. And even the two who paid their full share of the bill wouldn't stop complaining about how much they spent on parking and the babysitter and couldn't we have just gone to the TGI Friday's near their house instead? Never again, Andy … never again; I have now turned my back on hope and humanity — and I have *you* to thank for it."

Good, good. Despite my initial fears, this intro worked out very, very well.

IN BROAD STROKES

iTunes has built-in support for contacts and appointments. Click a few buttons on your desktop and the data appears on your iPod under their own dedicated menus.

No extra software is necessary. All you need to do is point iTunes towards your Microsoft Outlook addresses and calendars, if you're a Windows user. If you're on a Mac, iTunes will use the data you have in the Mac OS's standard, built-in calendar and address book apps. (These would be iCal and Address Book in Mac OS 10.4 [Jaguar] or earlier; what comes in Mac OS X 10.5 [Leopard] and later might be different.)

Mac or PC, the interfaces are dashed-near identical.

So if synchronizing this data is built-in, why

do these other apps even exist? Some of them are "all in one" iPod utilities that manage a whole gamut of features, and the developers just threw in addressing and calendaring because it's a fairly simple trick.

Others attempt to extend the iPod's capabilities beyond the standard contact and appointment managers, by including some of Outlook's more Jedi-like project-integration features or supporting standards that aren't nearly as ubiquitous, or include support for less-popular contact and appointment apps.

And the troubling thing is that there are so many of these utilities — and their individual advantages are so subjective, from user to user — that it's hard to single any recommendations. When it comes to synchronizing appointments and calendars, iTunes addresses the basic needs of most users.

Even if your favorite contact and appointment manager isn't supported, you can export that data into your iPod directly. (More on that at the end of the chapter.)

SYNCHING CONTACTS AND APPOINTMENTS

Like I said, Apple has greased the wheels for you. All you need to do is tell iTunes to start synching your contacts and appointments, and maybe be more specific and tell iTunes not to bother synchronizing *all* your data … just the *good* leads, the *Glengarry* leads. …

(Jack Lemmon? *Glengarry Glen Ross?* "Hey you!" Alec Baldwin barks at a clearly beaten-down-by-life Lemmon. "Put the coffee *down*. The free coffee's just for people who *sell*." Well, it was a great movie. You would have *loved* the way that this section's first paragraph ended if you'd seen it. …

Okay. Enough of that.)

You work this mojo through the Contacts and Calendars tabbed panes of iTunes' iPod Preferences dialog box. When your iPod is connected, you can bring up this box by either clicking the iPod button at the lower-right corner of the iTunes window or by selecting iPod Options from the contextual menu under your iPod's name on the left side of the window.

Contacts

Go to the Contacts pane of the iPod Settings window; whether Windows or Mac, you'll see nearly the same thing depicted in Figure 13-1.

Do note that iTunes for Windows sports a pop-up menu that isn't in the Mac flavor: You get to choose between the Outlook app and Outlook Express as the source of your data. If you're on a Mac, iTunes will grab

Figure 13-1
Who do you know? Activating address synch

your appointments from the Mac OS's built-in calendar tool.

To activate synchronization of your contacts to your iPod, just select Synchronize Contacts. If you have your contacts organized into groups or lists, select the Synchronize Selected Groups/Lists Only radio button, and check all the groups that you'd like to throw onto your iPod. Unchecked boxes will be left behind. It's the velvet rope of iPod, only the ones left behind don't smell quite so much of drugstore-bought perfume.

Calendars

Setting up calendar synch is just as simple. Go to the Calendars pane and select the Synchronize Calendars checkbox. If you're on a Mac, you'll be peeping Figure 13-2. If you're a Windows user, picture this window in frostier, cooler tones.

>TIDBIT

One note on to-dos: iTunes doesn't really appreciate how big tasks in Microsoft Outlook, so its support for them in Windows is microscopic. For this reason, folks who get a real aerobic workout from Outlook are doubly encouraged to give a third-party utility a try.

My recommendation: iPodSync (www.ipod-sync.com), which I've been talkling about elsewhere in the book. As a Windows-directed app, it allows an iPod to *fully* exploit the wealth of data you have tied up in Outlook.

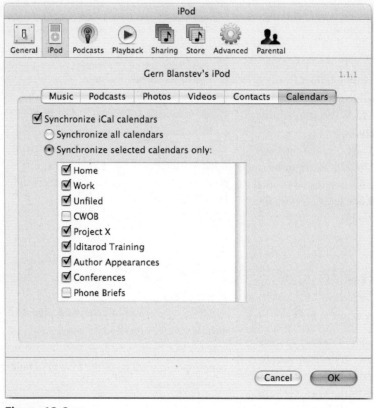

Figure 13-2
What's going on? Activating calendar synch

enchanted radish, a Land that Shadows Our Own That Shall E'er Remain Hinted in Mirrors and Sighs, and a witch-leaning princess who thought she ought to have been invited to some party or another. But the upshot is that all copies of iTunes are enchanted, and although there is indeed a To-dos pane in iPod Preferences, only the pure of heart, the keen of sense, and the clear of purpose can see it and click the Synchronize To-do's checkbox.

You'll see that you also have the option of selecting individual calendar groups as well. As in the Contacts pane, check the boxes of each of the groups you'd like to keep handy on your iPod.

To-Do Lists

Can your iPod also synch your ample Task and To-do lists? After all, those are built-in features to your calendar software. And there *does* appear to be a menu for them on your iPod.

Well, let me tell you a story (gather 'round, children). It's rather long, and it involves an

We peasants in our sackcloths await that day with great relish. Until then, we collect our twigs for the evening fire and stoke our mead and await the coming of the One whose coming was foretold by the Other One. We *thought* he was The One at first, but then he laughed and said that, yes, he gets that a lot, no apologies necessary.

Two points, from all that:

1. In fact, iTunes regards to-dos as part and parcel of the calendar experience, and if you activate Calendar synchronization,

you get to-dos along with it. There's nothing to activate or click. It's automatic.

2. You were nice enough to lay out good money for this book, and I felt kind of sheepish about just slapping in a sentence about getting to-dos for free. So I just kept right on typing, there.

But I hope you enjoyed my tale nonetheless. No, I've never been to a Renaissance fair. I've attended a couple of *Star Trek* conventions and the San Diego Comic-Con, though. Surely that counts?

UTILITIES BEYOND ITUNES

Simple, yes?

Hmm. Perhaps *too* simple. Yes, Mañao, my faithful friend, … I suspect that we may have stumbled straight into a *trap!*

(Sorry for the overly creative intro. I'm so sorry. It's just that usually, I schedule some days to work on the geek books and col-umns, and other days to work on novels and stuff. Once I get into Creative Writing mode, it's hard to turn it off, you know? I'll try to keep a closer eye on that sort of thing. It's tedious, I know.)

Remember those third-party iPod utilities I mentioned? The ones that take contacts and calendars from even the most bizarre, antique sources and sling them onto your iPod? Well, they work because contacts and calendars are two of the very few sorts of iPod data that sit on your iPod in folders, in plain view of both you and the OS, in a format that conforms to widely understood international standards:

> Contacts are stored in vCard format. This standard is more than ten years old and was developed by a consortium of companies (Apple included) that wanted to create a simple mechanism for moving address info from one app to another.

> Calendars are in the iCalendar (or iCal or ICS) format. Don't be distracted by the

Figure 13-3
Cramming appointments and contacts down your iPod's throat without iTunes' permission

> **TIP**

There are a variety of utilities that can export data to a standard format to put all sorts of strange information onto your iPod. Before the iPod had a Notes menu (and with it the ability to read text files), a common hack would be to export information from the Web as an iCal file. So to read all the news articles that were published on a certain day, you'd just go to January 21, and there, as an appointment at 5:21 p,m., would be an article that was posted to the Web site on that time and day.

Suffice to say, when the Apple's iPod team saw how much work people were going through just to get a simple page of text onto the device, it added Notes to the iPod's standard bag of tricks.

fact that one of Apple's built-in calendar apps is also called iCal: It's a popular standard supported by dozens of apps across many different operating systems.

And the iPod's built-in software isn't fussy about where those files come from. Toss any vCard file into the iPod's Contacts folder or any iCalendar file into its Calendars folder and the data will show up under the appropriate menus.

You get to those folders by enabling the iPod's Enable Disk Use mode. Just click the aptly named checkbox in the first pane of iPod Preferences and the device will appear on your desktop like any standard USB storage device (see Figure 13-3).

So even if you're using a contacts and calendar manager that isn't directly supported by iTunes, it's probably possible to export the data from the app into one of the two standard formats, and to save the data into the right iPod folder directly from the application itself.

I've just re-read that intro and I suppose that the manful thing for me to do at this stage would be to concede that many humans are indeed worth going out and meeting. Ricky Gervais, for example. He sounds like he'd be fun to hang around with. Uma Thurman? Oh, absolutely. Good call; thanks. You don't happen to have her e-mail, do you? … I've had a Pepperidge Farm Milano cookie and watched a Road Runner cartoon. My faith in humanity is restored. No need to call or write. I'm just fine.

Anyway, enjoy the "calendars and contacts" features.

Picture That

The Skim

It hardly seems fair. It used to be so *easy* to spot those people who were coming up to you with the express and malicious intent of badgering you with relentless family snapshots. Big 4-by-6-inch prints jutted out of their pockets like big, glossy Danger flags. Sure, there was no way to see a wallet-sized print coming, but in most social situations in which a wallet is being presented, there's a good chance it's a preamble to them picking up your bar tab. So at least there's a potential benefit to repressing all your (correct) urges to light the table on fire as a diversion and then run for the car.

But surely, nothing gold can stay. We've been trained to associate iPods with nothing but *good* things. Every album that The Who ever recorded. Podcasts in which Ricky Gervais or Penn Jillette thrill us with real-life monkey tales. Episodes of that cartoon edition of *Star Wars*. Then, suddenly, your "friend" hands the iPod over and you have every right to believe that you're going to be pleasantly entertained, but no, you're stuck there for twenty minutes, scrolling through pictures from his family car trip to the Yakov Smirnoff Dinner Theater in Branson, Missouri, while he narrates.

Well, fight fire with fire. It's spiteful to keep a huge pile of boring personal photos on your iPod just in case, but if there's one sure-fire way to

>TIP

As part of the ongoing system of subtle cruelty that underlies all modern technology, not all iPods can deal with pictures. If yours has a color screen (and this includes every screen on every iPod that Apple currently makes), welcome to the club. But if you have an older model with a black-and-white display, you'll have to activate the Solitaire game and pretend that the queens, kings, and jacks are your friends and family. Squint a little and you can make it work.

make sure you'll never have to pretend that someone's baby looks any smarter or cuter than any another baby is to immediately follow their presentation with a 50-shot photo essay about how easy it is to change the bags on this new vacuum cleaner you bought last month.

PHOTO LIBRARY SOFTWARE

Normally, iTunes is the warehouse that holds all your iPod's potential inventory.

But there's a snag: iTunes happily manages your music and your videos, but although it's charitably willing to acknowledge the existence of these things known as "pictures," it's not willing to store or organize them for you.

So whereas the concept of throwing music on an iPod requires explanations of a Willy Wonka Land–like assortment of colorful options and features, putting pictures on an iPod more or less boils down to telling iTunes where, specifically, you keep the things and how you'd like them stored on your device.

It's bleak and rainy as I write this, so to keep my own spirits up I shall continue the Wonka metaphor by describing the (by now familiar) iPod Options window as the big colorful candyland area with the chocolate river that Augustus Gloop tumbles into at the start of the picture (see Figure 14-1). Like the fabled movie set, this window is central to the entire operation. Also, it allows us to pause for a moment and envision gummybears as big as a Yorkshire terrier.

Click the Photos tab to fiddle with photo settings. By default, the Synchronize Photos From feature is unchecked, meaning that iTunes won't bother slapping pictures onto your iPod.

Click the checkbox to turn photo synchronization on. Then, you need to tell iTunes where to synchronize photos *from*. This boils down to two choices:

> **A spiffy, handy-dandy, nicely organized formal photo library.** Managed by a slick application that slurps pictures straight from your camera and slaps baby pictures into printed calendars faster than your friends can throw them away.

> **Any old folder.** Which is just what you think it means. You point iTunes at a folder and zap: Pictures in the folder become pictures on your iPod, automagically.

Photo Libraries

Clearly, this is the smoothest way to go, because that's how you naturally tend to organize your pictures on your computer. The simplest and most brainless way of managing photos on an iPod is to just let your photo library do most of the heavy lifting for you.

The bad news is that the relationship between iTunes and a photo library manager is a fairly intimate one and, as such, iTunes won't work with just *any* application.

If you're using a Mac, well, you definitely want to use iPhoto. It came with your computer, it works well, and when you plug anything that even *smells* like a digital camera into your Mac, the operating system has already been configured to automatically hand the microphone off to iPhoto and cue the orchestra to play the opening bars of "Moon River," so to speak.

On the Windows side, it's a bad news/exceptionally good news situation. PCs don't all ship with the same library app, and furthermore, there isn't *one* insanely popular app that everybody uses (like iPhoto on the Mac).

But the fab news is that Adobe has a terrific photo library manager called Photoshop Album. It's a commercial product, but it's cheap. And if "cheap" is too much money for you, there's a free edition that eliminates many of the sexier features but leaves its most important features intact. You can download it from www.adobe.com.

Either way, in iTunes, select your photo library app from the pop-up menu next to the checkbox (see Figure 14-2). And do take this

Figure 14-1
Setting your iPod's Photo preferences.

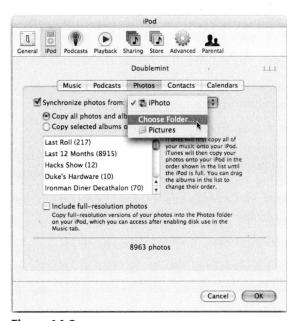

Figure 14-2
The dizzying array of photo sources available to iTunes

> **➤TIP**
>
> You can open your iPod's Options window in iTunes in one of two ways. One option is to choose Edit ➪ Preferences in Windows or iTunes ➪ Preferences on the Mac, and then click the iPod button. The second option is to use the contextual menu for your iPod in iTunes' Source list. You can bring up this menu by either clicking on your iPod's desktop icon with the right mouse button, or (if you have a Mac with just one mouse button) holding down the Control key while clicking.

opportunity to note that this list is populated with just the one app on your computer compatible with iTunes, and reflect that as it is so often in life, all choice is but an illusion.

Any Old Folder

Actually, I take back that whole "illusion of freedom" nonsense. You do indeed have infinite alternatives, including the ability to tell iTunes to synch pictures from any folder attached to your computer.

Figure 14-2 shows the Choose Folder option, which is straightforward enough that I'm only going to haul out the numbered-list format because I set up my word processor with a special button that generates them automatically:

1. Select Choose Folder from the pop-up list.

2. Navigate to the folder you'd like iTunes to synchronize from.

3. Click OK.

Charitably enough, iTunes populates this pop-up list with your computer's most likely spot for storing pictures: My Pictures for the Windows kids, Pictures for the Mac gang. But it can be any directory that your computer can see, even a remote folder on a network that everyone in the office uses as a collective photo dump.

NARROWING THE SYNCH

By default, iTunes selects the Copy All Photos and Albums, which means it'll attempt to copy the whole kit and caboodle and the horses they rode into town on. This is a Good Thing if you have no heart whatsoever, and you really believe that you're going to find a willing audience for (good Lord!) 8,963 of your personal photos.

I mean, honestly. Even thirty or forty are pushing it. There's maybe one good reason for making somebody sit through a slide show of hundreds or thousands of pictures, and even if you *do* find yourself in that sort of a position, you can usually get a confession out of the prisoner a lot faster by simply dropping your iPod into a sock and beating him with it. Which would still get you in trouble with the World Court as well as with karma, so that's another reason why you'll want to pare down the number of photos on your iPod.

There are more obvious reasons, of course. Photos take up space on your iPod that could be filled with more Dan Fogelberg music (though again, the iPod-in-a-sock technique is both a more effective means of torture and considered to be more humane as well).

But the most significant problem of synching lots of photos to an iPod is time. iTunes has to prep and copy each of those pictures. Go ahead and show up late for work with your hair and teeth unbrushed. Explain to your boss that you missed your train because it took iTunes ten minutes to update your iPod this morning with the 320 photos you shot of your dog trying to do his little trick last night.

Unless my advice means nothing to you, click the Copy Selected Albums/Folders Only button to tell iTunes to only copy a subset of your picture collection to the iPod during each synch.

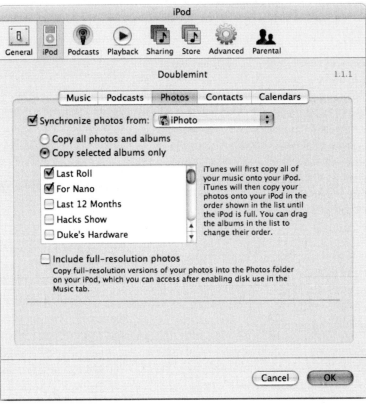

Figure 14-3
Choosing specific albums and subfolders for synchronization

Good: I'm glad my words are sinking in. Whether you're synching to a photo library or to a folder, iTunes offers you the same option for selecting elements of your picture collection. The list in Figure 14-3 contains all the photo albums in your photo library, or all the subfolders inside the folder you picked.

Select as few or as many of these as you like by clicking each checkbox.

You can also drag these items around to

>TIDBIT

iTunes doesn't even *pretend* that it loves pictures the same way it loves music and videos. Oprah Winfrey would have a fit if she learned about this poisonous family dynamic. When iTunes synchs your iPod, it first copies all the tunes and vids and only then, grudgingly, does it fill any leftover space with pictures. So if you care about which pix wind up on your iPod and which ones might get left behind, put the most important albums and photos at the top..

> **TIDBIT**

Okay, well, I guess I *should* acknowledge that for many members of our society — folks who have kids, I suppose; more and more states are passing laws allowing that sort of thing these days — having lots of pictures is a *good* thing. And I should also point out that many iPod models are compatible with a special cable that lets you plug it straight into a TV, so that a whole living room full of folks can enjoy the show.

change their order, whether you're synching every folder or album or just a few selected items. Selected albums/folders nearer the top of the list will be synchronized before the ones at the bottom.

Here we see one of the advantages of using a photo library manager. In Figure 14-3, I've selected two iPhoto albums: Last Roll and For Nano. iPhoto automatically populates Last Roll with the newest batch of pictures that I copied into the library. For Nano is an album that I maintain myself. It's a mixture of old and new pix that I like to have at all times … shots of my nieces and nephews, photos of me hanging out with fabulous celebrities (the "Time to Make the Donuts" guy from the Dunkin' Donuts commercial? met him) and other assorted eye candy.

So I get the best of both worlds. If last weekend's Newport Chowder Cook-Off happens to come up in conversation, it's likely that I can whip out a photo of my friend John and his stack of 40 empty cups to convince any doubters. And a man who walks with a photo of himself sitting in the Batmobile, even one taken three years ago, walks with

quiet power and serenity.

I've got the new pix and the important pix, and I leave the rest at home. Not coincidentally, I still have friends who are willing to hang out with me and who don't mind terribly if I bring out my iPod and start scrolling through pictures. (Though maybe that's just an indication of who my friends are.)

SUPER-SIZING YOUR PICTURES

That's about it. The next time iTunes synchs your iPod, it'll copy as many pix as it can from the sources you've defined, using whatever free space remains after it's done copying music and video. iTunes is (joyfully) aware that an iPod's screen isn't quite big enough to show off the VistaVision edition of *Ben-Hur*, so when it copies your photos to the device, the pictures are scaled down to a manageable size. Big enough to look good on an iPod screen, big enough to look good on a TV screen, but nowhere *near* the image's original size and detail.

That's good. Each photo shot by a modern digital camera takes up about as much room

> **TIP**

Many of those self-service photo kiosks at your local drugstore — those colorful machines that accept a memory card and spit out professional, glossy prints — also sport standard USB ports. They're *intended* for those little keychain memory drives, but (depending on the manufacturer) an iPod, tethered to a USB cable, will work just as well.

as a whole song, and costs time to copy from your computer to the iPod.

But there's a possible advantage to copying the original photo at full resolution. What if you're showing off your photo of Baby Tralfaz, and Grandma wants a copy of her very own?

Yes, we're on the same page: She's complimenting your infant son just to soften you up into giving her your iPod.

But you can wipe that faux-sincere look off her face if you clicked the Include Full-Resolution Photos option in Figure 14-3. "Why, I've got the original file right here on my iPod," you say. "Let me plug it into your computer and I can print your own copy in fifteen minutes."

Cool. If you've turned on your iPod's Enable Disk Use option (you can find it in the Music tab of your iPod's Settings window), your iPod will appear as a standard USB storage device when you hook up its USB cable and plug it into a Mac or PC. Your original photo files will appear in a folder marked Photos.

Still, use this feature wisely. If you've forgotten that you've even activated it, it can easily become the elusive answer to the question "Why does synch *take* so *freaking long?*"

Your iPod's Pictures feature is one of those tricks that blurs the line between a music player and a PDA. As you've seen in many of the chapters throughout this book, there are few limits to the sort of information you can carry around on an iPod, and you shouldn't ignore the power of a pocketful of pictures. I'm a multi-disciplinary geek, whose eudaemonic nerdiness expands across all borders and boundaries. Yes, I'm all about technology, but on a given Sunday you're likely to find me at the MIT Flea Market adding to my collection of vintage PCs, or poking around at a yard sale, or at a collectibles show.

And a fat folder of pictures on my iPod is one of my most effective tools. Hey, this lady has a whole bunch of Burger King *Star Wars* collectible glasses … do I already have the one with Luke Skywalker in his Bespin Cloud City pose? I unholster the iPod, scroll through an album named Star Wars and, a few thumb-flicks later, I hit across the photos of my *Empire Strikes Back* glasses. Yes, I already have that one.

I still *buy* the thing, of course. See, that way I have an extra one to trade. But it's nice to have a definitive answer right there at my fingertips.

Well, look, whatever you may think of *me* after that little story, you can't disagree that the iPod comes out smelling like a rose, right?

> > >

15

Documents and Books

The Skim

Documents. On your iPod.

Really?

And the source of your disbelief is not "Surely we live in an age of marvels, in which such miracles can and do occur." I sense that your eyebrows are knit and your lips are pursed in a manner that can only mean that you can't believe that anybody thought you'd ever be interested in doing such a thing.

And who can blame you? It's been a terrific book so far. If you've been working your way from front to back, you have music, TV shows, radio shows, and hundreds of pictures on your iPod.

Yet I appear to be trying to engage your enthusiasm about putting … documents. On your iPod.

Trust me. When I told you that you'd look ten years younger if you stopped bleaching your hair, you were mad, sure. But was I wrong? Of course not … if the opinion of that bartender who carded you last week matters.

THE FUNDAMENTALS

We covered most of the fundamentals of this back in Chapter 12, when we talked about Web pages. The iPod's built-in Notes menu will allow you to read any plain-text file that you've copied into the iPod's Notes folder.

But you can't get to the Notes folder until you've turned on your iPod's Enable Disk Use mode feature. You'll find this in iTunes' iPod Preferences (see Figure 15-1).

Once you've clicked that Enable Disk Use checkbox, any time you plug the iPod into one of your computer's USB ports, it'll appear as a standard USB storage device.

Figure 15-2 shows the iPod as it appears in Windows Explorer. Just copy or save text

Figure 15-1
Enable Disk Use mode lets your computer treat your iPod like any other storage device.

files into the Notes folder and you're done. For bonus points, you can even create folders *inside* the Notes folder. Each folder will appear as a submenu under the iPod's Notes menu, which makes it a snap to organize these notes by date or subject.

IPODDING A SHORT DOCUMENT

But we have some room to stretch out a bit here, so let's talk about what sort of text file your iPod can handle.

I'm shocked, stunned, and suffering from a dull stabbing pain in my left instep after looking at all the utilities out there that boast of their sorcerous ability to put your word-processing documents on your iPod (huzzah!).

The dull stabbing pain was due to the fact that these are a new pair of socks and when I snapped the tag off this morning, I left part of the little plastic thingy inside the sock.

If only my reaction to these utilities was so easy to deal with. One of these apps cost $30 … and yet none of them do anything that

> **TIP**
>
> You can mount your iPod on *any* computer, not just your own. If you've ever hooked up your iPod to a machine other than the one that stuffs it with iTunes content, you'd expect iTunes to throw out a not-at-all-friendly warning that this iPod's heart belongs to another, and that the only way this copy of iTunes could load stuff onto it would be if it were to erase everything from the device and start all over again.
>
> But that sort of mean-spirited possessiveness doesn't apply to files. You can copy files to your iPod from Desktop A and then copy them from the iPod onto Notebook B and Drugstore Photo Printing Kiosk C, no problem. We'll get into this a lot more in Chapter 20, which explores the niceties of using an iPod as a plain storage device.

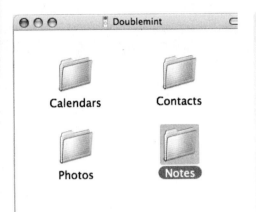

Figure 15-2
Like Sinatra at the Sands, when the iPod makes an appearance on your desktop, it's cause for joy.

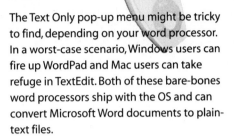

▶TIP

The Text Only pop-up menu might be tricky to find, depending on your word processor. In a worst-case scenario, Windows users can fire up WordPad and Mac users can take refuge in TextEdit. Both of these bare-bones word processors ship with the OS and can convert Microsoft Word documents to plain-text files.

your word processor can't do for free.

Two steps, for the love of God:

1. With the document open in your word processor, choose File ⇨ Save As.

2. Choose Text Only as the file format.

3. Save the file to the Notes folder of your iPod, which you have thoughtfully mounted on your desktop already.

All right ... *three* steps. But they're three *simple* steps. I've just gone to Amazon.com and confirmed that there are indeed about fifty DVDs I'd rather own than a $30 utility that saves me the trouble of selecting Text Only from a pop-up menu.

When you export your (lovely, printer-ready) word-processing document into a plain-text file, you strip the file of everything that makes it distinctive. Special fonts, italics, text columns, tables — it all becomes one single column of generic-looking text. But hey: At least you can *read* it.

Subtleties

Just to make sure we totally thrash out the subject of text files, hang your eyeballs on Figure 15-3, which shows Microsoft Word for Macintosh's array of file-export options.

I'm using Word for Mac as an example because it happens to collect the greatest number of text formats under one pop-up menu.

Let's see, here ... six of these menu items are, technically, text files, but only two will give us the file we want:

▷ **Text Only** is your basic, plain-vanilla text file and it'll work gangbusters on your iPod.

▷ **Unicode Text** is actually preferable, by a smidge. A Text Only file will strip all formatting from the file *and* it'll make sure that the file only contains the basic type-writer-style characters that were standardized back in an age when the continents of the Earth were all much closer together than they are now.

▷ Unicode is a vast improvement over the original (ASCII, if you collect jargon): in addition to classic hits like A, j, and who could forget &, it includes modern dingos

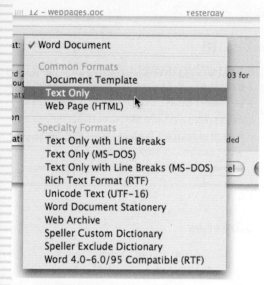

Figure 15-3

File formats: Even plain text isn't necessarily Just Text.

like bullets (•), symbols (™), and items that modern man has yet to find a use for (Œ, which might just be a smudge left by the printer).

>TIDBIT

The iPod's limitation on note length is indeed Incredibly Dopey. But by the time you read this, Apple will have released new, wide-screen iPods and the second-most rumored new feature will be formal support for long electronic texts.

Of course, the *single* most anticipated new feature will be a special little processor that automatically feeds the sound of an impatient sigh into your headphones any time a Grateful Dead song comes on and skips to the next track after the first seven measures.

You *don't* want text with line breaks. In plain text, each paragraph is a long line of text which the iPod's Notes reader can handily re-flow to fit the narrow screen. When your word processor adds line breaks that are hardwired to the width of a printed page, the results are borderline frustrating to read when poured into an iPod display.

IPODDING A LONG DOCUMENT

But maybe I shouldn't have slagged those commercial utilities so quickly. If you take your 200-page New Gonzo–style novel and export it to a file on your iPod — I don't know, to impress people sitting next to you on a plane where they can't possibly escape the conversation — you'll soon notice that the iPod doesn't show the entire file.

Not by a longshot.

Yeah, the notes feature is somewhat knee-capped by the fact that for now, there's a hard limit of 4,000 characters to every note file. That's a little less than two printed pages. Anything beyond that mark is ignored.

But this limit has spawned an assortment of utilities that automatically segment a long text into 4,000-character chunks and deposit them on your iPod in such a way that they feel like one single, chaptered piece.

My usual go-to resource for converting long texts to iPod electronic books is actually a free solution that works through a Web page. Figure 15-4 shows you the iPod eBook Creator page.

Whether you have a PC or a Mac, it works the same way:

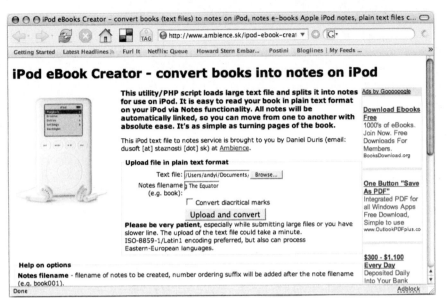

Figure 15-4
Converting a lonnnng text file into a series of linked and chaptered iPod Notes ...
with eBook Creator

1. Make sure the document you want to convert is a plain text file. If it's a Word document, just save it as Text. Name the file whatever you like, but make sure the filename ends with the .txt filename extension.

2. Open http://www.ambience.sk/ipod-ebook-creator with your usual Web browser.

3. Click the site's Browse button. A standard file browser window will appear. Select the text file and click OK.

4. Enter a name for the eBook in eBook Creator's Notes Filename field.

5. Click the Upload and Convert button. eBook Creator will percolate for a moment and then take you to a secondary Web page where you can download the con-verted eBook as a compressed Zip file.

6. Download the Zip file by clicking the link.

7. When the download's complete, double-click the Zip file to open it. All the individual 4,000-character "chapters" of the eBook will be sitting cozily inside a folder.

8. Copy the eBook folder to the Notes folder of your iPod.

HAVING YOUR IPOD READ TO YOU

"Tell me a story, Grampa."

"You got it, sport. 'The Three Bears'?"

"Naw."

"'Green Eggs and Ham'?"

➤TIP

I like eBook Creator because it's simple and it's free and it works like a treat. But there are many commercial iPod utilities that can convert more than plain text files; they can transmogrify Word files directly, along with PDF and other formats.

They're a trifle more complicated, because usually they're part of an all-in-one, "all the features missing from iTunes" utility. PocketMac iPod from www.pocketmac.net is a good app to try first. It offers quick and highly automated document conversion — like iTunes, it can synch automatically whenever you plug in your iPod — and it can handle text, Word, and RTF formats. It's also fairly cheap at about $20.

1. Launch the TextAloud app.

2. Choose File ➪ Open and select the file that you'd like converted to audio (see Figure 15-5). TextAloud will choose the title of the document as the title of the audio file. To change this, type something else in the Title field.

3. Click the Speak To File button.

4. Choose a location to save the new audio file and click OK to start the process. TextAloud will start grinding away, "speaking" each word of text into the file. Typically it finishes the job in about 10 percent of the time it would take to listen to the resulting audio file.

5. When the file is finished, drag it into your iTunes library.

"*Nuh*-uh. I want you to read me the quarterly RTU report on mid-Atlantic actuals, projected through 2008."

Yes, your iPod can read you a charming bedtime tale that'll nod you off to blissful slumberland, possibly while you're in the middle lane of the southbound side of Interstate 93 near Nashua, New Hampshire.

It's all thanks to text-to-speech utilities that can take a file of any length and "speak" it to a standard audio file that you can import straight into iTunes.

Documents-to-Speech in Windows

The app of choice here is NextUp.com's TextAloud (from www.nextup.com). You can read all about this handy utility in Appendix B. For now, let's get cracking and convert a novella that I downloaded a moment ago:

It's one of those glorious operations where you spend three minutes telling your intellectual inferior what to do and then twenty minutes trying to hit one of the empty soda cans on the far side of your office with a rubberband.

Documents-to-Speech on the Macintosh

On the Mac, you don't need an extra commercial utility to convert a document to an audio file. You can just slide together an Automator workflow and, presto!, you have a tool that's actually handier than the Windows utility.

Automator is a fantabulous utility that comes free with Mac OS 10.4 and later. It has this enormous pile of functional, self-contained Actions — and all you have to do is snap them together to form a sequence of steps

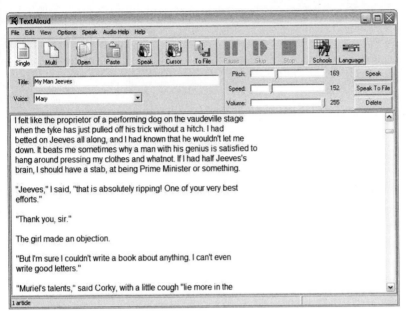

Figure 15-5
Converting document files to spoken-word audio files with TextAloud.

that you'd like your Mac to perform. Appendix A talks about Automator ad nauseum.

To create your Document-to-iPod solution, just create the Automator workflow you see in Figure 15-6, and save it as a plug-in for the Scripts menu.

Once it's in the Scripts menu, here's how you use it:

1. Open the document in TextEdit. TextEdit supports many file formats, including text-only, Word, and RTF.

2. Perform any last-minute changes or edits.

3. Go to the Scripts menu (it's the icon that looks like a thick, curly "S") and choose the document-to-iPod workflow.

The workflow will grind its way through the text and when it's done, the new audio file

will automatically be imported into your iTunes library.

E-BOOKS: HIDDEN GEMS

As a tech columnist, I see this sort of thing all the time: an idea for a product that's terrific, transforming, and powerful, so long as you don't try to get anybody to actually *pay* for it.

I agree with the public-policy wags who declared Reading Is Fundamental and backed up this assertion with a fleet of colorful vans that deployed books to neighborhoods all across America. I'd still rather eat a copy of *Ethan Frome* than have to read it again, but Wharton is an anomaly: Books are, on the whole, good things and reading them should be encouraged.

But *not* in electronic book (e-book) form.

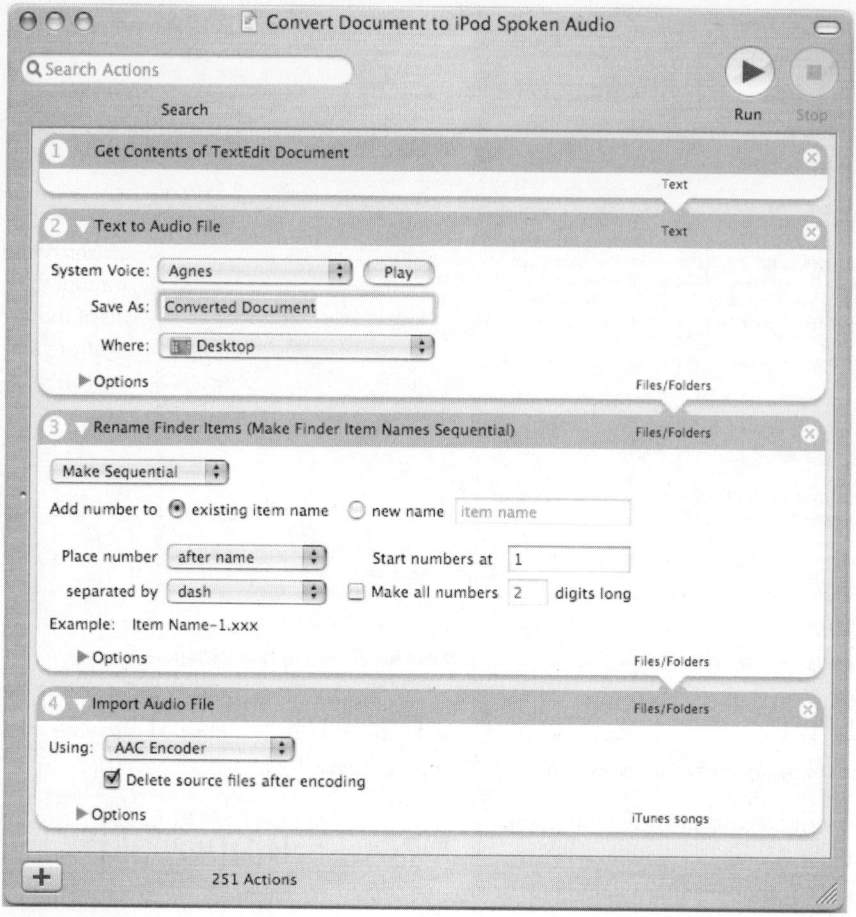

Figure 15-6
Your homemade Macintosh document-to-iPod solution

Please. At this writing, the only ideas that the tech industry has put forward are $300 handheld book readers that run for eight hours on batteries, and can only read $11 digital files that reproduce books you can buy for $4 at any secondhand bookstore.

All right, so those people are all idiots. Agreed? Now let's make them feel even worse about themselves by doing electronic books for free.

The copyright system, I was surprised to learn, wasn't set up for the purpose of protect-

ing an author's ability to sell a certain book.

Its true purpose is actually to make sure that at some point in the grand pageantry of human evolution, that book ultimately belongs to The People and can be freely reproduced.

That's the deal: The government will protect *Farmer Gord and the Infected Pinky Toe* throughout the lifetime of its author and then some. In return, the book becomes public domain eventually.

And public-domain books are precisely the sort of thing that the Internet is good at publicizing: free content distributed to all takers.

There are two central "libraries" so to speak for free electronic books:

> **Project Gutenberg** (www.gutenberg.org and www.gutenberg.net). This is the oldest and definitive source. This organization has been converting public-domain books to digital formats since well before the Web existed. It boasts tens of thousands of titles.

> **Archive.org**. The Internet's glorious center repository of free content. Whereas Gutenberg specializes in public-domain content, Archive.org also includes fiction, nonfiction, and scholarly texts that are still under copyright but that can be freely distributed nonetheless.

Take some time to browse their "shelves." Granted, you're unlikely to find the latest Oprah's Book Club selection, but there were more than a few great novels written before 1922, and many modern writers who are more than happy to put their out-of-print titles in front of a larger audience.

Of all the hassles I go through when I travel, by far the greatest tension hits me when I know that my bags are packed, the cab to the airport will be at the house in a few minutes, … and I haven't packed a book to read.

Ladies and gentlemen, I don't fear crashing shortly after takeoff and dying of asphyxiation amid an 800-degree fireball fed by hundreds of gallons of aviation fuel. I fear having to spend six hours from Boston to San Francisco with nothing to entertain me but the in-flight magazine and the whistling

>TIDBIT

Once again, I feel the need to sheepishly point out that one of you Readers of the Future will live in a world where Apple sells e-books in the iTunes store. I can only remind you that I am a hapless citizen of the past. I mean, come on. Just think about the lapels on the red corduroy jackets of those people from the Seventies. People from the past aren't as sophisticated as you are. We deserve your sympathy.

noise that the guy in the center seat makes through his nose while he sleeps.

Which is why I always have reading material

>TIDBIT

The free distribution of some copyright material is thanks to a recent intellectual-property innovation known as the Creative Commons license. Creative Commons is a carefully worded licensing agreement that allows a creator to offer certain freedoms on usage while keeping some for his or her own use. For example, giving you the freedom to download a book for free and post it on Web sites, so long as you don't sell it, modify it, or attempt to pass it off as your own work.

It's a fantastic concept and its influence is spreading far beyond books and music. Architects are releasing plans for low-cost housing under Creative Commons. If you want to build this house in the U.S., you have to pay the designer a license fee, but in developing nations? Take the plans with her compliments.

on my iPod. When videos fail to entertain, I go to podcasts and music. When even a Bill Evans album can't distract me from that image of the fuel and the smoke and the snoring guy next to me ... there's always Mark Twain's *Roughing It*.

16

E-Mail

The Skim

I'm going to come right out and say it: This is, without a doubt, the most *absolutely totally awesome* chapter in the whole book. The money you spent? Double it, ... *triple* it. By the time you get to the end of the chapter — no, the end of this *introduction* — you'll agree that it's the best dough you ever spent.

Every *other* file format and type of media we've discussed comes with the threat of a potential entertainment benefit. But not e-mail. No, not e-mail. E-mail is what you spend your entire day trying to *escape* from. E-mail is drudgery. E-mail is a burden. A responsibility.

To get right to it, just in case you didn't heed my advice to stop and think about it for a moment and you've yet to catch up with the rest of the class: E-mail is *work*!

Which means that the device you use to read it is a *work-related expense.* If you want your company to buy you a spiffy new video iPod, there's no need to hide it among months and months' worth of modestly inflated taxi vouchers. Put "Pocket e-mail reader: $300" on your expense report and hold your head high.

If the comptroller keeps asking stupid questions, hand him a copy of this book (buy it, of course; I just want to wet my beak here) and let him in on the scam. He'll be reaching for the Approved stamp with his left hand while his right hand mouses to www.apple.com for the address of the closest store.

And the thing is, this isn't even a scam. Apple doesn't officially include any sort of e-mail-synching features on the iPod. But whether you have a PC or a Mac, third-party utilities make e-mail just as simple to iPod as music, pictures, or notes. You can even go one step beyond and use software that will automatically turn your incoming e-mail into audio files that you can listen to during commutes or meetings.

IPODDING YOUR E-MAIL IN WINDOWS

Windows utilities that synch Microsoft Outlook mail to iPods are a cottage industry. What coal and iron were to western Pennsylvania during the Industrial Revolution, iPod utilities are to the world's community of .Net developers.

The Fancy Way: iPodSync

My favorite, though, is a cheerfully cheap app by the name of iPodSync, by ICC Software. You can download a free trial from www.ipod-sync.com. It's clean and pretty, and it really has a terrific sense of what you'd really want to use this sort of utility for. It doesn't complicate things by trying to be an all-in-one central enterprise B2B e-mail solution. "I want to keep my freshest e-mails on my

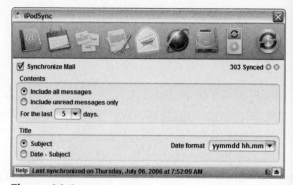

Figure 16-1

IPodSync: PC iPod synching as good as Apple should have made it

iPod" is the problem, and iPodSync is the solution.

Figure 16-1 shows you iPodSync's one and only window. iPodSync does much more than just e-mail — you'll find references to it elsewhere in the book — and each of its features

> **TIDBIT**

When I look at the name "iPodSync," I get that same shiver of dread you get during every slasher flick in which there's a rattling in the basement and one of the randy teens breaks away from the party to investigate. Apple doesn't like it when you sling the word "iPod" into a product name, and I'd be surprised if sometime during the life of this book, the company didn't have a Friendly Word with the developer, Mike Matheson, about its displeasure.

Still, it's a well-established, reliable product and I'm certain that even if there's a name change, the product will still be around. If www.ipod-sync.com ever disappears, plug the name of the app and the developer into a Google search and I'm sure you'll find it.

is nicely organized behind their own icons.

To set up e-mail synching, click the envelope pane to reveal e-mail settings. Here, iPodSync offers you two methods of limiting the amount of e-mail that gets synched to your iPod:

> Include Unread Messages Only does what it says. It'll only copy the messages that Outlook thinks you haven't read already. Good if your attitude is "I want to catch up on mail during my flight," not so good if it's "Hey, cool … all the information about my meeting was in that e-mail I read this morning; it'll be on my iPod after I synch it."

> For The Last Days lets you limit messages by age. Whether you've told iPodSync to synch everything or just the unread messages, this will set a cutoff from five days to four months. Last week's e-mail with the unlock code for the door to the regional warehouse: in. Your ex-boyfriend's apology for why he stood you up on the Millennium New Year party: out. Like the idiot jerk-faced freeloader himself.

So for example, I usually keep iPodSync set to synch every message, read and unread, from the past two days. I just like to have fresh information at hand.

If I'm in a situation where I truly need access to my whole e-mail store, I'll either already have my notebook with me or I'll just find a connection to the Internet and get it from a Web mail client. But you can configure iPodSync to suit your own needs.

Like all utilities of its ilk, iPodSync exports all your e-mails directly onto your iPod as individual notes. The Title section of the

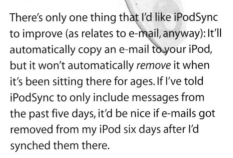

app's Options window lets you control how these e-mails are titled, which means that it controls how they show up in the iPod's Notes menu.

You have two titling types to choose from:

> **Subject** means that the e-mails will appear in the Notes menu as a list of message subject lines.

> **Date – Subject** means that a date/time stamp will precede the subject line, formatted in the style you've chosen in the pop-up menu to the right.

The "correct" settings will depend on how you'll be using these e-mails.

The iPod automatically organizes its Notes menu alphabetically, by title. So Date – Subject has a huge benefit: E-mails will appear in your iPod automatically sorted by

Figure 16-2
Cleaning house by deleting all the
e-mail from your iPod

date, just as they do in Outlook. One glance
and you can see the morning's messages.

More to the point, it seems like the basic
courtesy of making sure that message sub-
jects match message contents has gone the
way of gaslights and spats.

All too often I've needed to locate an e-mail
that told me where a beloved family member
was hospitalized, only to find it under the
subject "Re: RE: re: FWD: New Batman
movie ROCKS!!!" But I knew that it came in
on Monday or so. Zip to message 1,109 in
the list and, boom, there it is.

Subject is the way to go if you trust the
humans who send you e-mail. Dicey. But it's
a great thing if you have an iPod with a nar-
rower screen, like the Nano. When the date
and the time are the first 12 characters of the
title, it leaves precious room for an actual
description of the message content.

Once you've set your options and selected the
Synchronize Mail checkbox at the top of the
Options window, iPodSync is ready to go.

To synch e-mail, just connect your iPod and
click iPodSync's Sync iPod button, at the far
right of the window. When the synch is complete, eject your iPod either from iTunes or
Windows, or use the little Eject button at the
bottom corner of the iPodSync screen.

Ta-da! Your e-mails will appear in your iPod
as notes. You'll find them under a special new
Notes submenu titled "Email."

Note that because iPodSync works by copying files into the iPod's own folders, you have
to enable the iPod for disk use: With your
iPod connected, just go into iTunes and click
the iPod Options button at the bottom-right
of the iTunes window; it's a simple checkbox.

One caveat: It'd be nice if your e-mails were
synched automatically every time iTunes
synched the device. And it'd also be nice if this
keyboard were made of marzipan and, at the
end of the day, I could eat one of those keys
that I never use. Oh, well. Manual synching
of e-mail is better than *no* synching of e-mail.

The Cheap and Universal Way: Plain Text

Oh, dear. I'm not implying that people are
cheap for not using a commercial utility like
iPodSync. I'm offering this as a way to synch
your e-mail if you're *not* using Microsoft
Outlook.

Like, if you're using Microsoft Outlook
Express, or Mozilla Thunderbird, or … er
… other e-mail clients that, unlike Outlook,
you don't have to pay for.

Okay, you know what? Now I *am* implying
that you're cheap. You want quality, but you
don't want to have to underwrite the efforts
of those brave artists who struggle to create

it. I mean, *honestly!*

(Continuing.)

iPodSync works by transmogrifying your e-mails into text files and then copying them into your iPod's Notes folder, where the iPod's built-in software will add the file's title to the menu. If you can't do it automatically, you can do it by hand.

Here's how to do it in Outlook, though the steps are just about identical no matter which e-mail client you're using:

1. Connect your iPod to your PC and make sure Disk Mode has been enabled. Head on over to the iPod Options window in iTunes and turn it on if the iPod doesn't appear to Windows as a storage device under My Computer.

2. Open Outlook and select the e-mail that you want to export.

3. Choose File ⇨ Save As. A standard Windows file browser will appear.

4. Navigate from My Computer to the name of your iPod to your iPod's Notes folder.

5. Save the file into your Notes folder, choosing a title that'll be useful when you see it scrolling past you on your iPod's screen.

You can select multiple e-mails, but (in Outlook and most other mail apps) they'll all be combined into one huge file. And because the iPod has a 4,000-character limit on the size of note files, anything beyond the first couple of pages will get chopped off.

If your e-mails themselves are more than 4,000 characters long, you can, use an iPod utility that automatically segments long text files into notes-studly bites. An app like … oh, I guess iPodSync. Read more about this in Chapter 15.

The Really Cool Way: Turning Your E-Mail into Spoken Audio

"Any messages while I slumbered, Jeeves?"

"Only the one, sir. From Mrs. Travers."

"My aunt? What did she have to say?"

"She wishes you to visit an antiques shop on Brompton Road and, as she put it, 'Sneer at a cow-creamer.'"

Now *that's* the life. Lounge around and have servants read the mail to you. But a dollar doesn't go as far as it used to, so if you want to listen to new e-mails while you drive or commute, you'll need to buy MagneticTime. Download it from www.MagneticTime.com.

MagneticTime works with Outlook or Outlook Express and can automatically transmogrify e-mails into spoken text and export them directly into an iTunes playlist.

It's not quite as slick and simple as iPodSync, but nonetheless it's all stage-managed in a few simple steps, through one window (see Figure 16-3):

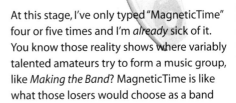

>TIDBIT

At this stage, I've only typed "MagneticTime" four or five times and I'm *already* sick of it. You know those reality shows where variably talented amateurs try to form a music group, like *Making the Band*? MagneticTime is like what those losers would choose as a band name. I mean … *brrr.*

Figure 16-3
Listen to your e-mail, thanks to MagneticTime.

1. Select the Import button.

   If you're using Outlook Express, MagneticTime will bring up a list of e-mails for you to choose from.

   If you're using Outlook, it'll automatically import all the messages found in the MagneticTime mail folder, which the app's installer automatically set up for you.

   The cool thing about the special mail folder is that like any Outlook folder, you can set up special automatic mail-processing rules so that, say, every message from your boss (but not a co-worker) or a friend (but not the so-called friends who borrow your tools and don't return them, or who seduce your boy- or girlfriend more times than might be considered socially permissible) lands

   in the folder and can be grabbed by MagneticTime.

2. The e-mails selected for import appear in MagneticTime's Library list, which you can preview by clicking the Library button. All the checked e-mails will be imported into iTunes.

3. Click the MT-iPod button at the top of the window. MagneticTime will start grinding on all those e-mails. One by one, they'll be converted into MP3 files and imported into iTunes, where they'll appear in a special iTunes playlist titled "MT-Emails."

Natcherly, if you've told iTunes to synch that playlist to your iPod automatically, all your imported e-mail will land on your device during your next synch.

IPODDING YOUR E-MAIL ON THE MAC

You don't need any external utilities to put your e-mail from the Mac's built-in mail client onto your iPod. True, iTunes doesn't have that feature, but you can *build* the correct utility yourself with Automator, which is included free with Mac OS X 10.4 and later editions.

Automator is a dirt-simple tool that allows the average user to string lists of pre-fabbed Actions together to perform a task. Turn to Appendix A for a complete discussion of how it works and how to use it.

iPodding Your E-Mail as Text

Figure 16-4 shows you a very simple, yet extremely flexible Automator workflow for converting e-mail into notes. As is, this workflow takes every e-mail in the mailbox iPodMail, combines it into a text file, loads it onto your iPod as a new note, and then updates the iPod. You'll need to have your iPod docked to your Mac for this to work, of course. What this workflow can *do* for you depends on how you set it up and save it:

> The Find Messages in Mail action can search for any mail anywhere in the app, using multiple search terms. In Figure 16-4, I've simply told it to grab everything from a specific mailbox. But by using standard Mac search items, you can configure this Action to just select Messages whose Sender is boss@yourwork.com, whose Date Sent is Since Yesterday, and whose Subject contains Emergency!

> If you choose Automator ➪ Save As Plug-In and select Script Menu as the destina-

>TIDBIT

Honestly, it's like when you've *just* read a fantastic book or seen the greatest movie you've seen in five years, and you're trying to get a friend to go try it. But as much as you want to tell them the whole story, that'll ruin it for them. So you just fall to the ground in some sort of seizure.

Here, instead of "I can't go into detail, because it'll ruin the story," it's "I can't go into detail, because I've promised to make this book come it at something under 700 pages and $50 cover price." But trust me: Automator is nine pounds of cool in a six-pound-capacity bag, and you should feel free to experiment.

tion, the workflow will appear in a menu right alongside Apple Mail's standard menu bar, and it will behave a lot like a built-in feature.

> If you choose Automator ➪ Save As Plug-In and select iCal Appointment, you can have this workflow run automatically every morning just before you leave for work — or at any other regular interval. So without really doing anything (except maybe for leaving your iPod docked to your Mac when you're not using it), when you unpocket your iPod on the morning train you'll discover that all e-mails of interest have magically been made available for reading.

And because this is just an Automator workflow document, you can create several instances of this workflow and have them all running.

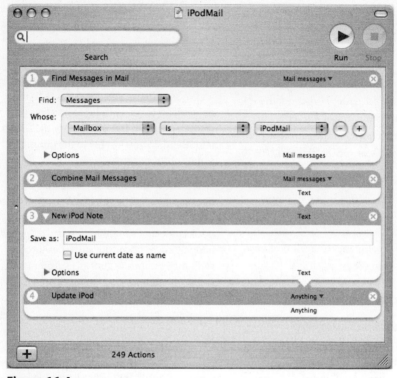

Figure 16-4
The iPodMail workflow

Instead of dragging this sequence of Actions in just once, drag in one set and set it up to save a note containing all your personal e-mail. Then drag in a second set, configured to save your work e-mail, under a totally separate title. A third workflow grabs anything from the past day that you haven't read under a *third* note.

iPodding Your E-Mail as Spoken Audio

Adapting the iPodMail Automator workflow so that it deposits audio files into iTunes instead of text files into your iPod's Notes folder just involves sliding in a few new Actions (see Figure 16-5).

Click Run, and every e-mail in the iPodMail folder will be converted into an AAC file, imported to iTunes, and copied to the iPod-Mail Spoken Email playlist. If you set up this playlist to synch automatically to your iPod, your e-mail will be deposited there with your next update.

The same notes and tricks apply to this workflow as with the previous one. You can easily customize it to convert message of any sort of specification, by modifying the Action named Find Messages in Mail. By repeating those Actions several times, you can have the workflow create several different audio files with different titles and specifications.

And yup, you can attach this to the menu

Figure 16-5
Garbo Speaks! Exporting Mac Mail to audio files

bar or an iCal appointment for close-as-a-heartbeat convenience.

ABOUT THAT EXPENSE REPORT ...

So that's the big scam: You now have precisely the weaponry you need to suggest — nay, *insist* — that the responsibilities of your position and the demands on your time are such that your company needs to reimburse you for that iPod you bought.

The *bad* news is that your boss might just go ahead and assume that you're actually listening to e-mails every morning on the drive in to the office. If that happens and he or she manages to trap you by asking you a ques-

> **TIP**

Mac text-to-speech isn't exactly *lightning*-quick. The only time it's a fast process is when you give it a few short e-mails. If you have more ambitious plans for this workflow — such as listening to an hour's worth of status reports in the car during your 90-minute commute — schedule this workflow to take place before you wake up, when it'll have plenty of time to grind through all that text.

tion about an e-mail that you *should* have listened to on the way to the office, don't take the coward's way out and admit that it was all just a scam.

Stand your ground: Insist that your current iPod's hard drive is too tiny to fit everything and demand that the company buy you a newer, *better* one.

17

Spreadsheets and Databases

The Skim

The Universe is inscrutable. We know this. At least five times a week, we have cause to wonder (aloud and with liberal use of profanity) just *what* the bloody hell it thinks is so damned funny, anyway. Yet we don't receive any sort of useful answer. Thus: inscrutable.

If you want a specific example, let me remind you of two facts. (1) Spreadsheets and databases are omnipresent tools for managing reams and reams of valuable information. (2) Your iPod is a handy pocket-sized device ideal for transporting and *reading* information. Clearly, like a congressperson and a purveyor of $13 haircuts, or a freshly painted park bench and the seat of a bridal gown twenty minutes before the service, or white rice and chunks of fresh pineapple — trust me, give it a try — iPods and this sort of data were meant to be together.

And yet it's a heavy trick to pull off. It's not like most of the other solutions in this book, where there's either a universal step-by-step process that works with anything or a "meat grinder" app that does the work for you. Toss in the data you want, turn the crank, and presto: An iPod-compatible file is spit out from the bottom of the machine.

So no, there's no automagic solution to converting spreadsheets and databases. But if it's any consolation, the difficulty of converting these files into iPod-readable formats is far exceeded by the difficulty of explaining it in a manner that'll be practical to tens of thousands of random readers. It's not like you're the worst off in this particular situation.

Yes, dear reader, the next time one of your local nonprofits holds some sort of fundraiser — PBS, Toys for Tots, Cheese for Nebraska — send them a check in any amount or used clothing in good condition, and tell them it's for me. They'll nod solemnly and make sure it finds its way to me in Boston.

THE BROAD PROBLEM AND THE BASIC SOLUTION

The problem we're dealing with here is that by its very nature, the data in a spreadsheet or a database is formatted in entirely unpredictable ways. You slap down numbers and information into cells and fields wherever and however you want, without a care in the world.

And that's spiffy from a self-empowerment point of view … but it makes it impossible for one simple utility or procedure to work on whatever data you throw at it. It'll have to be a do-it-yourself process.

So let's work with a general concept, here. Both spreadsheets and databases work with tables of information: databases in the form of a tabular report, spreadsheets through the row and cell format. Figure 17-1 is the sort of thing we're talking about here.

Both types of app can also export table data into a format known as "tab-delimited." It's a plain text file in which every line of text is a separate row of table data, and a tab char-

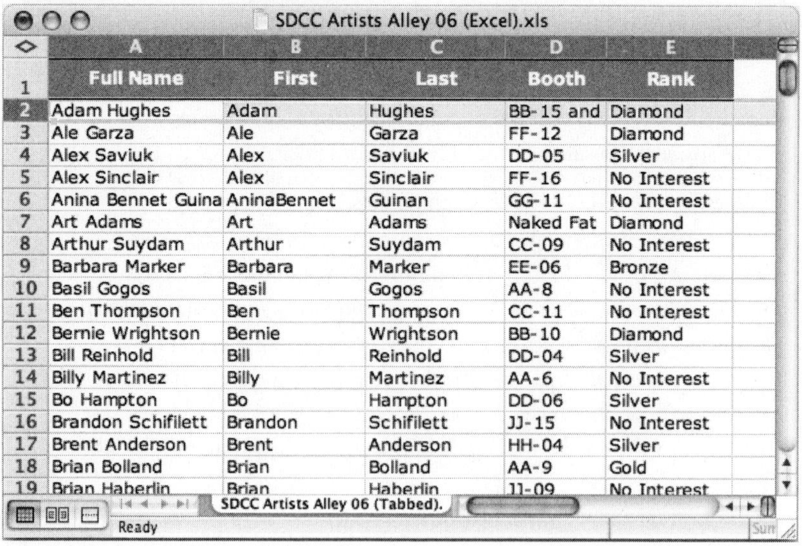

	A	B	C	D	E
1	Full Name	First	Last	Booth	Rank
2	Adam Hughes	Adam	Hughes	BB-15 and	Diamond
3	Ale Garza	Ale	Garza	FF-12	Diamond
4	Alex Saviuk	Alex	Saviuk	DD-05	Silver
5	Alex Sinclair	Alex	Sinclair	FF-16	No Interest
6	Anina Bennet Guina	AninaBennet	Guinan	GG-11	No Interest
7	Art Adams	Art	Adams	Naked Fat	Diamond
8	Arthur Suydam	Arthur	Suydam	CC-09	No Interest
9	Barbara Marker	Barbara	Marker	EE-06	Bronze
10	Basil Gogos	Basil	Gogos	AA-8	No Interest
11	Ben Thompson	Ben	Thompson	CC-11	No Interest
12	Bernie Wrightson	Bernie	Wrightson	BB-10	Diamond
13	Bill Reinhold	Bill	Reinhold	DD-04	Silver
14	Billy Martinez	Billy	Martinez	AA-6	No Interest
15	Bo Hampton	Bo	Hampton	DD-06	Silver
16	Brandon Schifilett	Brandon	Schifilett	JJ-15	No Interest
17	Brent Anderson	Brent	Anderson	HH-04	Silver
18	Brian Bolland	Brian	Bolland	AA-9	Gold
19	Brian Haberlin	Brian	Haberlin	JJ-09	No Interest

Figure 17-1
A table of data

acter separates each column of data. And we already know how to slap a plain-text file into an iPod as a note (that was covered in Chapter 15).

So all we really need to do is take that text file and make a few adjustments to it so that the text is easy to read on your iPod's narrow screen.

IPODDING A SPREADSHEET

Step 1 of iPodding a spreadsheet is to admit that you have a problem and put your faith in a higher power.

Er … no, sorry, wrong project. I mean, you need to set your expectations properly. You're obviously not going to have a "live" spreadsheet on your iPod. Every cell is going to be locked into whatever value it contained when you exported the spreadsheet.

Plus, if you have an ambitious sheet that commits to the idea of Manifest Destiny — spreading arrogantly across endless vistas, with data formatted into several separate tables and tabs — you're going to have to modify it so that all the info that you want to carry with you sits in a single square table. You might also want to delete any columns of data that you don't really want.

From there, it's just a matter of using your spreadsheet's Save As or Export command. In Microsoft Excel (for both PC and Mac), it's File ➪ Save As. Select Text – Tab Delimited as the file format and save it someplace convenient.

But we're going to have to fiddle around a bit with the text before it's truly useful. I would *hope* that by now, you just sort of trust me on these things, but (a) I suppose I shouldn't

```
Adam HughesAdamHughesBB-15 and 16No
Interest
Ale GarzaAleGarzaFF-12Diamond
Alex SaviukAlexSaviukDD-05Silver
Alex SinclairAlexSinclairFF-16No Interest
Anina Bennet
GuinanAninaBennetGuinanGG-11No
Interest
Art AdamsArtAdamsNaked Fat RaveDiamond
Arthur SuydamArthurSuydamCC-09No
Interest
```

Figure 17-2
Spreadsheet spaghetti: tab-delimited data before tweaking

just assume that I've earned your trust, and (b) another illustration will help break up the text and add some visual *zazz*. So I won't be offended if you take a look at Figure 17-2, which shows what the data from Figure 17-1 looks like on an iPod screen without any transmogrification.

It's a narrow screen, which is Problem 1, and the iPod's Notes reader ignores the tabs and mushes all the row's elements together, which is Problem 2. Alas, the only formatting that the iPod respects are the Return characters that separate each line of text.

The best solution to both problems is to put each row element on a separate line. For bonus points, let's also insert a blank line between each of the rows of data from our original spreadsheet. We can do this easily

≻TIP

If your spreadsheet program doesn't have a tab-delimited output option, try the text output option. The tab-delimited format is such a mainstay that sometimes, the person who threw together the menu just assumes that "text" always means "tab-delimited."

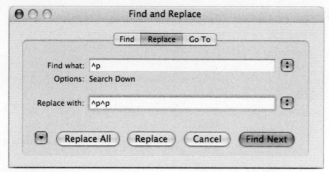

Figure 17-3

Search-and-replace becomes search-and-rescue.

Adam Hughes
Adam
Hughes
BB-15 and 16
Diamond

Ale Garza
Ale
Garza
FF-12
Diamond

Figure 17-4

The transmogrified table, on your iPod

enough right in Microsoft Word.

1. Open the tab-delimited file in Microsoft Word.

2. Bring up Word's Find and Replace window by choosing Edit ➪ Replace (see Figure 17-3).

   The first thing we want to do is make every line end with two Returns instead of just one (one Return to move to the next line, a second to create a blank line). In Word's search lingo, ^p means "new paragraph." If you just hit the Return or Enter key (as you would when typing text the regular way), Word would assume that you're using a shortcut to click the default button in the Search dialog. That's no good.

3. Type ^r into the Find box and ^p^p into Replace. Click the Replace All button.

   Now we change the tabs to returns. ("Oh, I see," you're thinking. "If we'd done this step first, then we'd be doubling-up *these* returns as well, which is bad. How clever.") Actually, you're probably just wishing that I got on with it. Off I go.

4. Type ^t into the Find box and ^p into the Replace box. Click Replace All.

5. Now just save this document as a plain-text file. If your iPod is docked to your computer, you can save it straight into its Notes folder.

That's all there is to it. The data will appear under your iPod's Notes menu looking something like Figure 17-4.

Remember that the iPod can only handle notes of 4,000 characters or less; anything above that will get cut off. If the file is over the limit, use a utility that automatically chops it up into separate chapters. (Info on that can be found in Chapter 15.)

IPODDING A DATABASE

A database app is a bit easier to deal with than a spreadsheet. Spreadsheets were designed to scroll infinitely downward (which the iPod can handle) and infinitely westward (which spells Trouble).

But databases are designed with no set formats in mind. All it cares about is the data, and giving you the power to express and output that data in whichever form suits your purpose.

The very simplest way to get data out of a database and into your iPod is to use the app's built-in Export features. Just as with your spreadsheet program, your database will support tab-delimited exports.

Some apps, like Microsoft Access, make you explicitly choose Tab as the character that separates individual data fields (as in Figure 17-5).

Others allow you to control what fields are included, but on the whole the procedure is almost exactly the same as the spreadsheet procedure described in the previous section: Export the database into a tab-delimited file, use a word processor to transmogrify the text so that each field is on its own line and a blank line separates each record, and then save it.

Custom iPod Database Report Format

But like I said, databases are supposed to be good at exporting data in just the way we want it. Putting every item on its own line rankles a bit, given that two of those items are narrow enough to share the same line.

So let's complicate our lives and create a report format just for our iPod export. Figure 17-6 shows you an iPod layout for our data, using Microsoft Access.

Regardez-vous, silver plate:

> I have collapsed both the Page Header and the Page Footer, to make sure that Access formats the output as one long stream. Otherwise, the app will add white space at the top and the bottom of every page.

⋗TIP

I'm using Microsoft Word as an example for searching and replacing because (a) it's exceedingly likely that you're using Excel as your spreadsheet, and (b) if you're using Excel, it's exceedingly likely that you have Microsoft Word as part of the Office package.

Most word processors can perform a search-and-replace on symbols such as tabs and returns — it's just that their search and replace boxes might use different symbols to stand in for those symbols. Many use \r for returns and \t for tabs. That's part of a standard form of lingo for searches.

Note that you might have to check a special box for Regular Expressions to make it work. That's how the Word-compatible word processor from OpenOffice.org works. If you don't have Word and don't want to buy it just to pull off a couple of iPod tricks, download it from that URL. It's a free, open-source suite of Microsoft-compatible office apps. And quite an awesome download no matter what your motivation.

> I've included empty space in the Detail section where the data lives. That'll become white space separating each of the records.

> I've left off the field labels, because I'm confident that I'll remember that this is a list of names, booth numbers, and rankings. But hey, this is a database; knock yourself out and label everything if you wish.

> I've smushed the field boxes representing the two individual lines of text as close together as I could make 'em. Otherwise, the app will insert white space between the lines, and that just ain't right.

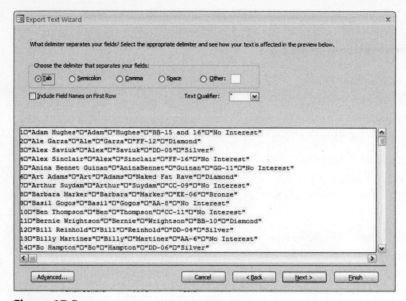

Figure 17-5
You must select a tab delimiter in Microsoft Access

For all your care and caution, preparing an iPod-specific report format is an arcane process, and success will hinge on whether or not the Universe believes that you're a kind and decent person who deserves to have nice things happen to you. If you've spent much of your life being mean and not returning your library books on time and talking in movie theaters, you're just going to have to keep switching between the Design view and the Preview view, making adjustments until you have what you want.

Finally, you close your eyes, commend your soul to God, and save this file as plain text. Figure 17-7 is pretty much what you'll see on your iPod.

The usual caveats apply:

> You need to activate the Enable Disk Use option on your iPod (see Chapter 15).

> And if the file is longer than 4,000 characters, you'll need to chop it down into chapters with a utility (again, return to Chapter 15 of this selfsame book for the whole story).

CALL IN THE GEEKS

I can't send you away without telling you how valuable a geek can be in a situation like this.

Spreadsheets and databases are power office tools, which means that the apps are wired for scripting and automation.

Take the database example above. I've given you an "export to tab-delimited" solution that works and a trial-and-error method of creating a custom report format that will work even better, but it requires some tweaking on your part. A database geek can write you a script or a macro that simply moves through all the records of your database,

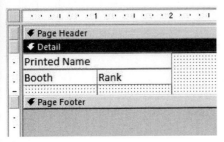

Figure 17-6
Putting fields right where you want them, with a custom report

Adam Hughes
BB-15 and 16   No Interest

Ale Garza
FF-12   Diamond

Alex Saviuk
DD-05   Silver

Alex Sinclair
FF-16   No Interest

Figure 17-7
Database to iPod: a little purtier

extracts the data you want, and exports it into a text file just the way that you and your iPod want it. Ditto for spreadsheets.

Chances are excellent that somebody in your office or circle of friends is a geek with the proper qualifications. And as spokesperson for my kind, I happily report that most geeks enjoy interacting with the humans. Geeks are social creatures. Even those who aren't are interested in observing a wide variety of human behavior, in the interests of making sure that the androids that they're building in

their basement can assimilate amongst society undetected and complete their missions.

Oh, and free meals. We like getting a free dinner. We show up at 5 p.m., you turn on the grill, and by the time the steaks and the corn are done; we have the whole iPod process reduced to a single button-press. Win-win. Operators are standing by. I have no known allergies or food restrictions.

18

Presentations

The Skim

The typical iPod commercial features reverse-silhouette images of folks in their teens and early twenties frooging and boogalooing to a hot soundtrack in a smart and lively fashion, their message being a simple one of Freedom and Joy.

Yes, if Apple decided to spotlight someone using an iPod for Microsoft PowerPoint presentations instead of music, the subject would be a frumpy middle-manager in a $130 suit meekly waving a laser pointer, his message being a tedious and complicated one that concludes "… and so, we'll be shutting down our Dayton operation in Q2, ahead of an 8 percent reduction in workforce across all divisions in Q4."

So Apple's probably making the right choice in not spotlighting this particular iPod capability. Besides, you can navigate through the iPod's menus as deeply and earnestly as you like … you won't find a Presentations menu.

But as you wearily prepare to lug your 17-inch notebook around for twelve hours, heaving it through four airports, two security checkpoints, four connecting flights, and two taxicabs, a few points might occur to you:

▷ You were definitely taking your iPod with you as well … and, gee, your iPod can be hooked up to any standard TV or video projector with a simple, cheap cable.

▷ The iPod can't display presentation files as readily as it can play music. But it *can* display pictures.

▷ You're going to be presenting to the freaking *Dayton* office, for crying out loud. They're all going to be fired in a few months anyway. Why bust your butt by hauling your entire mobile office down there?

On that basis, using an iPod as a presentation device is both morally sound (presuming that you've the morals of sphagnum moss) and easy to pull off. Just convert those

> ▷TIDBIT
>
> If you are indeed going out to downsize entire divisions, please don't take anything I've said in the introduction seriously. Enjoy your bonus, and cheer up; maybe there *isn't* such a thing as karma or Eternal Judgment or whatever. Maybe when you die, you utterly cease to exist. It's gotta be as likely as the possibility that you'll be made to account for all the wrongs you've committed in life, with a focus on every incident in which you willfully turned away from the basic instinct of Compassion. On that basis, there's every reason to believe that there's a slim chance that when the ballgame's over, you won't be cast down into the fire that never ends.
>
> That said, the fact that you parked in a handicapped spot before firing all those people … I mean, that was *cold*, dude.

presentation slides to a stack of image files, and the only thing left to decide is whether you'll buy your kid a T-shirt or a snowglobe at the airport gift shop, after you've indelibly downgraded the lives of 91 full- and part-time staffers. And their children. Please think of the children, won't you? Not of their welfare, certainly, though I'm sure I didn't need to remind you of that.

POWERPOINT AND YOUR CHOICE: WINDOWS OR MAC OS

Converting a PowerPoint presentation into a stack of iPod-friendly images is a piece of cake. PowerPoint — for both Windows and Mac OS X — has a built-in ability to export a presentation as a series of JPEG files, so you're done and dusted with no added expenditures necessary.

To convert a PowerPoint presentation to iPod-studly JPEGs:

1. Choose File ➪ Save As.

2. From the Save As Type pop-up menu, choose JPEG File Interchange Format.

3. Navigate to your My Pictures folder in Windows or Pictures on the Mac as the destination for the JPEGs, just to keep things tidy, and then click the Save button. PowerPoint will ask if you want to export the entire presentation, or just the one slide you're looking at right now (see Figure 18-1)

4. Click the Every Slide button.

5. Finally, tell iTunes to synch your presentation folder to your iPod the next time you update the device (skip ahead to

Figure 18-1
Telling PowerPoint to transmogrify the whole stack of slides

Figure 18-5). (Not sure how? Go back to Chapter 14 for the complete 411 on loading images on your iPod.)

And that's it. PowerPoint will grind its way through every one of your slides.

The end result will be a brand-new folder with the exact same title as your presentation file, which will contain a sequence of JPEGs named Slide1, Slide2, Slide3, etc., as Figure 18-2 shows.

And now you're done.

The presentation will appear under your iPod's Photos menu, listed by the name of the folder.

So if the title of your presentation is "Jeff Gorman Is a Big Stupid Cheating Idiot Loser, And Here's Why I Should Be Named the Commissioner of Our Fantasy Football League Instead of Him," you *might* want to shorten the title of that folder to something that'll fit in the width of your iPod's screen.

Figure 18-2
A big happy pile of JPEG slides

Figure 18-3

Plopping a presentation on your 'pod

UNIVERSAL TRANSMOGRIFICATION FOR WINDOWS

If you're a Windows user and your presentation needs go beyond PowerPoint, go to www.print-driver.com and download fCoder Group's Universal Document Converter.

As the URL implies, UDC isn't a standalone utility: It's a print driver that's available to you in all your Windows apps, via the print dialog box.

Choose Universal Document Converter as your printer, click a few options, and whatever-it-is will land on your hard drive as a series of JPEGs. Instead of landing on the floor in front of your printer, as a series of smudgy images on inkjet paper.

It ain't dirt-cheap (particularly compared to the no-cost solution that PowerPoint offers through its Save As option), but it's a pretty definitive answer: If your app can print, then it can create JPEGs that you can slap onto your iPod.

It's good to know about, at any rate, and there's a free demo version that you can play around with.

KEYNOTE AND MAC OS

Converting a Keynote presentation follows the same basic path as you'd use with Power-Point ... if of course you use PowerPoint. But you probably use Keynote, which is why you're reading this section.

Anyhow, Keynote has a built-in Export function that allows you to save a presentation as a pile of JPEGs.

1. Choose File ➪ Export.

2. Select Images as the file type (see Figure 18-4) and then click Next.

   You're then presented with a small group of options. You can choose to export the whole presentation or just a subset.

   And if you want Keynote to try to re-create all those slick build effects where bullets appear one at a time and a slide's pictures appear only after you've finished talking through its text, select Create an Image for Each Stage of Builds. Keynote will phony-up that slick build effect through a sequence of JPEGs. The results: A four-bullet slide will appear as a sequence of five incrementally complete JPEGs, for example. Otherwise, Keynote will just render the end state of the slide.

   Keynote also gives you several file-format options. JPEG (Medium Quality) is good enough for presentation purposes.

3. Click Next. You'll be whisked away to a magical — no, make that "boring, familiar, standard" Save box. Navigate to the folder where you'd like these JPEGs slides to land. Just to keep things nice and tidy, y'all ought to make a new folder for the presentation. Otherwise, you might lose

track of your slides, particularly if you're saving them in the same Pictures folder that contains hundreds or thousands of other clutter and flotsam.

4. Click the Export button to make the magic happen. Keynote will create a series of JPEGs.

   Each JPEG will be named with the title of the presentation file, followed by a three-digit number to keep them all in the proper order.

5. Finally, tell iTunes to synch your presentation files to your iPod with the next update. (Not sure how? Go back to Chapter 14 for the full story on this sort of thing.)

If you're as smart as everybody tells me you are (no need to be modest) you'll probably drag that JPEG presentation photo into iPhoto.

Then you'll create a new album containing these slides, double-check to make sure they're in the

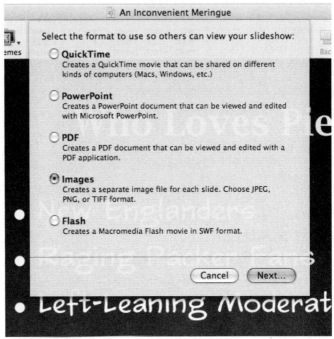

Figure 18-4

Exporting a Keynote presentation as a series of JPEG files

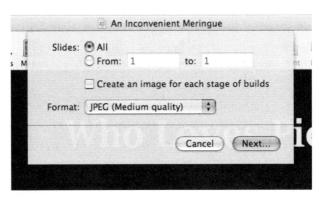

Figure 18-5

Your "blueprint" for an Automator tool that can take any document in any Mac app and turn it into an iPod-ready presentation

proper sequence, give the album a short memorable title that'll be easy to grok on the iPod's narrow screen, and then tell iTunes to synch that album to your iPod.

Voilà! You can access your presentation through the iPod's Photos menu. You'll find that the album is listed right under its proper title and everything, with all your slides in the same order in which they appeared in the iPhoto album.

BUILDING A UNIVERSAL MAC SOLUTION

Just as I showed you earlier for Windows, there's a way to print to a sequence of JPEGs from any Macintosh app. But unlike the

Windows solution, you don't have to buy a thing. Just build an Automator workflow to handle the whole process.

Figure 18-5 shows you what to build, and Appendix A will teach you everything you need to know about how to build it.

It's just two actions: Type the title of the action into the Search box to locate the actions and then drag them into the workflow, one after the other, until you see what you see in Figure 18-5. (Be sure to modify the Actions' setting so that they match what you see in the figure.)

When you're done, choose File ➪ Save As Plug-In in Automator and save it as a Print Workflow, giving it a good, saucy name like

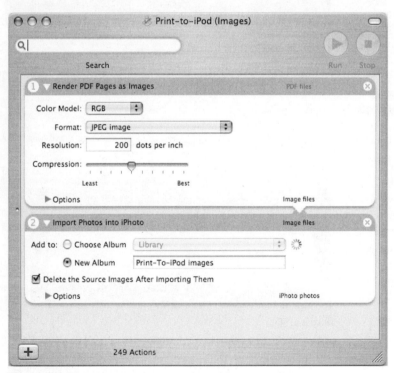

Figure 18-6
Creating a new presentation-slide paper size

"Print-to-iPod Presentation" or something similarly scandalous.

Presto: Your new workflow immediately appears in the standard Print dialog of every Mac application yet conceived by humanity. You can access it through the PDF pop-up button.

But before you take your new homemade toy out for a spin, you'll need to create one last thingamabob: a custom page size to ensure that your slides are the same shape as a video screen. Out of the box, your Mac is paper-trained for all kinds of formats. But a standard 4-by-3-inch video screen probably isn't one of them.

The Mac OS makes it simple to define new output sizes:

1. In whatever app you're printing from, choose File ➪ Page Setup.

2. Choose Manage Custom Sizes from the Page Size pop-up menu. You'll be presented with the little editing window seen in Figure 18-6.

3. Click the plus (+) button to create a new custom page size. Name it "Print-to-iPod Presentation" or somesuch.

4. Set the Page Size to 8 by 6 inches. These are the same proportions as a standard video screen.

5. Choose User Defined from the Printer Margins pop-up menu, and set all margins to zero.

6. Click OK to save your new custom page size.

Now you're ready to go. If you want to take a Web page (for example) and turn it into a stack of slides that you can present from your iPod, you just:

1. Select your custom screen size from Safari's Page Setup dialog box.

2. Using the Print command, choose Print-to-iPod Presentation (or whatever you named the workflow) from the Print dialog's PDF pop-up menu.

   Automator will grind on your request. In a moment, it'll open iPhoto and show you the new contents of the Print to iPod Images photo album.

3. Rename that photo album to the title of your new presentation.

   Be sure to rename the album; the next time you run this Automator action, it'll fill the Print-to-iPod Presentation (or whatever you called it) album with new slides.

4. Go into iTunes, and under iPod Options tell iTunes to synch this album to your iPod with the next update.

Yes, there was a bit of sweat equity involved there.

But this Mac solution also comes with a certain pride of accomplishment. In a world in which it's so hard to even lay claim to the small victories, this is no small feather in your cap.

TAKE A BOW

At the very end of all this, I should probably acknowledge that as easy as it is to create presentations that can be run straight off an iPod, part of the motivation for doing it is just the basic coolness of stepping onto a stage or into a conference room armed with nothing more than the same gizmo that addled your senses with relentless Beastie Boys tracks during the cab ride over.

Still, it's a very, very credible solution. All you need is Apple's iPod AV video cable, which ends in standard RCA video connectors that'll plug into any TV and most projectors. The video quality? A little worse than what you'd get if you ran a presentation at 800-by-600-pixel resolution. It's definitely usable, but if you brought your laptop you'd be able to take advantage of the super-high-resolution of a good projector.

At any rate, you can't beat it for convenience.

And, as I said, coolness. "Ain't it a beaut?" you'll want to marvel to the crowd. "Can you believe I'm showing you all this right off of my iPod?"

But try to stifle this impulse. You've just told 293 concerned parents at a school board meeting that if the state board's standardized test scores can be believed, their kids would have learned more algebra last year if they'd eaten their textbooks instead of reading them. At this moment, presentation equipment is the very last thing on their minds.

Travel Companionage

The Skim

When you're lost in an unfamiliar city, your iPod can help you in two or three ways that are immediately obvious:

1. You can walk up to a stranger and say, "This video-capable iPod cost me $300. It's yours if you can tell me how the *bloody hell* you get to 69 East Madison from here."

2. You can put your headphones on, start watching episodes of *Six Feet Under*, and just sort of hope that things will somehow work out all right in the end.

3. If approached by a squad of ne'er-do-wells, you can drop it in a sock and swing it over your head, converting it into a terrifying and effective close-quarters weapon.

   Remember that, if you are attacked by thugs, an iPod Nano is only an effective incapacitant if you can somehow convince the ne'er-do-well to try to swallow it. Sometimes smaller *isn't* better!

And those are just the tips that don't require any advance planning on your part. If you're willing to do a little legwork, all sorts of helpful abilities become available to you through your iPod.

NAVIGATE THE SUBWAY SYSTEM

If you have an iPod that's capable of displaying photos (that is, any iPod with a color screen) you can take advantage of the selfless labors of a plucky band of creative adventurers who are striving to convert the subway maps of every major world city into a series of iPod-tuned images and making these maps available via the Web.

And that's an ambitious goal. My personal rule is "Any subway system that's too complicated to fit onto a T-shirt is too complicated for humans to ride." Yet they're making a great success of the project, turning rats' nests of lines and bullets and names into clean, efficient maps that can be viewed on the iPod's tiny screen.

Just point your favorite Web browser to www.ipodsubwaymaps.com (see Figure 19-1) and select from any of two dozen world cities. A file containing a map collection will arrive on your hard drive.

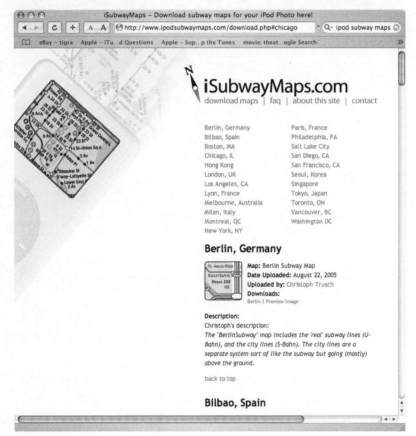

Figure 19-1
iPodSubwayMaps puts the underground world of drunks, panhandlers, and odd smells right in the palm of your hand.

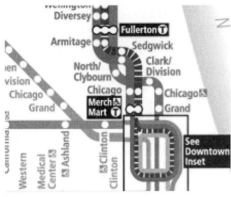

Figure 19-2
A page from the Chicago map. This is
definitely Lower Wacker Drive (not).

The files are simple JPEG images and you
can load them on your iPod the same way
you'd load a batch of photos. Turn to Chapter 13 for the full 411 on loading photos and
pictures onto your iPod.

Naturally, both the huge scale of a subway
map and the eensy scale of an iPod screen
means that the map has been cut up into

> **TROUBLE**
>
> Yes, people are volunteering their time and
> their creativity to create a service that ben-
> efits the millions of people served by public
> transportation systems. The public transpor-
> tation systems' response? Oftentimes, they
> get all lawyer-y. Amazing! The transit folks
> are correct *technically* — often, the maps
> found on these sites are adapted from the
> systems' copyrighted map images — but for
> pity's sake, when people volunteer to help
> you achieve your public mandate and they
> don't ask for a dime in return, the correct
> response is "Yes, thank you muchly."

a number of slices. But if you're not one of
those people who carry around a paper map,
it's quite usable (see Figure 19-2). And bravo
to your sense of priorities. You only have a
limited number of pockets, and space is far
too valuable to devote any of them to analog
technologies.

Some public transportation systems are
catching on, actively linking to iPodSubway-
Maps. Some are going one step further and
are providing even better iPod solutions.
For example, riders of San Francisco's BART
system can download an ambitious package
of maps and updated schedule information. Visit www.bart.gov to download the
QuickPlanner package. If you're not lucky
enough to be living in or visiting San Francisco, Google for the official Web site of your
public transportation system to see if it's as
ambitious about offering support for citizens
of the Push-Button World of Tomorrow.

NAVIGATE THE WHOLE PLANET

The subway maps illustrate the problems
of using an iPod as a mapping device. You
have a tiny screen, and you're using a fairly
basic feature that Apple designed with baby
pictures in mind. That is, every image will be
shrunk to fit the screen, and you can't scroll
from one section to another or zoom in for a
closer look at the details.

So if you want to load actual street maps on
your iPod, you need to prepare the map files
on your own, and you need to make sure
that you'll be able to read the street names
and other details. The Web is chockablock
with free online mapping services such as
Google Maps (maps.google.com) and Yahoo

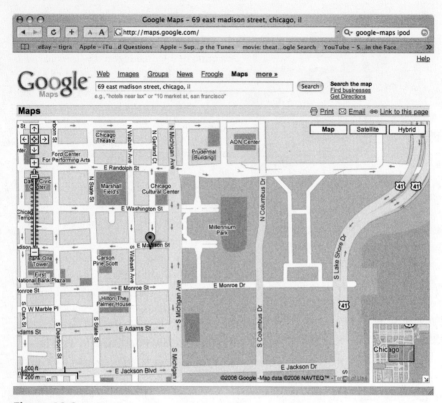

Figure 19-3
Map target acquired, sir

Maps (maps.yahoo.com).

Preparing a Map Detail from Google Maps

I'm using Google Maps for this example, but the basic idea is the same no matter what you use: Put a map on the screen and save a chunk of it as a JPEG file that can be synched to your iPod.

1. Give Google Maps the street address of the place you want to map.

2. Adjust the map's zoom settings to make sure that most of the street names around your target address are labeled

(see Figure 19-3).

3. Capture the screen to a file on your computer.

4. Crop the screen to focus just on the detail you need.

5. Save the image as a JPEG file.

Steps 3 and 4 will depend on what sort of machine you're using. And at this point in the narrative, we usher the Mac people into one room and the PC people into another room, to receive separate talks.

Macintosh Users
Good to be rid of those (shudder) Windows

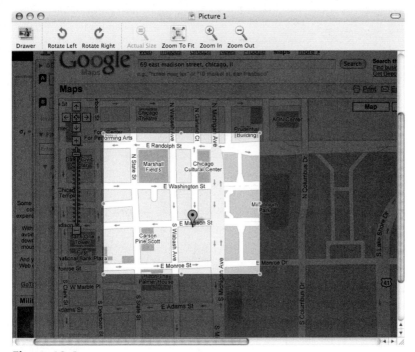

Figure 19-4
Homing in on your target

people, eh? Conventional-thinkers, never pushing the envelope … and how come they always smell like nail-polish remover?

Well, onward with the instructions. To save the entire contents of your Mac's screen as an image file, the easiest way is to use the Grab utility that comes with Mac OS X. (It's buried in the Utilities folder, inside the Applications folder.)

After launching the application, use the commands in the Capture menu to select what you want to, er, grab. Then choose File ➪ Save As to save the file; Grab automatically saves the file to the TIFF format. But you want it in JPEG format, so just double-click the TIFF file to launch Mac OS X's Preview utility (which you can also find in the Utilities folder) and choose File ➪ Export to create a copy in the JPEG format (just make sure JPEG is selected in the Format pop-up menu). That's it! (Well, not quite. You might want to crop the image if you hadn't done so while grabbing the image. Read on for that.)

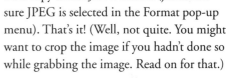

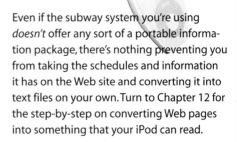

> **TIP**
>
> Even if the subway system you're using *doesn't* offer any sort of a portable information package, there's nothing preventing you from taking the schedules and information it has on the Web site and converting it into text files on your own. Turn to Chapter 12 for the step-by-step on converting Web pages into something that your iPod can read.

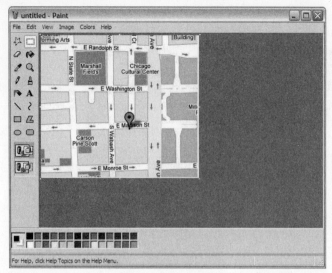

Figure 19-5
Creating a map in
Microsoft Paint

There is another way, familiar to long-time Mac users, those who saw The Light before the iMac, iTunes, iPod, and other i-stuff: Press Shift+⌘+3. You'll hear the sound of a camera clicking, which means the image has been saved to your Desktop with the name Picture followed by a number. Then crop it. Or press Shift+⌘+4, then drag to select just the portion of the screen you want — that takes care of the cropping! Either way, you'll get a PDF file that you can open in Preview and export to JPEG format.

How do you crop a screen image you've already taken, if you don't have an image editor like Adobe Photoshop? Easy. In the Preview utility, do this:

1. Drag a selection rectangle around what you'd like to see on your iPod screen (see Figure 19-4).

2. Choose Tools ⇨ Crop to erase everything but what you've selected.

3. Choose File ⇨ Save. Give the map image a name and be sure to select JPEG in the Format pop-up menu.

Windows Users

Good to be rid of those (shudder) Macintosh people, eh? Smug, self-satisfied jerks … and how come they always smell like coffee? Well, onward with the instructions:

To save the entire contents of your PC's screen as an image file:

1. Press the Print Screen key on your keyboard (it might be labeled PrtScr or something else cryptic) to save the contents of your screen into the Windows Clipboard.

2. Launch Windows's built-in Paint program. You'll find it in your Start menu's Programs submenu, under Accessories. (If you have another image editor such as Corel Photo-Paint, Jasc Paint Shop Pro, or Adobe Photoshop, use that instead.)

3. Choose Edit ⇨ Paste, or just press Ctrl+V. The window now contains the screen image.

Now you need to crop the image in Paint or your image editing app. In Paint:

1. Drag a selection rectangle around what you'd like to see on your iPod screen.

2. Choose Edit ➪ Copy or press Ctrl+C.

3. Choose File ➪ New, then paste the selection into the new image by choosing Edit ➪ Paste or pressing Ctrl+V (see Figure 19-5).

4. If necessary, resize the image canvas so that it's no larger than your map image. Click the gray background of the window to expose the canvas' resizing handles. Adjust until you can't see any more of that white stuff.

5. Choose File ➪ Save and give the map a name. Be sure to select JPEG as your file format in the Save As Type pop-up menu.

Come Together, Right Now

And now let us dance again as a harmonious joint community of PC and Mac users.

That's it. You can synch this JPEG map (see Figure 19-6) to your iPod as you would any other picture file (see Chapter 14 for a refresher).

Turn-by-Turn Directions

Do-it-yourself is (at this writing) the only method of producing iPod maps that always yield decent results. All the same, there's a free Web service that's worth looking at: www.ipod-directions.com (see Figure 19-7). This service interacts with Yahoo Maps. Enter a start address and an end address. iPod Directions will take Yahoo's resulting maps and the directions, convert them all to iPod-sized image files, and deposit them on your hard drive, ready to be synched.

The service works really well, but it's not

Figure 19-6
The finished iPod-ready Google Map.

for everybody. I wouldn't dare try reading directions off an iPod screen while driving, unless my ongoing curiosity about what an airbag deployment feels like became too great to control.

Even when you're just walking, there's a point where even the most hardcore geek has to admit that copying complicated directions onto an iPod is sometimes not as good a solution as copying them to traditional ana-

>TIP

Figure 19-6 demonstrates my rule of thumb for resizing these map images: I try to size them so that they're no bigger than roughly twelve times the width the narrowest labeled street. There's no magic number here, but this usually means that you'll be able to read all the labels and legends on your iPod screen. If you're using an iPod Nano with its thumbnail-sized screen ... um, maybe you're better off just printing a copy of the map instead.

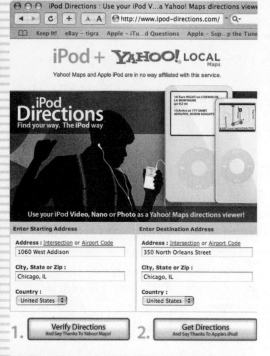

Figure 19-7
iPod Directions converts Yahoo Maps content into iPod-study files.

log mashed-pulp substrate.

In other words, just stop being Commander Future and *print* the bloody map and directions onto paper.

IPOD AS UNIVERSAL TRANSLATOR

Just because something's a simple idea, it doesn't mean that it's a *stupid* idea.

I'll give you a perfect example. There's absolutely nothing as stupid as a movie produced by Adam Sandler that stars Rob Schneider.

And yet, the *Deuce Bigalow* pictures took weeks to shoot, requiring hundreds of cast and crew, multiple tractor-trailerloads of highly technical equipment, and tens of millions of dollars. QED: a stupid idea that was actually quite complicated.

Actually, I've just demonstrated that just because something is *stupid* it doesn't mean that it's *simple*. But I'm leaving that in anyway. A few weeks ago I was hanging out with friends and they insisted that they put on *Deuce Bigalow: European Gigalo* and I suppose I'm still kind of resentful.

When you're a visitor to a foreign land, you should make an attempt to speak the local lingo. Even if the only phrase you really master is "That's a lovely necktie you're wearing; say … do you speak English?" it demonstrates a certain basic respect for the citizenry and an appreciation that they're not all employees of the Walt Disney Company.

I spent a week in Mexico recently, and I tried to speak Spanish as frequently as I possibly could. I'm certain that my success was partly due to the indulgence of kind people who mentally translated my American Tourist High-School Spanish to *actual* Spanish as I spoke, but I certainly had a better time than I would have if I'd arrived on those golden shores armed only with a library of pantomime skills and the endearing English phrase "Don't nobody here speak American?!?"

So when I got back to my hotel after my first day, I connected to Google's language tools (www.google.com/language_tools) and had Google translate every English phrase that I'd struggled to communicate over the course of the day (see Figure 19-8).

From "Could you please help me take a picture?" to "Is there a store nearby that sells comic books?" to "I just can't seem to get the song 'Tainted Love' by Soft Cell out of my head" and beyond — one by one, I got translations and pasted them into a text file, until I had dozens and dozens.

I dragged the file into my iPod's Notes folder and presto: For the rest of the week, I had a custom-made, highly Andy-centric phrasebook in my pocket at all times. (Turn to Chapter 12 for a more complete rundown of copying text files to your iPod.)

And there are plenty of online phrasebooks on the Web that you can download for free How do you find them? Wiki your way.

WikiTravel is a Web resource that tries to do for travel guides what Wikipedia does for online encyclopedias: become a definitive reference powered by contributions from thousands of visitors. A search for "phrasebook" reveals translations of common tourist phrases in dozens of different languages, from Afrikaans to Yonaguni. Just cut and paste the language you need into a text file, copy it to the Notes folder of your iPod, and you're good to go. Far.

I think I deserve a little credit for being so upfront about the limitations of the iPod here. As a navigational aid, is an iPod as valuable as a Global Positioning System receiver with a gigabyte of interactive scalable maps? No. As a translator, is it as useful as carrying around a thick phrasebook? Of course not. Have all these loaded, rhetorical questions left me a bit drained and in need of a soda? Indeed yes. Excuse me for a moment.

Ahh ... that's better.

> **TIP**

The trouble with software-based translation services is that (as the denouements in a metric ton of bad sci-fi stories agree) a machine has no soul. So it's entirely possible that Google's German translation of "Can you help me take a picture?" actually means "I want you to be an accomplice in an art heist." So it's usually a good idea to see what happens when you give the same phrase to another online translator, like the Babel Fish service available from AltaVista (babelfish. altavista.com).

But the point is this: you don't *carry* a GPS receiver with you everywhere you go, and a phrasebook is (a) overkill for most tourists and (b) makes you look about as tragic

Figure 19-8
Google Language Tools turn a tourist into a traveler.

s those pitiable unfortunates who wander around Times Square wearing green foam-rubber Statue of Liberty crowns.

But your iPod is something you carry with you everywhere. It's like your wallet and your keys. I didn't *plan* to listen to music while I walked the streets of Mazatlán, but I also didn't plan to get a photo of me standing in front of an enormous and gorgeous hand-painted Coca-Cola billboard. And thanks to my Universal Translator file, I have next year's Christmas card picture.

20

Bleeding the Fun Out of Your iPod

The Skim

Dumping Photos from your Digital Camera >
iPod as a Notebook Replacement? > Backing up Your Files >
But Wait! There's More!

It's been a fun 19 chapters so far, I hope you'll agree. If you've been trying out everything chapter by chapter, your iPod is now chockablock with content. Music, podcasts, movies, TV shows, books, Web sites, …

Incidentally, on the off chance that you *haven't* been trying everything chapter by chapter, and the reason *why* is because you've spent the past five or six hours in one of those huge comfy chairs at the bookstore reading this book and sipping at a $6 frappamochacuppacupertino or whatever the hell it is that they sell in the attached coffee shop … well, I don't know what to say. I suppose I'm flattered that you read the whole thing in one sitting, particularly in a place where you could just as easily have gone to the Humor aisle and grabbed one of those *Complete Peanuts* collections, or a copy of P.G. Wodehouse's *The Code of the Woosters*, possibly the greatest English novel published in the previous century (I mean the one before the last one — y'know, the 19th — hard to believe that the 1990s are already "previous century"!).

Still: *c'mon*, man. Enough is enough. This book is quite attractively-priced and delivers exceptional value for your book buying dollar/

pound/euro/bhat/ringgit.

Onward. It *has* been fun and your iPod is now loaded up with. ...

Oh good heavens, you're telling me that you saw a guy in here the other day *actually taking the book into the coffee shop* with his iPod and a notebook?

No, no, you're right ... this isn't about me, this is about you.

Your iPod is now loaded with all kinds of stuff to reduce the most frustrating morning commute, the most paralyzing wait at the Department of Motor Vehicles, or even the

Figure 20-1
The iPod Camera Connector

most self-deluded attempt to get back into shape by jogging a minimum of four miles every morning and turning it into an entertaining skip down the yellow brick road.

But I can't help but notice that you *still* have about nine gigabytes of space left on that thing. We've plowed through all the different ways you can fill your iPod with enjoyable or even Just Plain Useful things. In this, our final assault upon the principle of available storage space, we shall look at other ways to fill that drive.

The goal isn't to be a glutton. No, no. The goal is to manufacture an excuse to buy one of those *new* iPods with the larger hard drives. It's so important to have goals in life, isn't it?

DUMPING PHOTOS FROM YOUR DIGITAL CAMERA

Digital photography has completely changed the way I take pictures. I used to pack four or five rolls of film for a weeklong trip, and by Friday I'd curse that I'd already used up all 96 frames. Now, I slip a one-gigabyte memory card into the camera every morning and by 2 p.m. I curse that I could only get 533 shots on the thing. I hear my traveling companion complain, "But it's a *pigeon*. We see *thousands* of them back in Boston!" I hear, I laugh, I continue to shoot, this time turning the Bracketed Exposure feature on so I'm taking three shots at a time.

Memory cards are cheap enough that you can easily afford to buy enough storage to shoot them all day long. But if you're going to be out road-tripping for a few days and you don't want to drag your laptop with you, Apple's $30 iPod Camera Connector is a terrific buy (see Figure 20-1).

It's just a little nubby piece of plastic that clicks into the dock connector of any iPod with a color display. Plug your camera's USB cable into the jack at the bottom of the connector and a new menu springs to life on your iPod's screen. Click Import Photos and all the pictures on your camera will be copied into your iPod. When it's done, you're free to erase your memory card and keep shooting.

You can view the photos on your iPod just as though you'd synched them to the device from your desktop, and the next time you dock the iPod, the new pictures will automatically be added to your computer's photo library.

IPOD AS A NOTEBOOK REPLACEMENT?

Listen, I don't want you to use this as an excuse *not* to get your boss to buy you a $2,000 notebook. I simply want to call your attention to a few facts:

1. At the office, you have a wonderful desktop computer with expensive, name-brand apps fully loaded: Microsoft Office, Adobe Creative Suite, that World of Warcraft client app that your boss doesn't know about. Et cetera.

2. At home, you have an equally wonderful computer. It has nearly the same set of apps up and running on it.

3. Oh, and the branch office in New Mexico? The one that you have to jet out to once a month for a meeting? I'm going to take a guess that one of the computers over *there* has Microsoft Office installed on it as well.

4. As light and small as small computers

> **>TROUBLE**

One word of warning about using your iPod as a hard drive: Keep in mind that the iPod's designers never figured that its hard drive would be spinning constantly. When it's being used as a music player, the iPod spins up the hard drive, loads in the next music file, and then spins the drive back down again, both to extend the playtime of the battery and protect the drive against bumps and knocks.

So if you get terribly ambitious with backups — you choose to back up all ten gigabytes of your hard drive's files, instead of just a few critical folders — you run the risk of shortening the life of your iPod's drive. Seriously: Feel the iPod the next time you're copying a lot of music and video to it. After a few minutes, that sucker gets *warm*. There's your tipoff.

have become in the past twenty years, none of them are anywhere *near* as teensy as an iPod. You don't need a special bag for your iPod, and when you step up to airport security, the folks manning the conveyor belt don't demand that you remove your iPod from wherever you keep it and place it in its own separate tray away from everything else.

All together, it's a not-unconvincing argument that you don't actually *need* to lug a complete working computer around with you wherever you go, from home to office to conference and back again.

No, all you *really* need to carry with you are your files. And (as we've seen in Lord knows how many chapters) your computer can treat your iPod just like any other external

>TIP

If you're going to be storing all your critical business and personal information on an iPod (or any other pocket device, for that matter), it bears mentioning that the humans are imperfect creatures. iPods get left in taxis. Ne'er-do-wells also tend to pickpocket them on subways. So when you put important data on such a tiny device, you run a certain risk that those files will fall into the wrong hands.

The solution is to use a file-encryption utility, such as the products based on the PGP standard. When files are protected with strong encryption you can e-mail them directly to P. Nasty McIdentityTheft himself; he won't be able to read them without (a) the right piece of software and (b) your personal password.

Which makes it important that you have a copy of the encryption/decryption utility on all your computers. And that you never, ever, *ever* forget your password.

hard drive if you enable the iPod's Enable Disk Use mode: Just click the iPod button in iTunes when the device is docked and make sure that the Enable Disk Use checkbox has been checked. Bravo: Windows and the Mac OS will mount the iPod as a storage device.

The rules that link an iPod to one and only one iTunes library still apply:

> If it's linked to your home computer, your work computer won't be able to access any of its songs or playlists.

> If the other computer has a copy of iTunes installed, it'll ask if you'd like to erase all the iPod's music and link the thing to its own music library.

But other than that, it's a plain old USB hard drive and you can carry it from machine to machine with impunity. Copy your Documents folder (on the Mac) or My Documents (in Windows) folder to your iPod and make your music player into the hub of your digital experience. It might take you a while to train yourself to save files to the iPod instead of your desktop, but once you've acquired the knack, you've lightened your daily load considerably.

BACKING UP YOUR FILES

In all your eagerness to load up your four hours of Lovin' Spoonful studio bootlegs and all 211 episodes of *The Rifleman*, it's easy to overlook the fact that an iPod is a big honkin' hard drive that can be USB'd to a computer and be exploited like any other storage device.

Given that there're only *so* many alternate takes of "Did You Ever Have to Make Up Your Mind?" that any sane man or woman can tolerate, there's bound to be some empty space left on the device. And when the day comes that Murphy's Law and Karma both turn their attention to you and choose to wipe out your entire (My) Documents folder the night before an critical deadline (yes, that day is coming), those empty gigabytes will mock you like Marley's Ghost.

You *could* have filled it with a fresh backup of every document on your computer, but *no*: Once you had Zal Yanovsy's eleven-minute free-jazz guitar riff on "Do You Believe in Magic?" on the thing, your ambitions were complete ... and you unplugged your iPod.

If your computer sees your iPod as just another hard drive, any conventional backup app can store data onto it. But there are a couple of apps for PCs and Macs that can take special advantage of the iPod.

Backing Up in Windows

Amongst iPodSync's fearsome weaponry (download it from www.ipod-sync.com) is a simple and clean feature that allows you to keep folders synchronized between your PC and your iPod (see Figure 20-2).

iPodSync is easier to use than a traditional backup utility. You just point the app to specific PC folders that you'd like it to keep synchronized to your iPod:

1. Click the Files icon in iPodSync's toolbar.

2. Select the Synchronize Files checkbox.

3. Click the Add button to choose a folder for synchronization.

… And repeat until you start feeling better about the safety of your files. Every time iPodSync synchs your iPod, it'll make

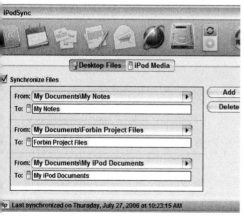

Figure 20-2

Preparing for the worst: backing up Windows files to your iPod with iSync

>TIDBIT

This must be the twentieth time I've praised iPodSync. One of the hassles of putting this book together was choosing the software that I was going to recommend. There are loads of iPod utilities out there; plenty of users have wished that the iPod could do this or that it could work with that, and there've been plenty of software developers eager to step in and answer the call.

But I couldn't recommend hundreds and hundreds of dollars' worth of extra software. Fortunately, iPodSync does *so* much for *so* little money and is *so* easy to use and *so* reliable that I can defiantly say that here, and nowhere else, should your iPod Software Dollar be spent.

Which isn't to say that there aren't any other decent iPod utilities on the market. But good heavens, any developer who tries to challenge iPodSync in the broad "Synch the kinds of data that iTunes forgot about" category has its work cut out for them.

One postscript, repeated from elsewhere: Apple has historically taken a dim view of companies that put the word "iPod" in product names. So don't be surprised if this utility ceases to exist some day under its original name. If you can't locate a copy at www.ipod-sync.com, Google for the old name; the new site and the new URL will pop right up, I bet.

sure that the contents of both the desktop's selected folder and the folder on your iPod are identical.

Backing Up on a Mac

There are a few iPod-specific utilities for per-

Figure 20-3
Backing up Mac files to an iPod through the magic of Automator

forming backups, but none provide the sort of value that iPodSync does on the PC.

These Mac utilities give you one or two features that you desperately need and then a huge bushel of features that just duplicate what iTunes can do on its own, or what you can do in Automator.

Figure 20-3 shows you an Automator work-

flow that you can easily modify to handle all your backup-to-iPod needs.

Read Appendix A for the full explanation of (a) what Automator is, (b) why it's so incredibly damned sexy, and most importantly (c) how to create, save, and use Automator workflows.

The workflow in Figure 20-3 is what I've

set up for my own use. (Yes, I actually do practice what I preach!) It copies two sets of things to the iPod ("Gern Blanstev's iPod") using the following workflow:

1. Selecting Get Selected Finder Items grabs three specific folders on my hard drive: my Documents folder, the folder that contains everything on my personal Web site, and my Mail folder. The three folders are then copied to my iPod. The Replacing Existing Files checkbox means that the workflow will replace the old backup folders with the new, fresh ones.

2. You can add your own folders to Get Specified Finder Items by clicking the plus (+) button in the Action and choosing the folder. Repeat as often as you wish.

3. Next, the Find Finder Items action does a search for all files on my hard drive that match a certain criteria. Honestly, everything I'm working on is going to be inside the three folders that I've already specified, but it's handy to have all the files I'm currently working on all gathered in the same place.

4. So the search I've set up collects all files of type Document that have been modified within the past 24 hours. These are copied to a special folder on my iPod named "Fresh Meat."

Because I've saved this workflow as an iCal plug-in, it runs every morning at 5 a.m. And because I'm in the habit of leaving my iPod docked to my Mac overnight to charge, my iPod automagically contains a backup of all my critical data.

And all I had to do was go to bed!

> **>TIDBIT**
>
> Hey, cool; you have a free Automator workflow that backs up your data. So you don't need to buy a "real" backup app, like (my favorite) Retrospect, or the free Apple Backup utility that comes with your .Mac account, right?
>
> Mmm … no. This workflow falls firmly under the category of "better than nothing." A "real" backup app can clone your entire hard drive to another volume either on your desktop, on another computer across the network, or on a server a thousand miles away.
>
> A guy I once rented a car from sold me the $12 supplemental insurance policy with the following pitch: "If you roll the car twelve times, crunch the roof and the front and rear end, blow out all the windows, and land in a swamp, so long as you get the car back to the lot, you can just hand me the keys and the whole incident will be behind you."
>
> That's what you get with a backup program. If your hard drive does a total firework or if your computer's stolen or a mudslide wipes out your vacation home, you simply retrieve your backup from where you safely stored it, let the backup app percolate for a moment, and when it's done, your files will be back on your (possibly replacement) computer as if nothing had ever happened.

BUT WAIT! THERE'S MORE!

And we've just scratched the surface of how you can exploit the fact that your $200 buys you not just a music and video player, but a pocketable, battery-powered hard drive. Export your favorites/bookmarks from your Web browser and carry them on your iPod, so that you can always visit your usual sites no matter whose machine you're sitting behind. Carry installation apps of your most critical software on there; if you desperately need a certain chat client on the machine you're poaching but it isn't pre-installed, just install a fresh copy from your iPod.

Et. Cet. Era.

I've always thought that one of the truly brilliant ideas that Apple put into the iPod was its name. It doesn't give away what the bloody hell the thing is supposed to *do*. In fact, you have to look pretty closely at the device before you can work out that it's even a music player: the Play/Pause and track

labels are small and discreet.

The whole idea of the iPod was to allow Apple to continue to evolve it in whatever direction made the most sense. And that same sort of power is in the hands of its users: Don't think of it as a mere mechanism for guaranteeing that four days' worth of southern rock are never far out of reach. Think of it as a physical wrapper for any-thing and everything in your home or office that you'd like to have with you as you explore The Big Room.

Automating Processes in Mac OS X

The Skim

Automationalization > Building a Workflow >
Working with Workflows > Shameless Plug

As a product, the iPod has found a certain degree of success in the marketplace. Millions of folks want to have an iPod in their pockets, which means that thousands of companies want to get their hands in the till. Result: hundreds and hundreds of utilities for expanding the capabilities of our little pearlescent pal.

Natcherly, this book discusses and endorses many of them. But there are way too many $20 utilities that do Just One Thing — and not terribly well, either. Better, I think, to learn about a couple of valuable all-purpose tools that can serve a wider range of functions.

That's why you're reading this appendix. Peppered throughout the book you'll spot references to tricks that require Automator, a somewhat awesome piece of software that's comes with every copy of Mac OS X 10.4 and later (sorry, Windows users). "Ihnatko seems to think that I already *know* about this stuff!" you probably fumed to your spouse, partner, or perhaps dog, at the time.

You would have been very correct to be upset with me. But in truth, Ihnatko just thinks and hopes that you'll read this here appendix, which gives you all the basics.

AUTOMATIONALIZATION

Automator is an application. You can find it right in your Utilities folder, inside the Applications folder (see Figure A-1).

Figure A-1
Automator: Resistance is futile.

Automator is, hands-down, one of my favorite things on any OS anywhere. It's a bold attempt to give the average computer user the ability to take a boring, complicated process and reduce it to a simple, one-click action. Tell Automator how to do something, step by step, and that's the last time you ever have to do it yourself.

Lots of utilities have made that promise. But only Automator actually delivers. It's as if Automator has a big box of Lego blocks.

>TIDBIT

So Mac OS 10.4 was still about a year away from being released and Apple was showing me Automator for the first time. "I understand why the icon is a little robot," I told the President of Automator. "But why is he holding a flashlight?"

"That's not a flashlight," he said. "It's a pipe. He's like a little plumber, going around building things."

I was a little embarrassed, but not as embarrassed as I would have been if I'd gone with my first reaction. "Why is he holding a home-made potato cannon?"

Each block represents an element of anything you could ever do on a Mac. Just snap these blocks into a stack, one on top of another, and bang: You've described a list of instructions for Automator to follow, starting at the top and working to the bottom.

Lawyers representing Apple, the Lego company, and the publishers of this book would all be pleased if I immediately started referring to these blocks by their proper name: Actions. But the principle is the same: Come up with a list of Actions for Automator to perform, and then trust that the system works.

BUILDING A WORKFLOW

In fact, Automator is so simple that there's no need for us all to head into a shabby conference room for three hours of orientation. Unlike clumsy and old-tech ideas such as, say, thoracic surgery, we can just dive right in.

When launched, Automator automatically creates a brand-new Automator document for you (see Figure A-2). We call these things "workflows."

All those Actions "belong" to existing apps on your hard drive. When you install Microsoft Word, you also unknowing install a whole collection of Microsoft Word–specific Actions that let you Automate that app.

There can be hundreds and hundreds of these Actions, so naturally Priority 1 for Automator is to organize all these things so you can readily put your hands on the Action you need. Hence the Library and Action pane of the Automator window. Library lists all the apps that can be Automated. Select one of 'em, and all their related Actions will appear in the Action list.

Nearly all these Actions have clear, helpful names. Update iPod. Good example; any need to elaborate on that one?

No, of course not. But Apple designed Automator so that it'd be attractive even to those of us who are violently opposed to any form of technology more advanced than a strike-anywhere match, so if you click on a specific Action, the pane just below Library and Action will offer additional details on what the action is and how it works.

That big empty space off to the right is your factory floor. You drag Legos — Actions, *Actions,* sorry — into this little tray and move them into their proper order. Automator does the rest.

Finally, there are a couple of controls at the very top of the window. To the left, you'll spot a Mac-standard Search box. If you want to find the Action that updates your iPod with fresh content, you can just go blindly through the Library list and trust to luck, or you can just type iPod into the Search box and see what happens.

Answer: the Action list is filled with every iPod-related Action that's available. Sweet.

To the right are Run and Stop buttons. As we'll see, there are many ways and places where you can run an Automator workflow,

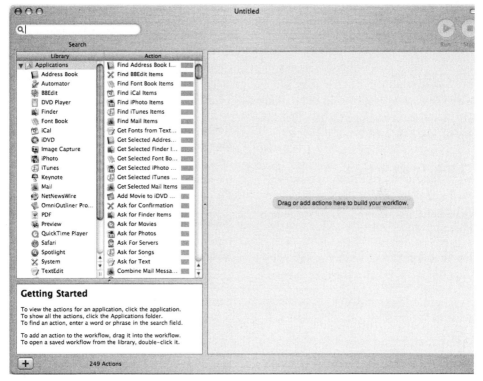

Figure A-2
A workflow that accomplishes nothing. Surely you've had a job that felt like this.

Figure A-3
Mr. Browseraction, I presume?
Finding Safari actions

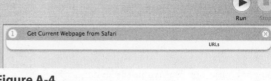

Figure A-4
The start of a beautiful workflow

but here are your boldest and most obvious targets. Run runs, Stop stops. These buttons work the same way on the $45 DVD player you bought at the gas station as they do on your $1,800 iMac.

WORKING WITH WORKFLOWS

So let's build us a workflow. I want to acquire the Godlike ability to take whatever Web page I'm viewing in Safari and add it to my iTunes library as an audio file that I can listen to in my car.

Think, Then Action

So the first step involves leaning back in the chair and adopting a thoughtful expression for a moment.

Yes, in Automator workflows — just as in acquiring a complicated back tattoo repre-

> **>TIP**
>
> To remove an Action from a workflow, just click the Close button at the top-right corner of the Action.

senting a popular movie — you avoid lots of trouble if you just spend some time Thinking Before Doing.

Here's what the workflow will have to do:

1. Get the current Web page.

2. Convert it to a sound file.

3. Import the sound file into iTunes, and add it to a playlist that I've already set up to synch automatically to the iPod.

Good plan. Onward.

The Big Drag

Okey-doke. So we start off with Step 1: Get the current Web page. Let's just type Safari into Automator's Search box and see what the browser can do through Automator (see Figure A-3).

Whaddya know … Get Current Webpage. Just the ticket. Just drag that Action into the workflow to the right (see Figure A-4).

The action expands a bit but it's still very human-friendly, no? See, it's even numbered as Step 1 for you and everything.

Next step: Convert the Web page to an audio file. Hmmm. I don't see anything like that in Safari's list of Actions. But I *do* spot Get Text from Webpage, and nearly any computer can convert text to synthetic speech. Drag the

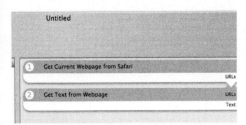

Figure A-5
Two actions: It's now officially a conspiracy!

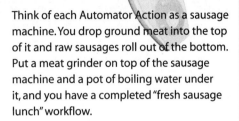

Figure A-6
Giving Automator a few specifics

Get Text from Webpage Action below Step 1 and see what happens (see Figure A-5).

You'll see the awesome simplicity of the user interface. Were you wondering why Get Current Webpage had the word "URLs" at the bottom of its box? Well, that's the "product" that this action spits out. The "input" for an individual action is labeled at the top of the box.

Onward. We need to convert this text to speech. Type Speech into the Search box and see what we get. Ah! "Text to Audio File." Perfect. Drag it under Step 2 (see Figure A-6).

Ah. Here, Automator needs us to fill in a few details. The Mac OS comes with lots of different synthetic voices, so pick one. We'll also need to tell the Action what to call

> **TIP**
>
> Think of each Automator Action as a sausage machine. You drop ground meat into the top of it and raw sausages roll out of the bottom. Put a meat grinder on top of the sausage machine and a pot of boiling water under it, and you have a completed "fresh sausage lunch" workflow.
>
> It's a gross metaphor if you're a vegetarian, but it's perfect for Automator. All this machinery is in a stack, and the output of one action becomes the raw material for the next one.

this new file and where to save it. Give it a generic name and stash it wherever you want. Doesn't particularly matter, because we're going to be importing the file into iTunes.

Oh! iTunes. A search on "iTunes import" yields "Import Audio File."

(For Heaven's sake … could this be any simpler? I'm sending Apple another five bucks right now.)

Drag Import Audio File to the end of the list as Step 4 and choose what sort of audio format you'd like to add to your library. And select the Delete Source Files after Encoding option — we're done with the original text-to-speech file, so we can get rid of it after it's been imported into iTunes' library.

For added convenience, I'd like to add the audio file to a special Audio Web Pages playlist. That way, I can tell iTunes to always synch that list to my iPod. Find the Add Songs to Playlist action and drag it to the end of the workflow as Step 6 (see Figure A-7).

Let's Go for a Spin

And take a moment to enjoy the sight there on the right of the workflow. Each of these boxes is an independent Action. All you did was drag 'em into a stack. And yet effortlessly and unerringly, URLs become text, text becomes a file, a file becomes an iTunes song, an iTunes song becomes a new item in a playlist. Kewl!

Let's take this workflow for a spin. Switch over to Safari, visit a nice, text-y sort of Web page (like what you get when you're visiting a newspaper article and click the Print This Article). Then switch back to Automator and click the Run button.

Watch in stunned admiration as Automator

works from top to bottom, executing each step in turn. A spinning dingoid appears in the lower-left corner of an Action while it's in progress, and a green checkbox appears when it's been completed successfully.

After a boring few minutes waiting for Text to Audio File to finish reading the text into an audio file (how fast can *you* speak?), the magical green checkbox will arrive at the bottom step. Lo and behold, a new song entitled "Converted Webpage" appears in my Converted Web Pages playlist.

Waitasec ...
Just One Small Change

One problem, though: The next time I run

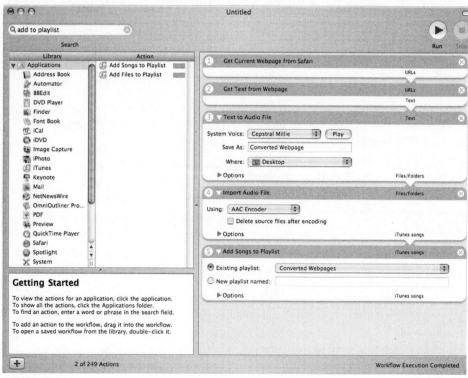

Figure A-7
The end of the assembly line

this workflow, *another* audio file with that same name will be dropped into the playlist. It'd be nice if the workflow stamped the file-name with the date and time so I could tell things apart.

It's easy as pie to edit a workflow. Want to insert a Rename Finder Items Action into the workflow? Just drag it where it needs to go, right between Steps 3 and 4. The Text to Audio File and Import Audio File Actions will skootch apart to make room for it. Figure A-8 shows the *final* final Import Web-page into iTunes Automator workflow.

>**TIP**

You can tinker with workflows until your spouse leaves you and your friends stage some sort of intervention. I don't keep my iPod docked to my Mac when I'm not using it, but if you do, you can tack an Update iPod Action to the end of the workflow. Bingo, the iPod's been freshened with no added labor necessary.

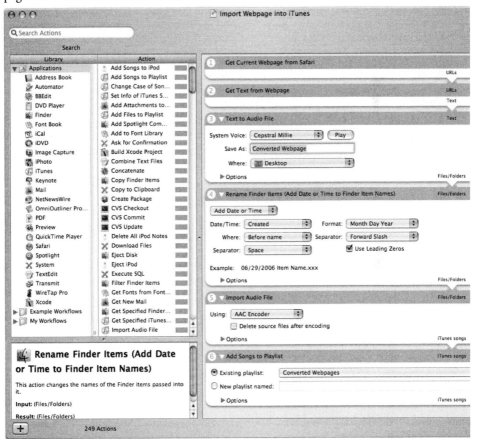

Figure A-8
No, seriously: the completed workflow

Save the workflow and we'll move on. I'll wait.

WORKING WITH WORKFLOW

So we've all been baptized into the First Church of Automator. But as is, our example workflow is merely ginchy. It's very nice, but every time we want to use it, we have to move away from Safari and click a Run button in the Automator app.

Automator workflows escalate into the mega-ginchy realm when you discover that you can trigger them from outside the Automator app. You can actually integrate them so well into outside apps that they almost work like built-in features.

Workflow as Plug-in

The heart of Automator's megaginchiness is its Save As Plug-In function, found under the File menu (see Figure A-9).

Each of these plug-in options will integrate your workflow into a different bit of the Mac experience.

Finder

The Action will appear under the Automator

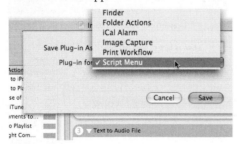

Figure A-9
Letting Workflows work for you outside of the Automator app

submenu, which pops up when you select an item in the Finder and activate its contextual menu (either by holding down the Control key while clicking, or by clicking the right-hand mouse button if your mouse has one).

Handy for point-and-shoot operations on individual files, like Copy This Picture to My iPod or Convert This Document to an MP3 Audio File and Put It in My iPod's 'Audio Documents' Playlist.

Folder Actions

When you attach a workflow to a Finder folder, the workflow will run any time new content is added to the folder. Create a folder named "iPod Document Wormhole" and attach a document-to-sound-file workflow to it. Every time you drop a document into it (or even just save a file there) — bango, it'll land in your iPod.

iCal Alarm

Oh, this one *kicks butt.* Save the workflow as an iCal Alarm and it'll become a recurring appointment in your iCal calendar. Make it run once, every day, every week, every month: at the designated time, the workflow will run automatically.

Lean back and figure out ways to abuse this. Every day on the drive to work, there's an audio file of the morning's top *New York Times* stories on your iPod. Every Monday, every score from every weekend football game is on there as a text file. On and on.

Image Capture

The Mac OS includes a utility called Image Capture, which is designed as a sort of centralized mechanism for bringing new images into your Mac. Whether they're coming in from a scanner, a digital camera, or a memory card, or wherever, you can set up your

Mac to automatically hand the chore over to Image Capture to acquire the image and stick it somewhere on your hard drive.

By attaching a workflow to the process, you can easily make Image Capture iPod-savvy. Every piece of artwork you scan goes to the database where you manage your art collection — *and* to your iPod's photo library. That sort of thing.

(Okay, so I've never found a personal reason to use Automator with Image Capture. I've *tried* it, and I'm qualified to *write* about it. Just leave me alone, all right?)

Print Workflow

The standard Mac OS X Print dialog box contains a pop-up button named PDF. This collects various features that tell the OS, "Pretend like you're going to be printing this document onto paper, but instead, take all the text and graphics and hand it off to this piece of software instead."

And yes indeed, you can install a workflow here (see Figure A-10).

Script Menu

Automator's big brother is a system called AppleScript. Where Automator is a user tool that lets the average user assemble a straight list of steps for automating a simple process, an AppleScript Script is something written by a programmer that can do practically anything, from duplicating a few files to making sure that 219 employees get their paychecks and three others get escorted to the parking lot by security.

But you don't need to know about that.

All you need to know is that there's a menu called Scripts and it's included in the menu bar of every Mac app. When you save your

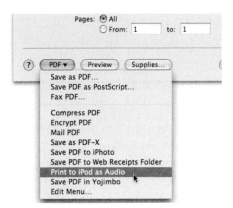

Figure A-10
Printing an item straight into an Automator workflow … and your iPod

workflow to the Scripts Menu, it'll appear in a special menu that's included inside the menu bar of every application (see Figure A-11).

If you can't find the Scripts menu, you can activate it through the AppleScript Utility app. It's sort of hidden away, in the Apple-Script subfolder of your Applications folder (see Figure A-12).

It's a handy place to put your iPod workflows because it's almost as though the folks who created Safari had a Send Web Page to iPod feature in mind all along.

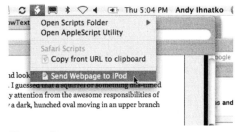

Figure A-11
The Scripts Menu, the handiest place to keep an Automator workflow

Figure A-12
Turning the Scripts menu on via the AppleScript Utility

SHAMELESS PLUG

I'm all edgy and worked-up right now, because I've spent about 3,000 words talking about Automator and muscle-memory is urging me to keep going. I want to spend another 10,000 words explaining how AppleScript has a wonderful plan for your life, if you'll only welcome it into your heart, et cetera, but this isn't a book about the Mac OS.

And besides … I wrote that book already. Buy it, please. Not because I want to add a moisture-controlled room to my house just for the comic-book collection — sure I do; I mean, I'd be weird if I *didn't,* wouldn't I? — but because Automator and Apple-Script truly are the sort of features that take a good thing like the Mac OS and truly make it Great.

As you've seen through the chapters of this book, it's the ultimate feature: it's a feature that lets you create new features. Windows users are going to have to buy almost a hundred bucks' worth of third-party utilities to get all the iPod-stuffing features that you can create for yourself with Automator.

And if you're saving $100, why not send twenty of that back to me? Seriously, the Mac OS book of mine is a good thing.

Text to Speech

The Skim

The iPod is a great device for listening to audio, but a not-so-great one for reading text. Well, nobody's perfect. As a ballplayer, I had a great glove but couldn't suss out semipro-level pitchers; yes, the dream died in tenth grade, but I still insist that I'm a good person with many valuable skills.

At least the iPod's text weakness can be addressed with some add-on software that takes any plain text and "speaks" it into an audio file. iPod + text-to-speech = mounds of wholesome crunchy goodness, including the ability to create your own audio books from free electronic texts available on the Net and listen to e-mails, reports, and Web pages during your morning drive.

Oh, and I lacked the explosive speed necessary to stretch those singles and doubles into doubles and triples. At least that's what the third-base coach told me when he asked for my uniform. I'm very nearly over it now. Well, "nearly," definitely.

TEXT-TO-SPEECH IN WINDOWS

Windows has a text-to-speech engine built-in, but it isn't terribly flexible. It's there so that folks with poor vision can use a PC by having text, menus, buttons, and anything else read to them.

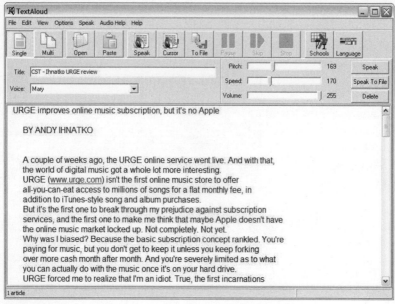

Figure B-1

Speak, Mishkin! TextAloud delivers useful speech services to Windows.

No, we're going to have to rely on some higher firepower. NextUp's TextAloud (www.nextup.com) is just the ticket. It's not a one-use, one-job utility … it pitches in as your go-to answer whenever there's some text that you'd like to carry around on your iPod as spoken audio. And it's affordable. Figure B-1 shows you TextAloud's main window.

Speaking Up

TextAloud can speak any text that's inside its window.

Sure, go ahead: Type "I don't know what

your mother was talking about; your new hairstyle doesn't make you look *anything* like a mail-order bride or a Steely Dan groupie." Click the Speak button and you'll receive the soothing words that you needed to hear.

But that's not what we came for. TextAloud can slurp text into this window from a bunch of different sources:

> **Files**. Most of the usual suspects can be opened directly by the app: text files, Rich Text Format (RTF) files, Word documents, PDFs, and even HTML files.

Figure B-2

A bunch of new buttons in your browser, courtesy of TextAloud

> **Web pages**. TextAloud installs a new bunch of buttons into your Web browser (see Figure B-2). If the TextAloud app is running, clicking the Add Article button will spit the contents of that window's Web page into TextAloud's speech window and switch you over to the app. You can also select one of TextAloud's voices from the pop-up menu before clicking Add Article to tell TextAloud to use that voice when converting.

> **The Clipboard**. Select any text in any application, choose Copy from that app's menu bar (or tap Ctrl+C) and TextAloud will leap immediately into action, slapping up the window seen in Figure B-3. Click the New button to copy the text to TextAloud as a new article, or Append to add it to the end of the current one.

Okay, this Clipboard-selection feature can get pretty freaking annoying pretty damned quickly. Which is why you'll want to fine-tune the options available through that window. If you tell TextAloud to ignore any Clipboard text that contains fewer than, say, 600 characters, it's less likely to come up when you're just doing basic word processing. And by shortening the prompt down to just a few seconds, the window won't bother you for long on those occasions when it *does* pop up at the wrong time.

And, of course, you can eliminate this feature entirely by unchecking the Watch Clipboard checkbox. You can still bring text into TextAloud through the Clipboard by the traditional way: Select the text, copy it, press Alt+Tab to go to the TextAloud app, and paste the text into the window.

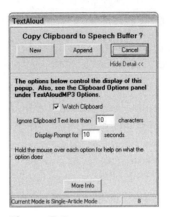

Figure B-3
Importing speakable text from the Clipboard

Working with Multiple Articles

TextAloud has a (very slightly) confusing approach to dealing with multiple items. By default, you're dealing with a single window and a single article; everything you import into the app either replaces, or is appended to the end of, the text that's already there.

By selecting Multiple Articles from TextAloud's Options menu, you can have the app handle each one of those items separately. You can spend the day adding stuff to TextAloud and then have all those things exported to separate audio files one after the other, while you're away at lunch, say.

Fabulous. But by default, TextAloud will export those separate articles into *one* audio file. Which seems to defeat the entire purpose. To make TextAloud turn your 11 articles and clippings into 11 independent, stand-alone audio files, choose Options ⇨ TextAloud Options and click the Multiple Files radio button in the Article Options tab of the window (see Figure B-4).

Speaking to a File

Once you have the text in TextAloud, converting the text to an audio file takes just a moment:

1. Type a title in the window's Title field. If you've imported text into multiple articles, you'll have to provide a name for each article via the Title field's pop-up menu.

2. Click the Speak to File button.

3. Choose a destination for the audio file(s) and click OK.

4. Wait.

▶TIDBIT

When you're processing text for speech, yet again your computer is forcing you to wait, wait, wait for results. This used to annoy me a lot more than it does now. When I realized how much time I spend sitting in front of a keyboard waiting for a process to finish, I started keeping a spool of dental tape in a desk draw. So now, while I wait, ... I floss.

This worked out so well — no cavities, and Mr. Gingivitis knows not to come knocking on my office door — that I bought a ukulele and kept *that* on my desk as well. And now it's two years later and I know about a dozen chords, five different styles of strumming, and nine or ten songs.

Next, I'm going to put a textbook on thoracic surgery next to the monitor. Well, who knows? If my computers continue to annoy me as regularly as they have since 1979, I could be board-certified inside of three years.

TextAloud will zip through the text, highlighting each word as it's spoken into the file. You don't need to sit back and witness the spectacle. You can switch to another task and allow TextAloud to process everything in the background.

When your toast pops up (metaphorically speaking), just drag the file into iTunes and you're good to go.

Audio File Settings

TextAloud works well straight out of the box — assuming you got it in a box instead of downloading it from the company's site — but you can make a few tweaks to suit your own tastes, temperament, and obsessive need to stick your nose into everything and maintain the illusion that you're the most important person in the whole world.

Check out TextAloud's Voices and File Options window, which you can access from the Options menu (see Figure B-5).

Three items here bear your kind attention:

> **Bit/Sample Rate**. By default, TextAloud chooses some pretty conservative quality settings. They result in nice, tiny sound files, but jeez ... you have a mount of space on your iPod and you don't need to be so utterly stingy. I like to goose those settings up to 48Kbps/32kHz. Above that, there isn't a terribly great improvement in sound quality.

> **Write to File Speed**. TextAloud is pretty zippy as is, but by selecting a faster conversion speed via the pop-up menu you can triple and even quadruple it. But nothing's free. At the default 10× speed, TextAloud can work in the background

➤TIDBIT

"It sounds like a drunken Norwegian who lost half his vocal cords in a bizarre lutefisking accident two years ago."

That's usually what people think of synthetic speech. I blame Stephen Hawking, for being (a) the most famous user of text-to-speech on the planet and (b) the very last user of text-to-speech who's still using 1980s speech technology.

Neither Apple nor Microsoft seem to think of speech as a huge priority … though Apple has made some big promises for Mac OS X 10.5. But for now, although Mac OS and Windows include powerful infrastructure for synthetic voices, the actual voice systems included with the OS are rather wretched. No, if you get into this at all, head over to NextUp.com and click the links for online stores where you can buy Windows– and Mac-compatible voices that are based on the very latest technology, such as AT&T Natural Voices.

It's like night and day. Your PC or Mac's built-in voices are … okay. Credible. But with a $30 voice installed, your computer can generate speech that sounds, at the very worst, like a New Yorker who's had maybe one beer. Two, tops.

Figure B-4
Telling TextAloud to split multiple articles into multiple audio files

Figure B-5
Tweaking options for the audio files

an entry for "Audio"? Just to keep your hard drive tidy, change that default to My Music. Better still, steer everything to a new TextAloud folder inside your music folder.

TEXT-TO-SPEECH ON A MACINTOSH

If you have a Mac, you don't need any sort of third-party utility to convert just about any text in any app to an audio file on your iPod. It doesn't come with an app as handy as TextAloud. Instead, it comes with a whole bunch of text-to-speech actions that work

while you're off surfing the Web or grinding your iron boot heel into the backs of the proletariat. You'll hardly notice. But faster speeds make greater demands on the CPU. At 40× speed, really, everything else grinds to a complete halt.

➤ **Audio Output Directory**. Great gravy … TextAloud defaults to the *My Documents* folder when it saves those audio files? *Really?* Does its dictionary not *have*

in Automator, a built-in utility that lets any user snap pre-built Actions together into a series of steps that the Mac can then perform on its own.

Check out Appendix A for a full discussion of Automator and what it can do for you. Sneak preview answer: anything and everything.

Appendix A shows you how to build an Automator action that converts any Safari Web page into iPod audio, for example. Not "an MP3 file that you can then import into iTunes," either. Load a Web page. Click a menu. Wait a minute or two. Presto: It's on your iPod. And additional handy Automator speech tricks are peppered throughout the book.

You really ought to give text-to-speech a shot.

Sure, there are some people who will never ever *ever* be able to tolerate synthetic speech. Partly this is for very good reasons (the biggest being that it's not perfect) and partly this is true for subconscious and silly ones (it reminds you of spending thirty minutes navigating through your cell phone company's automated support system).

But if your ear finds synthetic speech palatable, it truly opens up the iPod. If it doesn't, … keep checking back. Perfection is on the agenda.

Index

W

X

Y

➤ ➤ ➤